taste of home.
POTLUCK!

chicken stuffing casserole (p. 159)

taste of home. Reader's Digest

A TASTE OF HOME/READER'S DIGEST BOOK

Editor in Chief	Catherine Cassidy
Vice President, Executive Editor/Books	Heidi Reuter Lloyd
Creative Director	Howard Greenberg
North American Chief Marketing Officer	Lisa Karpinski
Food Director	Diane Werner RD
Senior Editor/Books	Mark Hagen
Editor	Janet Briggs
Associate Creative Director	Edwin Robles, Jr.
Art Director	Rudy Krochalk
Content Production Manager	Julie Wagner
Design Layout Artist	Emma Acevedo
Proofreader	Linne Bruskewitz
Recipe Asset System Manager	Coleen Martin
Premedia Supervisor	Scott Berger
Recipe Testing & Editing	Taste of Home Test Kitchen
Food Photography	Taste of Home Photo Studio
Administrative Assistant	Barb Czysz

The Reader's Digest Association, Inc.

President and Chief Executive Officer	Mary G. Berner
President, North American Affinities	Suzanne M. Grimes
President/Publisher Trade Publishing	Harold Clarke
Associate Publisher	Rosanne McManus
Vice President, Sales and Marketing	Stacey Ashton

For other Taste of Home books and products, visit us at tasteofhome.com.

For more Reader's Digest products and information, visit
rd.com (in the United States) or see rd.ca (in Canada).

International Standard Book Number (10): 0-89221-837-3
International Standard Book Number (13): 978-0-89821-837-4
Library of Congress Control Number: 2010932788

Cover Photography

Photographer	Dan Roberts
Food Stylist	Alynna Malson
Set Stylist	Jennifer Bradley Vent

Pictured on front cover: Italian Pasta Bake (p. 74) and Super Brownies (p. 201).

Pictured on back cover: Spinach Penne Toss (p. 184),
Berry Cheesecake Pie (p. 211) and White Chicken Chili (p. 67).

Printed in U.S.A.
3 5 7 9 10 8 6 4 2

Table of Contents

appetizers, snacks & beverages.... 5

breakfast buffets. 27

soups & sandwiches. 45

main dishes 71

casseroles. 115

quick & easy. 141

salads & sides 163

sweet endings 185

for a crowd. 215

indexes 246

Dig into a Smorgasbord of Flavor with *Taste of Home Potluck!*

96

103

Whether you need a dish for a charity buffet, church supper, family reunion, pancake breakfast or bake sale, *Potluck* has you covered.

The editors of Taste of Home, the world's #1 cooking magazine, assembled this mouthwatering collection of 336 recipes—each perfect for serving a crowd. In addition, every dish travels well, offers mass appeal and comes together with ingredients you likely have on hand.

Want an impressive appetizer to share with your book club? How about a savory nibble to bring to a football party? With *Potluck,* you'll find dozens of crowd-pleasing finger foods, dips, snack mixes and beverages that are sure to satisfy.

When the sign-up sheet comes around for your next bring-a-dish event, you'll gladly volunteer to supply an entree. That's because you'll find more than 100 main dishes, casseroles, sandwiches and other hearty specialties in this colorful cookbook...each perfect for large get-togethers.

Just consider Taco-Filled Pasta Shells (p. 84), Home-Style Chicken Potpie (p. 91), Tender Beef 'n' Bean Stew (p. 108) and Pizza Hot Dish (p. 121). They each serve 10 or more hungry guests.

When warm weather rolls in, so do the invites for backyard barbecues, neighborhood block parties, graduation celebrations and more. You'll never arrive empty handed thanks to recipes for taste-tempters such as Fancy Fruit Salad (p. 167), Buttery Corn Bread (p. 177) and Country Baked Beans (p. 179).

Even as the kitchen clock counts down the minutes to your party, *Potluck* helps you whip up an impressive edible. Simply see the chapter "Quick & Easy" (p. 141) for a delicious assortment of no-fuss recipes that will garnish praise on any buffet table.

If desserts are your specialty, you'll adore the selection of sweet treats found here. From cookies and bars to cakes and pies, there's a nibble to delight kids of all ages. See "Sweet Endings" (p. 185) for everything from swift classroom treats to dinner finales perfect to top off meals in your own home.

In addition, *Potluck* offers a chapter of recipes for any extra-large get-togethers or events you might volunteer for. See the chapter "For a Crowd" (p. 215) for Scalloped Potatoes and Ham (p. 217), Chicken Supreme with Gravy (p. 233) and Chocolate Chip Cookies (p. 242). These recipes yield 40, 70 and 84 servings respectively.

So whether you're looking for a quick contribution to an award ceremony or a sweet surprise for your holiday open house, *Taste of Home Potluck* makes sure the perfect bring-a-dish delight is at your fingertips!

appetizers, snacks & beverages

crab wonton cups
page 11

Jeanie Carrigan, Madera, California
I simplify party preparation by using my slow cooker to create this thick, cheesy dip. Your guests won't believe how good it is!

hot chili cheese dip

- 1 medium onion, finely chopped
- 2 garlic cloves, minced
- 2 teaspoons canola oil
- 2 cans (15 ounces *each*) chili without beans
- 2 cups salsa
- 2 packages (3 ounces *each*) cream cheese, cubed
- 2 cans (2-1/4 ounces *each*) sliced ripe olives, drained

Tortilla chips

In a small skillet, saute onion in oil until tender. Add garlic; cook 1 minute longer.

Transfer to a 3-qt. slow cooker. Stir in the chili, salsa, cream cheese and olives. Cover and cook on low for 4 hours or until heated through, stirring occasionally. Stir before serving with tortilla chips. **yield: 6 cups.**

chicken skewers with cool avocado sauce

- 1 pound boneless skinless chicken breasts
- 1/2 cup lime juice
- 1 tablespoon balsamic vinegar
- 2 teaspoons minced chipotle pepper in adobo sauce
- 1/2 teaspoon salt

SAUCE:
- 1 medium ripe avocado, peeled and pitted
- 1/2 cup fat-free sour cream
- 2 tablespoons minced fresh cilantro
- 2 teaspoons lime juice
- 1 teaspoon grated lime peel
- 1/4 teaspoon salt

Flatten chicken to 1/4-in. thickness; cut lengthwise into sixteen 1-in.-wide strips. In a large resealable plastic bag, combine the lime juice, vinegar, chipotle pepper and salt; add the chicken. Seal bag and turn to coat; refrigerate for 30 minutes.

Meanwhile, for the sauce, place remaining ingredients in a food processor; cover and process until blended. Transfer to a serving bowl; cover and refrigerate until serving.

Drain chicken and discard marinade. Thread meat onto four metal or soaked wooden skewers. Using long-handled tongs, moisten a paper towel with cooking oil and lightly coat the grill rack.

Grill, covered, over medium heat or broil 4 in. from the heat for 8-12 minutes or until no longer pink, turning frequently. Serve with sauce. **yield: 16 skewers (3/4 cup sauce).**

Veronica Callaghan
Glastonbury, Connecticut
I'm always looking for lighter recipes to take on tailgate outings, and this one works great. Just whip up the marinade, add chicken and take it along to grill at your pregame festivities.

Tracy Golder
Bloomsburg, Pennsylvania
This crunchy mix is great for a late night snack or any gathering. The chocolate-peanut butter combination will satisfy any sweet tooth.

chocolate wheat cereal snacks

- 6 cups frosted bite-size Shredded Wheat
- 1 cup milk chocolate chips
- 1/4 cup creamy peanut butter
- 1 cup confectioners' sugar

Place cereal in a large bowl; set aside. In a microwave, melt chocolate chips and peanut butter; stir until smooth. Pour over cereal and stir gently to coat. Let stand for 10 minutes.

Sprinkle with confectioners' sugar and toss to coat. Cool completely. Store in an airtight container. **yield: 6 cups.**

warm ham and cheese spread

- 4 pita breads (6 inches), split
- 1/4 cup olive oil
- 4 cups ground fully cooked ham
- 1 cup (4 ounces *each*) shredded Swiss, American and cheddar cheeses
- 1/4 cup mayonnaise
- 1/2 teaspoon ground mustard
- 2 tablespoons minced fresh parsley

Additional shredded Swiss cheese, optional

Cut each pita half into eight wedges; brush rough sides with oil. Place on ungreased baking sheets. Bake at 350° for 10-12 minutes or until golden brown, turning once. Remove to wire racks.

In a large bowl, combine the ham, cheeses, mayonnaise and mustard. Transfer to a shallow 1-qt. baking dish.

Bake, uncovered, at 350° for 15-20 minutes or until edges are bubbly. Sprinkle with parsley and additional Swiss cheese if desired; serve with pita wedges. **yield: 3-1/2 cups.**

Patricia Prescott
Manchester,
New Hampshire
I'm always looking for creative yet family-pleasing ways to stretch my tight grocery budget. I usually make this dish with ham "ends" that are available at the deli counter.

Lily-Michele Alexis
Louisville, Kentucky
When you want a more "meaty" appetizer for your holiday buffet, reach for these finger-licking-good ribs!

honey garlic ribs

- 6 pounds pork baby back ribs, cut into two-rib portions
- 2 cups water, *divided*
- 3/4 cup packed brown sugar
- 2 tablespoons cornstarch
- 1 teaspoon garlic powder
- 1/4 teaspoon ground ginger
- 1/2 cup honey
- 1/4 cup soy sauce

Place ribs bone side down in a large roasting pan; pour 1 cup of water over ribs. Cover tightly and bake at 350° for 1-1/2 hours.

In a small bowl, combine the brown sugar, cornstarch, garlic powder and ginger. Stir in the honey, soy sauce and remaining water until smooth. Drain fat from roasting pan; pour sauce over the ribs.

Bake, uncovered, for 45 minutes or until meat is tender. **yield: 24 servings.**

homemade lemonade

Rebecca Baird
Salt Lake City, Utah
This old-fashioned thirst-quencher is one I serve often during hot summer months. Club soda gives a little fizz to this sweet and tart beverage.

3 cups sugar
2 cups water
1 cup lemon peel strips (about 6 lemons)
3 cups lemon juice (about 14 lemons)
1 bottle (1 liter) club soda, chilled

In a large saucepan, heat sugar and water over medium heat until sugar is dissolved, stirring frequently. Stir in lemon strips. Bring to a boil. Reduce heat; simmer, uncovered, for 5 minutes. Remove from the heat. Cool slightly. Stir in lemon juice; cover and refrigerate until chilled. Discard lemon strips. Pour mixture into a pitcher; gradually stir in club soda. **yield: 10 cups.**

pigs in a blanket

3 cups all-purpose flour
1 tablespoon sugar
2 teaspoons baking powder
1/2 cup shortening
1/2 cup cold butter, cubed
1 cup milk
10 crushed Zwieback *or* Holland rusks (1-1/4 cups)
1/4 teaspoon salt
1/4 teaspoon pepper
1-3/4 pounds ground beef
1-3/4 pounds bulk pork sausage
Dijon mustard, optional

In a large bowl, combine the flour, sugar and baking powder. Cut in shortening and butter until mixture resembles coarse crumbs. Gradually add milk, tossing with a fork until dough forms a ball. Divide dough into three portions. Refrigerate until chilled.

Meanwhile, for filling, in a large bowl, combine the Zwieback crumbs, salt and pepper. Crumble beef and pork over mixture and mix well. Shape rounded tablespoonfuls of meat mixture into 3-in. logs.

On a floured surface, knead one portion of dough 8-10 times. Roll dough to 1/8-in. thickness; cut with a floured 3-in. round cutter. Place one log in the center of each circle. Brush edges of dough with water; fold dough over filling and pinch edges to seal. Reroll scraps. Repeat with remaining dough and filling.

Place on greased racks in shallow baking pans. Bake at 350° for 35-40 minutes or until meat is no longer pink. Serve with mustard if desired. **yield: about 4-1/2 dozen.**

Cyndi Fynaardt
Oskaloosa, Iowa
Here's an awesome update on classic pigs in a blanket. Pork-and-beef logs are wrapped up in a from-scratch pastry dough. Bet you can't eat just one of them!

sausage-stuffed mushrooms

    35   large fresh mushrooms
    1/2 pound bulk pork sausage
    1/2 cup shredded part-skim mozzarella cheese
    1/4 cup seasoned bread crumbs

Remove stems from mushrooms and finely chop; set caps aside. In a large skillet, cook sausage and mushrooms over medium heat until meat is no longer pink; drain.

Remove from the heat. Stir in cheese and bread crumbs. Fill each mushroom cap with about 1 tablespoon of filling.

Place on foil-lined baking sheets. Bake at 400° for 16-20 minutes or until mushrooms are tender. **yield: 35 appetizers.**

Kathryn Schumacker
Batesville, Indiana
My family eats these as fast as I can make them, and with just four ingredients, they couldn't be easier to prepare. Guests will love the taste, and you'll love the simplicity.

asiago chicken spread

    3/4 pound boneless skinless chicken breasts, cut into
         1/2-inch cubes
    1/4 teaspoon salt
    1/8 teaspoon pepper
      2 tablespoons butter
      2 garlic cloves, minced
    1/3 cup salted cashew halves
    1/3 cup mayonnaise
    1/2 cup chopped onion
    1/4 cup shredded Asiago cheese
    1/4 cup minced fresh basil
    1/2 teaspoon hot pepper sauce
Assorted crackers *or* toasted baguette slices

Season chicken with salt and pepper. In a large skillet, saute chicken in butter for 5-6 minutes or until chicken is no longer pink. Add garlic; cook 1 minute longer. Stir in cashews. Remove from the heat; cool.

In a food processor, combine the mayonnaise, onion, cheese, basil, pepper sauce and chicken mixture; cover and process until blended. Press into a 2-cup bowl; cover and refrigerate for at least 2 hours.

If desired, unmold onto a serving platter; serve with crackers or baguette slices. **yield: 2 cups.**

James Korzenowski
Fennville, Michigan
This fabulous recipe is perfect for when you want to make something ahead of time. Friends with hearty appetites will love the chunks of chicken, crunchy cashews and Asiago cheese.

crab wonton cups

32 wonton wrappers
Cooking spray
1 package (8 ounces) cream cheese, softened
1/2 cup heavy whipping cream
1 egg
1 tablespoon Dijon mustard
1 teaspoon Worcestershire sauce
5 drops hot pepper sauce
2 pouches (3.53 ounces *each*) premium crabmeat, drained
1/4 cup thinly sliced green onions
1/4 cup finely chopped sweet red pepper
1 cup grated Parmesan cheese

Press wonton wrappers into miniature muffin cups coated with cooking spray. Spritz wrappers with cooking spray. Bake at 350° for 8-9 minutes or until lightly browned.

Meanwhile, in a small bowl, beat the cream cheese, cream, egg, mustard, Worcestershire sauce and pepper sauce until smooth. Stir in the crab, green onions and red pepper; spoon into wonton cups. Sprinkle with Parmesan cheese.

Bake for 10-12 minutes or until filling is heated through. Serve warm. Refrigerate leftovers. **yield: 32 appetizers.**

Connie McDowell
Greenwood, Delaware
These tasty little crab tarts make excellent appetizers served warm and crispy from the oven. You can also add them to your list of holiday finger food as well. They are truly crowd-pleasers.

Cindy Steffen
Cedarburg, Wisconsin
This is a refreshing punch that isn't as sweet as most. My family loves the tart "wake-you-up" flavor!

golden fruit punch

4 maraschino cherries
1 medium navel orange, thinly sliced
1 small lemon, thinly sliced
1 small lime, thinly sliced
1 can (12 ounces) frozen lemonade concentrate, thawed
1 can (12 ounces) frozen limeade concentrate, thawed
1 can (12 ounces) frozen pineapple-orange juice concentrate, thawed
2 liters diet ginger ale, chilled

Arrange fruit in a 5-cup ring mold; add 3/4 cup water. Freeze until solid. Add enough water to fill mold; freeze until solid.

Just before serving, in a punch bowl, combine juice concentrates with 2 cups water. Stir in ginger ale. Unmold ice ring by wrapping the bottom of the mold in a hot, damp dishcloth. Invert onto a baking sheet; place fruit side up in punch bowl. **yield: 21 servings (4 quarts).**

bacon-cheddar biscuit snackers

- 1 pound sliced bacon
- 2 cups all-purpose flour
- 2 cups (8 ounces) finely shredded cheddar cheese
- 1 teaspoon salt
- 1/2 cup shortening
- 1/3 cup milk

Cut each bacon strip in half widthwise. In a large skillet, cook bacon over medium heat until partially cooked but not crisp. Remove to paper towels to drain; keep warm.

In a large bowl, combine the flour, cheese and salt. Cut in shortening until mixture resembles coarse crumbs. Stir in milk just until moistened. Turn dough onto a lightly floured surface; knead 8-10 times.

Divide dough in half. Roll one portion into a 12-in. x 9-in. rectangle. Cut in half, forming two 9-in. x 6-in. rectangles; cut each rectangle into nine 1-in. strips. Repeat with remaining dough.

Place a piece of bacon on each biscuit strip; carefully roll up jelly-roll style. Place seam side down on ungreased baking sheets. Bake at 450° for 8-10 minutes or until golden brown. Serve warm. Refrigerate leftovers. **yield: 3 dozen.**

Ann Robertson
Smyrna, Tennessee
These "rollers" are great to take to parties or to enjoy at home for dessert. The spirals are simply delicious and come together in minutes.

Terri Newton
Marshall, Texas
Make this fun, easy snack mix in the microwave for a treat anytime. Add extra red pepper sauce for more "kick."

texas snack mix

- 3 cups *each* Corn Chex, Wheat Chex and Rice Chex
- 1 cup unsalted peanuts
- 1 cup miniature pretzels
- 1 cup cheese-flavored snack crackers
- 1/4 cup butter, melted
- 1 tablespoon Worcestershire sauce
- 2-1/2 teaspoons hot pepper sauce
- 1-1/4 teaspoons seasoned salt

In a large bowl, combine the cereal, peanuts, pretzels and crackers. In a small bowl, combine the butter, Worcestershire sauce, pepper sauce and seasoned salt; pour over cereal mixture.

Microwave in batches on high for 2 minutes, stirring three times. Spread onto waxed paper-lined baking sheets to cool. Store in an airtight container. **yield: 3 quarts.**

editor's note: This recipe was tested in a 1,100-watt microwave.

Carolyn Butterfield, Lake Stevens, Washington
I entered this recipe in a local fair, and it took first place! This is one of my favorites because all of the ingredients (except for the lime juice) came directly from my garden and beehives.

watermelon salsa

2	cups seeded finely chopped watermelon
1/2	cup finely chopped peeled cucumber
1/4	cup finely chopped red onion
1/4	cup finely chopped sweet red pepper
1	jalapeno pepper, seeded and minced
1/4	cup minced fresh cilantro
1	tablespoon minced fresh basil
1	tablespoon minced fresh mint
2	tablespoons honey
1	teaspoon lime juice

Baked tortilla chip scoops

In a large bowl, combine the melon, cucumber, onion, peppers and herbs. Drizzle with the honey and the lime juice; gently toss to coat.

Refrigerate for at least 1 hour. Serve with chips. **yield: 3 cups.**

editor's note: When cutting hot peppers, disposable gloves are recommended. Avoid touching your face.

easy entree

If you have any of the Watermelon Salsa left after serving it with chips at your get-together, try spooning a little over grilled tilapia for a refreshing spring or summer meal. It's also tasty with pork or even chicken.

special cheese balls

2	packages (8 ounces *each*) cream cheese, softened
2	cups (8 ounces) shredded sharp cheddar cheese
2	cups (8 ounces) shredded mild cheddar cheese
4	ounces crumbled blue cheese
4-1/2	teaspoons prepared horseradish
1	teaspoon Worcestershire sauce
1/8	to 1/4 teaspoon onion powder
1/8	teaspoon garlic powder
1/3	cup finely chopped pecans, toasted
1/3	cup finely chopped salted peanuts

Assorted crackers, grapes *and/or* apple slices

In a large bowl, combine the cheeses, horseradish, Worcestershire sauce, onion powder and garlic powder. Shape into two balls. Cover and refrigerate for 15 minutes.

Combine pecans and peanuts; press onto cheese balls. Cover and refrigerate for at least 2 hours. Serve with crackers, grapes and/or apple slices. **yield: 2 cheese balls (2 cups each).**

Margaret Nichols
White Hall, Illinois
Coated with nuts, these cheese balls are impossible to pass up on a buffet table. I've even served them with crackers and fruit at morning meetings.

spinach-corn bread bites

1	package (8-1/2 ounces) corn bread/muffin mix
1/2	cup grated Parmesan cheese
1/8	teaspoon garlic powder
2	eggs
1/2	cup blue cheese salad dressing
1/4	cup butter, melted
1	package (10 ounces) frozen chopped spinach, thawed and squeezed dry
1/2	cup shredded cheddar cheese
1/2	cup finely chopped onion

In a large bowl, combine the muffin mix, Parmesan cheese and garlic powder. In another bowl, whisk the eggs, salad dressing and butter; stir into dry ingredients just until moistened. Fold in the spinach, cheddar cheese and onion.

Fill greased miniature muffin cups two-thirds full. Bake at 350° for 12-14 minutes or until a toothpick inserted near the center comes out clean. Cool for 5 minutes before removing from pans to wire racks. Serve warm. Refrigerate leftovers. **yield: 4 dozen.**

Laura Mahaffey
Annapolis, Maryland
Although this recipe makes a big batch of savory bites, there are never any left over. Whether served as a snack or a change-of-pace side dish, they are always popular!

pepperoni pinwheels

- 1/2 cup diced pepperoni
- 1/2 cup shredded part-skim mozzarella cheese
- 1/4 teaspoon dried oregano
- 1 egg, *separated*
- 1 tube (8 ounces) refrigerated crescent rolls

In a small bowl, combine the pepperoni, cheese, oregano and egg yolk. In another small bowl, whisk egg white until foamy; set aside. Separate crescent dough into four rectangles; seal perforations.

Spread pepperoni mixture over each rectangle to within 1/4 in. of edges. Roll up jelly-roll style, starting with a short side; pinch seams to seal. Cut each into six slices.

Place cut side down on greased baking sheets; brush tops with egg white. Bake at 375° for 12-15 minutes or until golden brown. Serve warm. Refrigerate leftovers. **yield: 2 dozen.**

Vikki Rebholz
West Chester, Ohio
These golden-brown rounds have lots of pepperoni flavor. They're easy to make and are really good, too!

hot buttered coffee

- 1/4 cup butter, softened
- 1 cup packed brown sugar
- 1 teaspoon vanilla extract
- 1/2 teaspoon ground cinnamon
- 1/4 teaspoon ground nutmeg
- 1/4 teaspoon ground allspice
- 1/8 teaspoon ground cloves

EACH SERVING:
- 1 cup hot brewed coffee (French *or* other dark roast)

Cinnamon sticks and whipped cream, optional

In a small bowl, beat butter and brown sugar until crumbly, about 2 minutes. Beat in vanilla and spices.

For each serving, stir 1 tablespoon butter mixture into 1 cup coffee. Garnish with cinnamon stick and whipped cream if desired.

Cover and refrigerate leftover butter mixture for up to 2 weeks. **yield: 20 servings (1-1/4 cups mix).**

Taste of Home
Test Kitchen
Rich and rewarding, this coffee is sure to warm your spirits. To save time at a potluck, dish up the butter mixture with a small scoop and let guests mix up their own beverages. It's great for fall events.

sour cream and beef turnovers

2	cups all-purpose flour
1	tablespoon sugar
1	teaspoon salt
1/2	cup shortening
1	cup (8 ounces) sour cream
1	egg yolk

FILLING:

3/4	pound ground beef
1	large onion, finely chopped
1/4	cup finely chopped fresh mushrooms
1/2	cup sour cream
1/2	teaspoon salt
1/2	teaspoon dried oregano
1/4	teaspoon pepper
1	egg
2	teaspoons water

In a large bowl, combine the flour, sugar and salt. Cut in shortening until crumbly. Stir in sour cream and egg yolk just until moistened. Shape into a ball. Cover and refrigerate for 2 hours or until easy to handle.

In a large skillet over medium heat, cook the beef, onion and mushrooms until meat is no longer pink. Remove from the heat; drain. Stir in the sour cream, salt, oregano and pepper.

On a floured surface, roll out dough to 1/8-in. thickness. Cut with a floured 3-in. round cutter. Place a rounded teaspoon of filling on one side of each circle; fold dough over filling. Press edges with a fork to seal. Prick tops with a fork. Reroll scraps; repeat.

Place on greased baking sheets. Beat egg with water; brush over turnovers. Bake at 450° for 12-15 minutes or until lightly browned. **yield: about 4-1/2 dozen.**

Elva Kelly
Prince George,
British Columbia
I always serve these turnovers at large get-togethers. If you like, however, you can add a tossed green salad and serve them for dinner. They freeze well, too.

confetti snack mix

Jane Bray
Temple, Terrace Florida
I've made this party mix for many years, and I usually double the recipe. It makes a wonderful gift, and everyone always asks for the recipe.

4	cups Golden Grahams
1	cup dry roasted peanuts
1	cup dried banana chips
1	cup raisins
1	cup milk chocolate M&M's

In a large bowl, combine all ingredients. Store in an airtight container. **yield: 7 cups.**

asparagus ham roll-ups

16   fresh asparagus spears, trimmed
1   medium sweet red pepper, cut into 16 strips
8   ounces Havarti cheese, cut into 16 strips
8   thin slices deli ham *or* prosciutto, cut in half lengthwise
16   whole chives

In a large skillet, bring 1 in. of water to a boil. Add asparagus; cover and cock for 3 minutes. Drain and immediately place asparagus in ice water. Drain and pat dry.

Place an asparagus spear, red pepper strip and cheese strip on each slice of ham. Roll up tightly; tie with a chive. Refrigerate until serving. **yield: 16 servings.**

Rhonda Struthers
Ottawa, Ontario
Havarti cheese, asparagus and red peppers make these tasty roll-ups ideal for a summer celebration. Fresh chive ties give them a fussed-over look, but they're a cinch to make.

Sandra Fisher
Missoula, Montana
I came up with this recipe when I got tired of the same old wings. These are baked with onion and garlic, then broiled and basted with a mixture of raspberry jam, barbecue sauce and jalapeno peppers. The sauce is also excellent on pork...and is great for dipping.

raspberry barbecue wings

2/3   cup barbecue sauce
2/3   cup seedless raspberry jam
3   tablespoons finely chopped onion
1   to 2 jalapeno peppers, seeded and finely chopped
2   teaspoons minced garlic, *divided*
2   teaspoons Liquid Smoke, optional, *divided*
1/4   teaspoon salt
15   chicken wings (about 3 pounds)
1   small onion, sliced
1   cup water

In a small bowl, combine the barbecue sauce, jam, chopped onion, peppers, 1 teaspoon garlic, 1 teaspoon Liquid Smoke if desired and salt; mix well. Cover and refrigerate for at least 2 hours.

Cut chicken wings into three sections; discard wing tip section. Place the chicken wings in a greased 15-in. x 10-in. x 1-in. baking pan. Top with sliced onion and remaining garlic. Combine the water and remaining Liquid Smoke if desired; pour over wings. Cover and bake at 350° for 30 minutes or until juices run clear.

Transfer wings to a greased broiler pan; brush with sauce. Broil 4-6 in. from the heat for 20-25 minutes, turning and basting every 5 minutes or until wings are well coated. **yield: 2-1/2 dozen.**

editor's note: Uncooked chicken wing sections (wingettes) may be substituted for whole chicken wings. When cutting hot peppers, disposable gloves are recommended. Avoid touching your face.

Laura Metzger, York, Pennsylvania
I like to entertain a lot and have used these tasty cups on several occasions as an appetizer. I also like how it is easy to switch around the ingredients to give it a different flavor.

chili ham cups

    1 package (3 ounces) cream cheese, softened
    1 cup finely chopped fully cooked ham
    1 cup (4 ounces) shredded cheddar cheese
    1 can (4 ounces) chopped green chilies, drained
  1/4 cup sliced ripe olives, drained
    1 tube (10.2 ounces) refrigerated biscuits
Salsa and sour cream, optional

In a small bowl, combine the cream cheese, ham, cheese, chilies and olives. Separate dough into 10 biscuits; press each biscuit onto the bottom and up the sides of a greased muffin cup. Fill with ham mixture.

Bake at 375° for 20-25 minutes or until cheese is melted and crust is golden brown. Let stand for 2 minutes before removing from pan. Serve warm. Garnish with salsa and sour cream if desired. **yield: 10 servings.**

bubbly cranberry punch

Rebecca Cook Jones
Henderson, Nevada
Tart and refreshing, this sparkling nonalcoholic punch will add pizzazz to holiday parties, bridal showers and other festive occasions. My mother-in-law gave me the recipe for this beverage.

2	cans (16 ounces *each*) jellied cranberry sauce
1-1/2	cups orange juice
1/2	cup lemon juice
2	bottles (1 liter *each*) ginger ale, chilled

Ice cubes

In a large pitcher or punch bowl, whisk cranberry sauce until smooth. Whisk in orange and lemon juices. Just before serving, slowly stir in ginger ale. Add ice cubes. **yield: 14 servings.**

crispy baked wontons

1/2	pound ground pork
1/2	pound extra-lean ground turkey
1	small onion, chopped
1	can (8 ounces) sliced water chestnuts, drained and chopped
1/3	cup reduced-sodium soy sauce
1/4	cup egg substitute
1-1/2	teaspoons ground ginger
1	package (12 ounces) wonton wrappers

Cooking spray
Sweet-and-sour sauce, optional

In a large skillet, cook the pork, turkey and onion over medium heat until meat is no longer pink; drain. Transfer to a large bowl. Stir in the water chestnuts, soy sauce, egg substitute and ground ginger.

Position a wonton wrapper with one point toward you. (Keep remaining wrappers covered with a damp paper towel until ready to use.) Place 2 heaping teaspoons of filling in the center of wrapper. Fold bottom corner over filling; fold sides toward center over filling. Roll toward the remaining point. Moisten top corner with water; press to seal. Repeat with the remaining wrappers and filling.

Place on baking sheets coated with cooking spray; lightly coat wontons with additional cooking spray.

Bake at 400° for 10-12 minutes or until golden brown, turning once. Serve warm with sweet-and-sour sauce if desired. **yield: about 4 dozen.**

Brianna Shade
Beaverton, Oregon
These quick, versatile wontons are great for a savory snack or paired with a bowl of soothing soup on a cold day I usually make a large batch, freeze half on a floured baking sheet, then store in an airtight container.

shrimp cocktail

3	quarts water
1	small onion, sliced
1/2	medium lemon, sliced
2	sprigs fresh parsley
1	tablespoon salt
5	whole peppercorns
1/4	teaspoon dried thyme
1	bay leaf
3	pounds uncooked large shrimp, peeled and deveined (tails on)

SAUCE:

1	cup chili sauce
2	tablespoons lemon juice
2	tablespoons prepared horseradish
4	teaspoons Worcestershire sauce
1/2	teaspoon salt

Dash cayenne pepper

In a Dutch oven, combine the water, onion, lemon, parsley, salt, peppercorns, thyme and bay leaf. Bring to a boil. Add shrimp. Reduce heat; simmer, uncovered, for 4-5 minutes or until shrimp turn pink.

Drain shrimp and immediately rinse in cold water. Refrigerate for 2-3 hours. In a small bowl, combine the sauce ingredients. Refrigerate until serving.

Arrange shrimp on a serving platter; serve with sauce. **yield: about 6 dozen (1-1/4 cups sauce).**

Peggy Allen
Pasadena, California
I serve this easy-to-make appetizer for every special occasion and for "munchie meals" on big-game days. My neighbors look for it whenever we get together.

garlic garbanzo bean spread

1	can (15 ounces) garbanzo beans *or* chickpeas, rinsed and drained
1/2	cup olive oil
2	tablespoons minced fresh parsley
1	tablespoon lemon juice
1	green onion, cut into three pieces
1	to 2 garlic cloves, peeled
1/4	teaspoon salt

Assorted fresh vegetables and baked pita chips

In a food processor, combine the first seven ingredients; cover and process until blended. Transfer to a bowl. Refrigerate until serving. Serve with vegetables and pita chips. **yield: 1-1/2 cups.**

Lisa Moore
North Syracuse, New York
My friends and family always ask me to prepare this dip. I guarantee you'll be asked for the recipe. You can serve it as a party starter or even as a filling for sandwiches.

caramel apple dip

1 package (8 ounces) cream cheese, softened
1/2 cup packed brown sugar
1/4 cup caramel ice cream topping
1 teaspoon vanilla extract
1 cup marshmallow creme
3 medium tart apples
2 tablespoons lemon juice
2 tablespoons water

Taste of Home
Test Kitchen
This sweet, smooth and fluffy dip is really a crowd-pleaser.

In a small bowl, beat the cream cheese, brown sugar, caramel topping and vanilla until smooth; fold in marshmallow creme. Cut apples vertically into thin slices.

In a small bowl, combine lemon juice and water; toss apples in lemon juice mixture. Drain. Using Halloween cutters, cut out the center of each slice. Serve apple slices and cutouts with dip. **yield: 2 cups.**

easy party bruschetta

1-1/2 cups chopped seeded tomatoes
2/3 cup finely chopped red onion
2 tablespoons minced seeded jalapeno pepper
2 garlic cloves, minced
1/2 teaspoon dried basil
1/4 teaspoon salt
1/4 teaspoon coarsely ground pepper
2 tablespoons olive oil
1 tablespoon cider vinegar
1 tablespoon red wine vinegar
3 dashes hot pepper sauce
1 loaf (8 ounces) French bread, cut into 1/4-inch slices
2 tablespoons grated Parmesan cheese

Del Mason
Martensville,
Saskatchewan
This colorful bruschetta packs plenty of fresh flavor and a hint of heat from the jalapeno peppers. It is perfect for a casual summer buffet when tomatoes are at their best.

In a small bowl, combine the first seven ingredients. In another bowl, whisk the oil, vinegars and pepper sauce; stir into tomato mixture.

Place bread slices on an ungreased baking sheet. Broil 3-4 in. from the heat for 1-2 minutes or until golden brown. With a slotted spoon, top each slice with tomato mixture. Sprinkle with cheese. **yield: 2-1/2 dozen.**

editor's note: When cutting hot peppers, disposable gloves are recommended. Avoid touching your face.

cowboy beef dip

- 1 pound ground beef
- 4 tablespoons chopped onion, *divided*
- 3 tablespoons chopped sweet red pepper, *divided*
- 2 tablespoons chopped green pepper, *divided*
- 1 can (10-3/4 ounces) condensed nacho cheese soup, undiluted
- 1/2 cup salsa
- 4 tablespoons sliced ripe olives, *divided*
- 4 tablespoons sliced pimiento-stuffed olives, *divided*
- 2 tablespoons chopped green chilies
- 1 teaspoon chopped seeded jalapeno pepper
- 1/4 teaspoon dried oregano
- 1/4 teaspoon pepper
- 1/4 cup shredded cheddar cheese
- 2 tablespoons sour cream
- 2 to 3 teaspoons minced fresh parsley

Tortilla chips

Jessica Klym
Killdeer, North Dakota
A group of us in a foods class developed this recipe for the North Dakota State Beef Bash Competition. We won the contest, and now my family requests this dip for all our special gatherings!

In a large skillet, cook the beef, 3 tablespoons onion, 2 tablespoons red pepper and 1 tablespoon green pepper over medium heat until meat is no longer pink; drain. Stir in the soup, salsa, 3 tablespoons ripe olives, 3 tablespoons pimiento-stuffed olives, chilies, jalapeno, oregano and pepper. Bring to a boil. Reduce heat; simmer, uncovered, for 5 minutes.

Transfer to a serving dish. Top with the cheese, sour cream and parsley; sprinkle with the remaining onion, peppers and olives. Serve with tortilla chips. **yield: 3 cups.**

editor's note: When cutting hot peppers, disposable gloves are recommended. Avoid touching your face.

fruity iced tea

Beverly Toomey
Honolulu, Hawaii
I like to garnish glasses of this iced tea with some wedges of our sweet Hawaiian pineapple. It is oh-so refreshing!

- 1 gallon water
- 24 individual tea bags
- 6 fresh mint sprigs
- 3-1/3 cups sugar
- 3 cups unsweetened pineapple juice
- 1 cup lemon juice

In a Dutch oven, bring water to boil. Remove from the heat. Add tea bags; steep for 10 minutes. Discard tea bags; add mint. Steep 5 minutes longer; discard mint.

Stir in the sugar, pineapple juice and lemon juice until sugar is dissolved. Cover and refrigerate until chilled. **yield: 4 quarts.**

picnic stuffed eggs

12	hard-cooked eggs
1/2	cup mayonnaise
1/4	cup sweet pickle relish, drained
1	tablespoon honey mustard
1	teaspoon garlic salt
1/2	teaspoon Worcestershire sauce
1/4	teaspoon pepper

Fresh parsley sprigs, optional

Slice eggs in half lengthwise; remove yolks and set whites aside. In a small bowl, mash yolks with a fork. Add the mayonnaise, pickle relish, mustard, garlic salt, Worcestershire sauce and the pepper; mix well.

Stuff or pipe into the egg whites. Refrigerate until serving. Garnish with parsley if desired. **yield: 2 dozen.**

Rebecca Register
Tallahassee, Florida
Stuffed eggs are a Southern favorite, and this version is one of my original recipes. My dad loves the tasty creation.

Susan Seymour
Valatie, New York
Want a change from spicy buffalo sauce...then try these wings. They have a good chance of becoming your new all-time favorite!

honey-mustard chicken wings

4	pounds whole chicken wings
1/2	cup spicy brown mustard
1/2	cup honey
1/4	cup butter, cubed
2	tablespoons lemon juice
1/4	teaspoon ground turmeric

Line two 15-in. x 10-in. x 1-in. baking pans with foil; grease the foil. Cut chicken wings into three sections; discard wing tips. Place wings in prepared pans.

In a small saucepan, combine the mustard, honey, butter, lemon juice and turmeric. Bring to a boil. Pour over chicken wings; turn to coat.

Bake at 400° for 1 to 1-1/4 hours or until chicken juices run clear and glaze is set, turning once. **yield: about 3 dozen.**

spicy crab dip

1/3	cup mayonnaise
2	tablespoons dried minced onion
2	tablespoons lemon juice
2	tablespoons white wine *or* white grape juice
1	tablespoon minced garlic
1/2	teaspoon cayenne pepper, optional
1/2	teaspoon hot pepper sauce, optional
2	packages (8 ounces *each*) cream cheese, cubed
1	pound imitation crabmeat, chopped

Assorted crackers *or* fresh vegetables

In a food processor, combine the first eight ingredients. Cover and process until smooth. Transfer to a large microwave-safe bowl. Stir in crab; mix well.

Cover and microwave on high for 2-3 minutes or until bubbly. Serve warm with crackers or vegetables. **yield: 4 cups.**

Carol Forcum
Marion, Illinois
With cayenne pepper and hot sauce, this delicious dip doubles up on the heat.

editor's note: This recipe was tested in a 1,100-watt microwave.

saucy asian meatballs

2	garlic cloves, minced
1/2	teaspoon ground ginger
1	teaspoon plus 1/4 cup reduced-sodium soy sauce, *divided*
1	pound lean ground turkey
1/4	cup rice vinegar
1/4	cup tomato paste
2	tablespoons molasses
1	teaspoon hot pepper sauce

Lisa Varner
Charleston, South Carolina
This meatball recipe originally called for beef and pork and a different combination of ingredients. I used ground turkey and altered the herbs for a healthy dish.

In a large bowl, combine the garlic, ginger and 1 teaspoon soy sauce. Crumble the turkey over mixture and mix well. Shape into 1-in. balls.

Place in a 13-in. x 9-in. baking dish coated with cooking spray. Bake, uncovered, at 350° for 20-25 minutes or until meat is no longer pink.

In a large saucepan, combine the vinegar, tomato paste, molasses, pepper sauce and remaining soy sauce. Cook and stir over medium heat for 3-5 minutes. Carefully add the meatballs; heat through. **yield: 3 dozen.**

honey-tangerine chicken skewers

Lily Julow
Gainesville, Florida
I created these skewers one day when I was trying to think of something new to do with chicken. The bite-size pieces are fabulous for parties.

2 pounds boneless skinless chicken breasts, cut into 1-inch cubes
1/4 teaspoon salt
1/4 teaspoon pepper
1/2 cup tangerine juice
1/4 cup butter, melted
1/4 cup honey
4 teaspoons dried oregano
4 teaspoons ground cumin
2 to 4 teaspoons hot pepper sauce
2 tablespoons canola oil

Sprinkle chicken with salt and pepper. In a large bowl, combine the tangerine juice, butter, honey, oregano, cumin and hot pepper sauce. Add chicken and toss to coat.

Thread chicken onto 16 metal or soaked wooden appetizer skewers. In a large skillet, cook skewers in oil in batches over medium-high heat for 4-5 minutes or until chicken is no longer pink. **yield: 16 servings.**

apple citrus cider

8 cups unsweetened apple juice
3/4 cup pineapple juice concentrate
3 tablespoons sugar
1 medium lemon, thinly sliced
3 cinnamon sticks (3 inches)
6 whole allspice
6 whole cloves
4 cups lemon-lime soda

In a large saucepan, combine the apple juice, pineapple juice concentrate, sugar and lemon slices. Place the cinnamon sticks, allspice and cloves on a double thickness of cheesecloth; bring up corners of cloth and tie with kitchen string to form a bag. Add to pan.

Bring to a boil over medium heat. Reduce heat; simmer, uncovered, for 10-15 minutes. Discard spice bag. Stir in lemon-lime soda; cook for 4-6 minutes or until heated through (do not boil). **yield: 12 servings (3 quarts).**

Patricia Aurand
Findlay, Ohio
My comforting cider with a yummy twist of pineapple and citrus is perfect for large events. The tangy treat is sure to warm hands of all sizes, big or little.

lemon-lime punch

- 2 quarts water
- 2 cups sugar
- 2 envelopes unsweetened lemon-lime soft drink mix
- 1 can (46 ounces) unsweetened pineapple juice
- 1 liter ginger ale, chilled
- 1 quart lime sherbet

In a punch bowl, combine the water, sugar and soft drink mix; stir until dissolved. Stir in pineapple juice. Refrigerate until chilled. Just before serving, stir in ginger ale and top with scoops of sherbet. **yield: 6 quarts.**

Mary Ray
Raccoon, Kentucky
This frothy refresher topped with lime sherbet is a longtime family favorite and the best punch I've ever had. It's fast and festive and easy to mix up for a variety of occasions.

tangy marinated mushrooms

- 1 pound small fresh mushrooms
- 1 small onion, thinly sliced
- 1/3 cup white wine vinegar
- 1/3 cup canola oil
- 1 teaspoon salt
- 1 teaspoon ground mustard

In a large saucepan, combine all ingredients. Bring to a boil over medium-high heat. Cook, uncovered, for 6 minutes, stirring once. Cool to room temperature. Transfer to a large bowl; cover and refrigerate overnight. **yield: 3 cups.**

Mark Curry
Buena Vista, Colorado
Add these flavorful mushrooms to an antipasto platter, toss in a salad or just serve the bites by themselves.

breakfast
buffets

hash brown
egg brunch
page 35

Mary Bilyeu, Ann Arbor, Michigan
This is ridiculously easy to make and has lots of healthy ingredients. It's a great way to start your day and keep you going. With clever packaging, it makes a nice bake sale item.

good-morning granola

4	cups old-fashioned oats
1/2	cup toasted wheat germ
1/2	cup sliced almonds
2	teaspoons ground cinnamon
1/8	teaspoon salt
1/2	cup orange juice
1/2	cup honey
2	teaspoons canola oil
1	teaspoon vanilla extract
1	cup dried cherries
1	cup dried cranberries

Reduced-fat plain yogurt, optional

In a large bowl, combine the first five ingredients; set aside. In a small saucepan, combine the orange juice, honey and oil. Bring to a boil, stirring constantly. Remove from the heat; stir in vanilla. Pour over oat mixture and mix well.

Transfer to a 15-in. x 10-in. x 1-in. baking pan coated with cooking spray. Bake at 350° for 20-25 minutes or until golden brown, stirring every 10 minutes. Cool completely on a wire rack.

Stir in dried fruits. Store in an airtight container. Serve with yogurt if desired. **yield: 7-1/2 cups.**

easy add-on

Try adding flaxseed or mini chocolate chips to this recipe. Or, consider raisins instead of the dried cranberries and cherries. Sprinkle a little on your morning yogurt or cereal, or pack it as a snack.

hawaiian fruit salad

3-1/2 cups cubed fresh pineapple
3 cups honeydew balls
1-1/2 cups cantaloupe balls
1 medium mango, peeled and cubed
1 cup green grapes
1 cup halved fresh strawberries
1 kiwifruit, peeled, quartered and sliced
BANANA DRESSING:
2 small bananas, cut into 1-inch pieces
1 cup (8 ounces) reduced-fat sour cream
1/4 cup packed brown sugar
1-1/2 teaspoons lemon juice

In a large bowl, combine the first seven ingredients. In a food processor, combine the bananas, sour cream, brown sugar and lemon juice. Cover and process until smooth. Serve with fruit. **yield: 14 servings.**

Pat Habiger
Spearville, Kansas
This light, colorful salad easily jazzes up a buffet table. The banana dressing really adds a unique touch. It's great served with grilled items, too. Use a little extra sour cream for an extra-pretty presentation.

Pat Waymire
Yellow Springs, Ohio
These tasty morsels are perfect with almost any egg dish or as finger foods that party guests can just pop into their mouths. Try them as an accompaniment to fondue.

sausage bacon bites

3/4 pound sliced bacon
2 packages (8 ounces *each*) brown-and-serve sausage links
1/2 cup plus 2 tablespoons packed brown sugar, *divided*

Cut bacon strips widthwise in half; cut sausage links in half. Wrap a piece of bacon around each piece of sausage. Place 1/2 cup brown sugar in a shallow bowl; roll sausages in sugar. Secure each with a toothpick. Place in a foil-lined 15-in. x 10-in. x 1-in. baking pan. Cover and refrigerate for 4 hours or overnight.

Sprinkle with 1 tablespoon brown sugar. Bake at 350° for 35-40 minutes or until bacon is crisp, turning once. Sprinkle with remaining brown sugar. **yield: about 3-1/2 dozen.**

raspberry-rhubarb coffee cake

1	cup sugar
1/3	cup cornstarch
3	cups chopped fresh *or* frozen rhubarb
1	cup fresh *or* frozen raspberries, mashed
2	teaspoons lemon juice

BATTER:

3/4	cup butter-flavored shortening
1-1/2	cups sugar
3	eggs
3	cups all-purpose flour
1-1/2	teaspoons baking powder
3/4	teaspoon baking soda
1-1/2	cups (12 ounces) sour cream

TOPPING:

1/2	cup all-purpose flour
1/2	cup sugar
1/2	cup quick-cooking oats
1/2	teaspoon ground cinnamon
1/4	cup cold butter, cubed
1/2	cup flaked coconut
1/2	cup chopped walnuts

Carol Ross
Anchorage, Alaska
Sweet raspberries and tart rhubarb are great partners in this classic coffee cake. For a mid-morning snack, I enjoy a piece alongside a glass of milk.

In a large saucepan, combine sugar and cornstarch; stir in rhubarb and raspberries. Bring to a boil over medium heat; cook for 2 minutes or until thickened, stirring constantly. Remove from the heat. Stir in lemon juice. Cool slightly.

In a large bowl, cream shortening and sugar until light and fluffy. Beat in eggs. Combine the flour, baking powder and baking soda; add to creamed mixture alternately with sour cream.

Spread two-thirds of the batter into a greased 13-in. x 9-in. baking dish. Top with rhubarb mixture. Drop remaining batter by tablespoonfuls over filling.

In a small bowl, combine the flour, sugar, oats and cinnamon. Cut in butter until crumbly. Stir in the coconut and walnuts. Sprinkle over the batter.

Bake at 350° for 60-65 minutes or until a toothpick inserted near the center comes out clean. Cool on a wire rack. **yield: 12 servings.**

egg scramble

1-1/2	cups diced peeled potatoes
1/2	cup chopped sweet red pepper
1/2	cup chopped green pepper
1/2	cup chopped onion
2	teaspoons canola oil, *divided*
2	cups cubed fully cooked ham
16	eggs
2/3	cup sour cream
1/2	cup milk
1	teaspoon onion salt
1/2	teaspoon garlic salt
1/4	teaspoon pepper
2	cups (8 ounces) shredded cheddar cheese, *divided*

Place potatoes in a small saucepan and cover with water. Bring to a boil. Reduce heat; cover and simmer for 10-15 minutes or until tender. Drain.

In a large skillet, saute half of the peppers and onion in 1 teaspoon oil until tender. Add half of the ham and potatoes; saute 2-3 minutes longer.

Meanwhile, in a blender, combine the eggs, sour cream, milk, onion salt, garlic salt and pepper. Cover and process until smooth. Pour half over vegetable mixture; cook and stir over medium heat until eggs are completely set. Sprinkle with 1 cup cheese. Repeat with remaining ingredients. **yield: 10 servings.**

Vicki Holloway
Joelton, Tennessee
Perfect for a special-occasion breakfast or large brunch, this easy egg scramble is warm and hearty with potatoes, ham, cheese and colorful sweet red and green peppers.

baked oatmeal

Kathy Smith
Butler, Indiana
My mom liked this recipe because it was quick and simple and made enough to fill up all seven of us hungry kids. Now I prepare it for my own family of five.

12	cups quick-cooking oats
2	cups sugar
2	cups packed brown sugar
4	teaspoons salt
2	teaspoons baking powder
4	cups milk
2	cups canola oil
8	eggs, lightly beaten

Additional milk

In a large bowl, combine the first eight ingredients. Pour into two greased 13-in. x 9-in. baking dishes. Bake, uncovered, at 350° for 30-35 minutes or until set. Serve with additional milk. **yield: 18 servings.**

breakfast burritos

- 12 bacon strips, diced
- 12 eggs, lightly beaten
- Salt and pepper to taste
- 10 flour tortillas (8 inches)
- 1-1/2 cups (6 ounces) shredded cheddar cheese
- 1/2 cup thinly sliced green onions

In a large skillet, cook bacon until crisp; remove to paper towels. Drain, reserving 1-2 tablespoons drippings. Add eggs, salt and pepper to drippings; cook and stir over medium heat until the eggs are completely set.

Spoon about 1/4 cup of egg mixture down the center of each tortilla; sprinkle with cheese, onions and reserved bacon. Fold bottom and sides of each tortilla over filling. Wrap each in waxed paper and aluminum foil. Freeze for up to 1 month.

To use frozen burritos: Remove foil. Place waxed paper-wrapped burritos on a microwave-safe plate. Microwave at 60% power for 1 to 1-1/2 minutes or until heated through. Let stand for 20 seconds. **yield: 10 burritos.**

editor's note: This recipe was tested in a 1,100-watt microwave.

Audra Niederman
Aberdeen, South Dakota
Here is our favorite brunch contribution. Try it with sausage instead of bacon.

Floyce Thomas-Larson
Silver Spring, Maryland
When the grandchildren came to visit, my mother made them this version of her Heartland fried cakes. They gobbled up every bit.

orlando orange fritters

- 2 cups all-purpose flour
- 1/2 cup sugar
- 2 teaspoons baking powder
- 1/2 teaspoon salt
- 2 eggs
- 1/2 cup orange juice
- 2 tablespoons butter, melted
- 1 tablespoon grated orange peel
- Oil for deep-fat frying
- Confectioners' sugar

In a small bowl, combine the flour, sugar, baking powder and salt. Whisk the eggs, orange juice, butter and orange peel; stir into dry ingredients just until moistened.

In an electric skillet or deep-fat fryer, heat oil to 375°. Drop batter by rounded tablespoonfuls, a few at a time, into hot oil. Fry until golden brown, about 1-1/2 minutes on each side. Drain on paper towels. Dust warm fritters with confectioners' sugar. **yield: 20 fritters.**

raspberry-filled poppy seed muffins

2-1/4 cups all-purpose flour
1-1/4 cups sugar
   2 teaspoons baking powder
1/4 teaspoon salt
1/8 teaspoon baking soda
   3 eggs
1/2 cup canola oil
1/2 cup buttermilk
3/4 cup chopped pecans
   2 tablespoons grated lemon peel
   2 teaspoons poppy seeds
   3 tablespoons seedless raspberry preserves

GLAZE:
3/4 cup confectioners' sugar
1/4 cup lemon juice

In a large bowl, combine the flour, sugar, baking powder, salt and baking soda. In another bowl, whisk the eggs, oil and buttermilk. Stir into dry ingredients just until moistened. Fold in the pecans, lemon peel and poppy seeds.

Fill greased or paper-lined muffin cups with a rounded tablespoonful of batter. Drop 1/2 teaspoon of preserves in the center of each; top with remaining batter.

Bake at 350° for 15-20 minutes or until a toothpick inserted near the center comes out clean.

Combine glaze ingredients. Poke holes in warm muffins; drizzle with glaze. Cool for 5 minutes before removing from pans to wire racks. Serve warm. **yield: 1-1/2 dozen.**

Carolyn Schmeling
Brookfield, Wisconsin
Each bite of these golden muffins is packed with poppy seeds, lemon flavor and raspberry preserves. They're great at coffee get-togethers.

buttermilk basics

For each cup of buttermilk a recipe calls for, you can use 1 tablespoon of white vinegar or lemon juice plus enough milk to measure 1 cup. Stir, then let the mixture stand 5 minutes before using.

banana-pecan sweet rolls

4-3/4 to 5 cups all-purpose flour
1/4 cup sugar
2 packages (1/4 ounce *each*) active dry yeast
1 teaspoon salt
1 cup milk
1/4 cup butter, cubed
1 cup mashed ripe bananas (about 3 medium)
1 egg
1 teaspoon vanilla extract

FILLING:
3 tablespoons butter, melted
1/2 cup chopped pecans
1/4 cup sugar
1/2 teaspoon ground allspice

ICING:
2 cups confectioners' sugar
1 tablespoon lemon juice
1 to 2 tablespoons milk

Dorothy Pritchett
Wills Point, Texas
Banana adds fun flavor to standard sweet rolls in this recipe. I've been known to serve these mouthwatering rolls for dessert, too!

In a large bowl, combine 2 cups flour, sugar, yeast and salt. In a small saucepan, heat milk and butter to 120°-130°. Add to dry ingredients; beat just until moistened. Add the bananas, egg and vanilla; beat until smooth. Stir in enough remaining flour to form a soft dough (dough will be sticky).

Turn onto a floured surface; knead until smooth and elastic, about 6-8 minutes. Place in a greased bowl, turning once to grease top. Cover and let rise in a warm place until doubled, about 1 hour.

Punch dough down. Turn onto a lightly floured surface; divide in half. Roll each portion into a 16-in. x 6-in. rectangle. Brush with butter to within 1/2 in. of edges. Combine the pecans, sugar and allspice; sprinkle over dough to within 1/2 in. of edges.

Roll up jelly-roll style, starting with a long side; pinch seam to seal. Cut each into 16 slices. Place cut side up on greased baking sheets. Cover and let rise in a warm place until doubled, about 30 minutes.

Bake at 400° for 12-15 minutes or until golden brown. Remove from pans to wire racks.

In a small bowl, combine the confectioners' sugar, lemon juice and enough milk to achieve desired consistency. Drizzle over warm rolls. Serve warm. **yield: 32 rolls.**

Barb Keith, Eau Claire, Wisconsin
Here's a recipe that combines slow cooking with brunch. It's a wonderful treat to take to a covered dish event or a morning get-together with friends.

hash brown egg brunch

1	package (32 ounces) frozen shredded hash brown potatoes
1	pound bacon strips, cooked and crumbled
1	medium onion, chopped
1	medium green pepper, chopped
1-1/2	cups (6 ounces) shredded cheddar cheese
12	eggs
1	cup whole milk
1/2	teaspoon salt
1/2	teaspoon pepper

Layer a third of the potatoes, bacon, onion, green pepper and cheese in a 5-qt. slow cooker coated with cooking spray. Repeat layers twice. In a large bowl, whisk the eggs, milk, salt and pepper; pour over top.

Cover and cook on high for 30 minutes. Reduce heat to low; cook for 3-1/2 to 4 hours or until a thermometer reads 160°. **yield: 10 servings.**

safety first

When serving on a buffet, try to keep hot egg dishes hot, and cold egg dishes cold. Casseroles and other dishes containing eggs should be cooked to 160°. Use a food thermometer to be sure.

cheese sausage strata

- 1-1/2 pounds bulk pork sausage
- 9 eggs, lightly beaten
- 3 cups milk
- 9 slices bread, cubed
- 1-1/2 cups (6 ounces) shredded cheddar cheese
- 1/2 pound sliced bacon, cooked and crumbled
- 1-1/2 teaspoons ground mustard

In a large skillet, cook sausage over medium heat until no longer pink; drain. Add the eggs, milk, bread, cheese, bacon and mustard. Transfer to a greased shallow 3-qt. baking dish. Cover and refrigerate overnight.

Remove from the refrigerator 30 minutes before baking. Cover and bake at 350° for 60-65 minutes or until a knife inserted near the center comes out clean. Let stand for 5 minutes before serving. **yield: 12 servings.**

Teresa Marchese
New Berlin, Wisconsin
Sausage provides lots of pizzazz in this hearty morning casserole. It's a great addition to a brunch buffet because it's assembled the night before to cut down on last-minute fuss.

Diane Halferty
Corpus Christi, Texas
Topped with fresh strawberries and chocolate whipped cream, these tender breakfast treats are rich and luscious enough to be served as dessert. They're sure to delight kids of all ages at large get-togethers.

chocolate pecan waffles

- 3/4 cup semisweet chocolate chips
- 3/4 cup butter, cubed
- 2 cups all-purpose flour
- 1/2 cup sugar
- 3 teaspoons baking powder
- 3/4 teaspoon salt
- 3 eggs
- 1-1/2 cups milk
- 3 teaspoons vanilla extract
- 1/2 cup chopped pecans, toasted

Chocolate whipped cream in a can and sliced fresh strawberries, optional

In a microwave, melt chocolate chips and butter; stir until smooth. Cool to room temperature.

In a large bowl, combine the flour, sugar, baking powder and salt. In another bowl, whisk the eggs, milk and vanilla; stir into dry ingredients until smooth. Stir in pecans and chocolate mixture (batter will be thick).

Bake in a preheated waffle iron according to manufacturer's directions until golden brown. Garnish with whipped cream and strawberries if desired. **yield: 20 waffles.**

sage breakfast patties

- 2 teaspoons rubbed sage
- 2 teaspoons minced chives
- 3/4 teaspoon salt
- 3/4 teaspoon white pepper
- 1/4 teaspoon onion powder
- 1/4 teaspoon chili powder
- 1/8 teaspoon dried thyme
- 1 pound ground turkey
- 1/2 pound ground pork

In a large bowl, combine the first seven ingredients. Crumble turkey and pork over mixture and mix well.

Shape into eighteen 2-in. patties. In a large skillet, cook patties over medium heat for 3-4 minutes on each side or until meat thermometer reads 165° and juices run clear. Drain on paper towels. **yield: 1-1/2 dozen.**

Laura McDowell
Lake Villa, Illinois
You'll want to skip store-bought breakfast patties when you try this simple recipe. It combines ground turkey and pork with sage and other seasonings for terrific flavor.

Jan Mead
Milford, Connecticut
These bite-size quiches are loaded with sausage and cheese, plus their crescent roll base makes preparation a snap. You can serve the cute, savory bites at any potluck gathering.

mini sausage quiches

- 1/2 pound bulk hot Italian sausage
- 2 tablespoons dried minced onion
- 2 tablespoons minced chives
- 1 tube (8 ounces) refrigerated crescent rolls
- 4 eggs, lightly beaten
- 2 cups (8 ounces) shredded Swiss cheese
- 1 cup (8 ounces) 4% cottage cheese
- 1/3 cup grated Parmesan cheese

Paprika

In a large skillet, brown sausage and onion over medium heat for 4-5 minutes or until meat is no longer pink; drain. Stir in chives.

On a lightly floured surface, unroll crescent dough into one long rectangle; seal seams and perforations. Cut into 48 pieces. Press onto the bottom and up the sides of greased miniature muffin cups.

Fill each with about 2 teaspoons of sausage mixture. In a large bowl, combine the eggs and cheeses. Spoon 2 teaspoonfuls over sausage mixture. Sprinkle with paprika.

Bake at 375° for 20-25 minutes or until a knife inserted in the center comes out clear. Cool for 5 minutes before removing from pans to wire racks. Serve warm. Refrigerate leftovers. **yield: 4 dozen.**

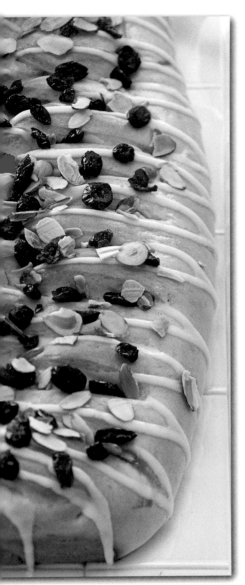

festive fruit ladder

1	package (1/4 ounce) active dry yeast
1	cup warm fat-free milk (110° to 115°)
1/2	cup sugar
2	tablespoons butter, softened
1	egg
1/2	teaspoon salt
3-1/2	to 4 cups all-purpose flour

FILLING:

1/2	cup sugar
2	tablespoons plus 2 teaspoons cornstarch
3/4	teaspoon ground cinnamon
2/3	cup apple cider *or* unsweetened apple juice
4	cups thinly sliced peeled tart apples
2/3	cup dried cranberries
1	egg
1	tablespoon water

ICING:

1	cup confectioners' sugar
4	teaspoons water
1/2	teaspoon almond extract
1/4	cup dried cranberries
2	tablespoons sliced almonds, toasted

In a large bowl, dissolve yeast in warm milk. Add the sugar, butter, egg, salt and 3 cups flour. Beat on medium speed for 2 minutes. Stir in enough remaining flour to form a soft dough.

Turn onto a lightly floured surface; knead until smooth and elastic, about 6-8 minutes. Place in a large bowl coated with cooking spray, turning once to coat the top. Cover and let rise in a warm place until doubled, about 45 minutes.

In a large saucepan, combine the sugar, cornstarch, cinnamon and cider. Bring to a boil; cook and stir for 1 minute or until thickened. Stir in apples; cook 5-10 minutes longer or until crisp-tender. Remove from the heat; stir in cranberries. Cool to room temperature.

Punch dough down; roll into a 15-in. x 12-in. rectangle. Place on a baking sheet coated with cooking spray. Spread filling lengthwise down center of dough. On each long side, cut 1-in.-wide strips 3 in. into center. Fold strips at an angle across filling; seal ends. Cover and let rise until doubled.

Beat egg and water; brush over dough. Bake at 350° for 25-30 minutes or until golden brown. Cool on a wire rack. Combine the confectioners' sugar, water and extract; drizzle over the loaf. Sprinkle top of loaf with the cranberries and the almonds. **yield: 1 loaf (24 slices).**

Cathrine Emerson
Arlington, Washington
Festive is the ideal word used to describe this heavenly delight. I am also going to try it with apricots and cinnamon or even some of my home canned plums!

almond berry muffins

1-1/4 cups sliced almonds, *divided*
1 egg white, lightly beaten
1-1/2 cups sugar, *divided*
1/4 cup shortening
1/4 cup butter, softened
2 eggs
1 teaspoon vanilla extract
1/2 teaspoon almond extract
2 cups all-purpose flour
1 teaspoon baking powder
1/2 teaspoon salt
1/4 teaspoon baking soda
3/4 cup buttermilk
1-1/4 cups fresh strawberries, chopped

In a large bowl, combine 1 cup almonds and the egg white. Add 1/2 cup sugar; toss to coat. Spoon into a greased 15-in. x 10-in. x 1-in. baking pan. Bake at 350° for 9-11 minutes or until golden brown, stirring occasionally.

In a large bowl, cream the shortening, butter and remaining sugar until light and fluffy. Add eggs, one at a time, beating well after each addition. Beat in extracts. Combine the flour, baking powder, salt and baking soda; add to the creamed mixture alternately with buttermilk. Fold in the strawberries and remaining almonds.

Fill greased or paper-lined muffin cups two-thirds full. Sprinkle with sugared almonds. Bake at 350° for 20-25 minutes or until a toothpick inserted near the center comes out clean. Cool for 5 minutes before removing from pans to wire racks. Serve warm. **yield: 1-1/2 dozen.**

Deborah Feinberg
East Setauket, New York
I made these moist muffins to take to the office, and they were a hit. Sugared almonds give them a crunchy topping. When strawberries aren't in season, I use individual frozen cut strawberries directly from the freezer.

hot fruit compote

Joyce Moynihan
Lakeville, Minnesota
This sweet and colorful fruit compote is perfect with an egg casserole at a holiday brunch. It can bake right alongside the eggs, so everything is conveniently done at the same time.

2 cans (15-1/4 ounces *each*) sliced pears, drained
1 can (29 ounces) sliced peaches, drained
1 can (20 ounces) unsweetened pineapple chunks, drained
1 package (20 ounces) pitted dried plums
1 jar (16 ounces) unsweetened applesauce
1 can (21 ounces) cherry pie filling
1/4 cup packed brown sugar

In a large bowl, combine the first five ingredients. Pour into a 13-in. x 9-in. baking dish coated with cooking spray. Spread pie filling over fruit mixture; sprinkle with brown sugar.

Cover and bake at 350° for 40-45 minutes or until bubbly. Serve warm. **yield: 20 servings.**

mocha-cinnamon coffee cake

3/4	cup chopped walnuts
1/3	cup sugar
1	tablespoon baking cocoa
1	teaspoon instant coffee granules
1	teaspoon ground cinnamon

BATTER:

3/4	cup butter, softened
1-1/2	cups sugar
4	eggs
1	teaspoon vanilla extract
2-1/4	cups all-purpose flour
2	teaspoons baking powder
1	teaspoon baking soda
1-1/2	cups (12 ounces) sour cream
1/2	cup semisweet chocolate chips

In a small bowl, combine the first five ingredients; set aside. In a large bowl, cream butter and sugar until light and fluffy. Add eggs, one at a time, beating well after each addition. Beat in vanilla. Combine the flour, baking powder and baking soda; add to creamed mixture alternately with sour cream just until combined. Stir in chocolate chips.

Pour a third of the batter into a greased 10-in. fluted tube pan. Sprinkle with half of the walnut mixture; repeat layers. Top with remaining batter.

Bake at 350° for 40-45 minutes or until a toothpick inserted near the center comes out clean. Cool for 10 minutes before removing to a wire rack. **yield: 12-16 servings.**

Bette Mintz
Glendale, California
This tender coffee cake is so yummy and sweet, it doesn't even need frosting.

strawberry syrup

1	cup sugar
1	cup water
1-1/2	cups mashed unsweetened strawberries

In a saucepan, bring sugar and water to a boil. Gradually add strawberries; return to a boil. Reduce heat; simmer, uncovered, for 10 minutes, stirring occasionally. Serve over pancakes, waffles or ice cream. **yield: about 2-1/2 cups.**

Nancy Dunaway
Springfield, Illinois
This recipe is a spin-off of my dad's homemade syrup. Our son requests it with fluffy pancakes whenever he and his family come to visit.

Roger Hawley, Valley Park, Missouri
*This bread bakes up soft and chewy with a hint of sweetness. It's great to
give as a gift or to accompany a meal with lots of friends.*

ezekiel bread

      3   packages (1/4 ounce *each*) active dry yeast
      5   cups warm water (110° to 115°), *divided*
      1   tablespoon plus 2/3 cup honey, *divided*
    2/3   cup canola oil
    1/2   cup sugar
      2   teaspoons salt
      4   cups whole wheat flour
      1   cup toasted wheat germ
      6   to 8 cups bread flour

In a large bowl, dissolve yeast in 3/4 cup warm water and 1
tablespoon honey. Add the remaining water and honey, oil, sugar,
salt, whole wheat flour, wheat germ and 3 cups bread flour. Beat
until smooth. Stir in enough remaining bread flour to form a soft
dough (dough will be sticky).

Turn onto a lightly floured surface; knead until smooth and elastic,
about 6-8 minutes. Place in a bowl coated with cooking spray,
turning once to coat the top. Cover and let rise in a warm place
until doubled, about 1 hour.

Punch dough down. Shape into four loaves. Place in 9-in. x 5-in.
loaf pans coated with cooking spray. Cover and let rise until nearly
doubled, about 30 minutes.

Bake at 350° for 30-35 minutes or until golden brown. Remove
from pans to wire racks to cool. **yield: 4 loaves (16 slices each).**

save money

You may just stop
buying bread at the
store once you begin
making this recipe! It
produces four lovely
loaves and freezes very
well. Simply stash the
extras in the freezer
until you need them.

Michelle Sheldon, Edmond, Oklahoma
My mother-in-law shared the recipe for these golden waffles with me. Our daughter,
Kayla, loves them. Just add a few ingredients to the mix and you'll be enjoying their
homemade whole-grain flavor in minutes.

whole-grain waffle mix

    4   cups whole wheat flour
    2   cups all-purpose flour
    1   cup toasted wheat germ
    1   cup toasted oat bran
    1   cup buttermilk blend powder
    3   tablespoons baking powder
    2   teaspoons baking soda
    1   teaspoon salt
ADDITIONAL INGREDIENTS:
    2   eggs
    1   cup water
    2   tablespoons canola oil
    2   tablespoons honey

In a large bowl, combine the first eight ingredients. Store in an airtight
container in the refrigerator for up to 6 months. **yield: 8-1/2 cups mix (about
4 batches).**

To prepare waffles: Place 2 cups waffle mix in a bowl. Combine the eggs,
water, oil and honey; stir into waffle mix just until moistened. Bake in a
preheated waffle iron according to manufacturer's directions until golden
brown. **yield: 5 waffles (about 6 inches) per batch.**

editor's note: Look for buttermilk blend powder next to the powdered milk
in your grocery store.

pennsylvania dutch potato doughnuts

2-1/2 cups mashed potatoes *or* riced potatoes (without added milk, butter *or* seasonings)
   1 cup milk
   3 eggs, lightly beaten
   2 tablespoons butter, melted
   2 cups sugar
   2 tablespoons baking powder
   5 cups all-purpose flour
   Oil for deep-fat frying

GLAZE:
   2 cups confectioners' sugar
   5 tablespoons half-and-half cream
   1/2 teaspoon vanilla extract

In a large bowl, combine the potatoes, milk, eggs and butter. Combine the sugar, baking powder and 2 cups flour; stir into potato mixture. Add enough remaining flour to form a soft dough. Divide dough in half.

Turn onto a lightly floured surface; roll each half to 1/2-in. thickness. Cut with a 2-3/4-in. doughnut cutter.

In an electric skillet or deep-fat fryer, heat the oil to 375°. Fry doughnuts, a few at a time, until golden brown on both sides. Drain on paper towels.

In a small bowl, combine glaze ingredients until smooth; drizzle over warm doughnuts. **yield: about 4 dozen.**

Marlene Reichart
Leesport, Pennsylvania
My relatives have been making these tasty doughnuts for years. The potatoes keep them moist, and the glaze provides just the right amount of sweetness.

make ahead

If you don't have time to make baked goods for bake sales, try to devote 1 day to making a large batch in advance. Place the goods in heavy-duty resealable plastic bags and freeze for up to 2 months.

christmas fruit kabobs

- 1/2 fresh pineapple, trimmed and cut into 1-inch chunks
- 4 kiwifruit, peeled and cut into 1-inch pieces
- 3 navel oranges, peeled and sectioned
- 3 medium apples, cut into 1-inch pieces
- 3 medium firm bananas, cut into 1-inch pieces
- 1 jar (10 ounces) maraschino cherries, drained

SAUCE:
- 1 egg yolk
- 1/4 cup maple syrup *or* honey
- 2 tablespoons lemon juice
- 3/4 cup heavy whipping cream, whipped

Alternately thread fruit onto wooden skewers. Cover and refrigerate until serving.

In a small saucepan over low heat, cook and stir the egg yolk and syrup until a thermometer reads 160° and is thick enough to coat the back of a metal spoon. Remove from the heat; stir in lemon juice. Cool completely. Fold in the whipped cream. Serve with fruit for dipping. Refrigerate any leftovers. **yield: 20 kabobs (about 1 cup sauce).**

Lois Rutherford
St. Augustine, Florida
My chunky fruit skewers are always a hit at potlucks and brunches. In fact, they make great appetizers at just about any get-together. I like this particular combination, but you should feel free to use whatever fruits are in season.

monterey quiche

- 10 eggs
- 4 cups (16 ounces) shredded Monterey Jack cheese
- 2 cups (16 ounces) 4% cottage cheese
- 2 cans (4 ounces *each*) chopped green chilies
- 1/2 cup butter, melted
- 1/2 cup all-purpose flour
- 1 teaspoon baking powder

Dash salt
- 2 unbaked deep-dish pastry shells (9 inches)

In a large bowl, combine the first eight ingredients. Pour into pastry shells.

Bake at 400° for 10 minutes. Reduce heat to 350°; bake 30 minutes longer or until a knife inserted near the center comes out clean. Let stand for 10 minutes before cutting. **yield: 2 quiches (6 servings each).**

Pam Pressly
Beachwood, Ohio
Buttery quiches filled with fresh vegetables and a blend of eggs and cheese are perfect for fall events. This version relies on Monterey Jack cheese to give the dish a rich flavor.

soups & sandwiches

shredded beef
sandwiches
page 61

Trina Bigham, Fairhaven, Massachusetts
When I turned 40, I decided to live an improved lifestyle, which included cooking healthier for my family. I make this soup every week, and everyone loves it. It's nutritious, too.

colorful chicken 'n' squash soup

- 1 broiler/fryer chicken (4 pounds), cut up
- 13 cups water
- 5 pounds butternut squash, peeled and cubed (about 10 cups)
- 1 bunch kale, trimmed and chopped
- 6 medium carrots, chopped
- 2 large onions, chopped
- 3 teaspoons salt

Place chicken and water in a stockpot. Bring to a boil. Reduce heat; cover and simmer for 1 hour or until chicken is tender.

Remove chicken from broth. Strain broth and skim fat. Return broth to the pan; add the squash, kale, carrots and onions. Bring to a boil. Reduce heat; cover and simmer for 25-30 minutes or until vegetables are tender.

When chicken is cool enough to handle, remove meat from bones and cut into bite-size pieces. Discard bones and skin. Add chicken and salt to soup; heat through. **yield: 14 servings (5-1/2 quarts).**

meatball sub sandwiches

2 eggs, lightly beaten
1 cup dry bread crumbs
2 tablespoons grated Parmesan cheese
2 tablespoons finely chopped onion
1 teaspoon salt
1/2 teaspoon pepper
1/2 teaspoon garlic powder
1/4 teaspoon Italian seasoning
2 pounds ground beef
1 jar (28 ounces) spaghetti sauce
Additional Parmesan cheese, and sliced onion and green peppers, optional
12 sandwich rolls, split

In a large bowl, combine the first eight ingredients. Crumble beef over mixture and mix well. Shape into 1-in. balls. Place in a single layer in a 3-qt. microwave-safe dish.

Cover and microwave on high for 3-4 minutes. Turn meatballs; cook 3-4 minutes longer or until no longer pink. Drain. Add the spaghetti sauce.

Cover and microwave on high for 2-4 minutes or until heated through. Top with additional cheese, onion and green peppers if desired. Serve on rolls. **yield: 12 servings.**

Deena Hubler
Jasper, Indiana
Making these saucy meatballs in advance and reheating them saves me precious time when expecting company. These sandwiches are great casual fare for any get-together.

---

editor's note: This recipe was tested in a 1,100-watt microwave.

Jennifer Middlekauff
New Holland, Pennsylvania
We have used this recipe countless times for family gatherings and birthday parties. The sandwiches are so easy to make, and they taste great.

ham barbecue

2 pounds thinly sliced deli ham
1 cup water
1 cup ketchup
1/4 cup packed brown sugar
1/4 cup Worcestershire sauce
2 tablespoons white vinegar
2 teaspoons prepared mustard
12 hamburger buns, split and toasted

Place the ham in a greased 3-qt. slow cooker. In a large bowl, combine the water, ketchup, brown sugar, Worcestershire sauce, vinegar and mustard; pour over ham and stir well. Cover and cook on low for 4-5 hours or until heated through. Serve on buns. **yield: 12 servings.**

hot crab hero

- 2 cans (6 ounces *each*) crabmeat, drained, flaked and cartilage removed
- 1/2 cup mayonnaise
- 1/4 cup minced fresh parsley
- 1/4 cup sour cream
- 1 tablespoon lemon juice
- 1/2 teaspoon garlic powder
- 1/8 teaspoon salt
- 1 loaf (8 ounces) French bread
- 2 tablespoons butter, softened
- 4 slices Swiss cheese

In a large bowl, combine the first seven ingredients. Slice bread horizontally in half; spread cut sides with butter. Top with cheese; spread with crab mixture.

Place on an ungreased baking sheet. Bake at 350° for 20-25 minutes or until browned. **yield: 12-14 slices.**

Beverly Mix
Missoula, Montana
These rich sandwich slices make great appetizers, whether you're entertaining at home or taking a special dish to a carry-in dinner.

hot colby ham sandwiches

Sherry Crenshaw
Fort Worth, Texas
This yummy recipe is a favorite with friends and family. Not only are the warm specialties easy to assemble, but they smell so good when baking that no one can resist them. They're a staple at our get-togethers.

- 1/2 cup butter, melted
- 2 tablespoons prepared mustard
- 1 tablespoon dried minced onion
- 1 tablespoon poppy seeds
- 2 to 3 teaspoons sugar
- 15 dinner rolls (about 3-inch diameter), sliced
- 15 slices Colby cheese
- 15 thin slices deli ham (about 1 pound)
- 2 cups (8 ounces) shredded part-skim mozzarella cheese

In a small bowl, combine the butter, mustard, onion, poppy seeds and sugar. Place roll bottoms, cut side up, in an ungreased 15-in. x 10-in. x 1-in. baking pan. Top each with Colby cheese, ham and mozzarella. Drizzle with half of the butter mixture.

Replace roll tops. Drizzle with remaining butter mixture. Bake, uncovered, at 350° for 10-15 minutes or until cheese is melted. **yield: 15 servings.**

beefy tomato pasta soup

- 1 pound ground beef
- 2 medium green peppers, cut into 1-inch chunks
- 1 medium onion, cut into chunks
- 2 garlic cloves, minced
- 5 to 6 cups water
- 2 cans (14-1/2 ounces *each*) Italian diced tomatoes, undrained
- 1 can (6 ounces) tomato paste
- 1 tablespoon brown sugar
- 2 to 3 teaspoons Italian seasoning
- 1 teaspoon salt
- 1/4 teaspoon pepper
- 2 cups uncooked spiral pasta

Croutons, optional

In a Dutch oven, cook the beef, green peppers and onion over medium heat until meat is no longer pink. Add garlic, cook 1 minute longer. Drain. Add the water, tomatoes, tomato paste, brown sugar, Italian seasoning, salt and pepper. Bring to a boil. Add pasta.

Cook for 10-14 minutes or until the pasta is tender, stirring occasionally. Serve with croutons if desired. **yield: 10 servings (about 2-1/2 quarts).**

Nancy Rollag
Kewaskum, Wisconsin
If you're a fan of Italian fare, then you'll like this chunky combination. I really enjoy this satisfying soup, and it's easier to fix than lasagna.

homemade crunch

Save the heels from bread or leftover hot dog or hamburger buns. Cube the bread, spritz with nonstick cooking spray and season with garlic powder, parsley and basil or oregano. Bake on a baking sheet at 250° until the croutons are crisp and golden.

cheesy corn chowder

- 6 bacon strips, chopped
- 3/4 cup chopped sweet onion
- 2-1/2 cups water
- 2-1/2 cups cubed peeled potatoes
- 2 cups sliced fresh carrots
- 2 teaspoons chicken bouillon granules
- 3 cans (11 ounces *each*) gold and white corn, drained
- 1/2 teaspoon pepper
- 7 tablespoons all-purpose flour
- 5 cups 2% milk
- 3 cups (12 ounces) shredded cheddar cheese
- 1 cup cubed process cheese (Velveeta)

In a Dutch oven, cook bacon and onion over medium heat until onion is tender. Add the water, potatoes, carrots and bouillon; bring to a boil. Reduce heat; cover and simmer for 15-20 minutes or until potatoes are tender.

Stir in corn and pepper. In a large bowl, whisk flour and milk until smooth; add to soup. Bring to a boil; cook and stir for 2 minutes or until thickened. Reduce heat. Add the cheeses; cook and stir until cheeses are melted. **yield: 15 servings (3-3/4 quarts).**

Lola Comer
Marysville, Washington
I've had this chowder recipe for 30 years, and the whole family really enjoys its cheesy corn taste. It makes a big pot that's great for a crowd.

italian sausage hoagies

Craig Wachs
Racine, Wisconsin
In southeastern Wisconsin, our cuisine is influenced by both Germans and Italians who immigrated to this area. When preparing this recipe, we usually substitute German bratwurst for the Italian sausage, so we blend the two influences with delicious results.

- 10 Italian sausage links
- 2 tablespoons olive oil
- 1 jar (26 ounces) meatless spaghetti sauce
- 1/2 medium green pepper, julienned
- 1/2 medium sweet red pepper, julienned
- 1/2 cup water
- 1/4 cup grated Romano cheese
- 2 tablespoons dried oregano
- 2 tablespoons dried basil
- 2 loaves French bread (20 inches)

In a large skillet over medium-high heat, brown sausage in oil; drain. Transfer to a 5-qt. slow cooker. Add the spaghetti sauce, peppers, water, cheese, oregano and basil. Cover and cook on low for 4 hours or until sausage is no longer pink.

Slice each French bread lengthwise but not all of the way through; cut each loaf widthwise into five pieces. Fill each with sausage, peppers and sauce. **yield: 10 servings.**

Denise Davis, Porter, Maine
Honey and ground ginger are the flavor boosters behind my no-stress
sandwiches. A bottle of barbecue sauce ties it all together in a pinch.

pulled pork subs

1	small onion, finely chopped
1	boneless pork shoulder butt roast (2-1/2 pounds)
1	bottle (18 ounces) barbecue sauce
1/2	cup water
1/4	cup honey
6	garlic cloves, minced
1	teaspoon seasoned salt
1	teaspoon ground ginger
8	submarine buns, split

Place onion and roast in a 5-qt. slow cooker. In a small bowl, combine the barbecue sauce, water, honey, garlic, seasoned salt and ginger; pour over meat. Cover and cook on high for 5-6 hours or until meat is tender.

Remove meat; cool slightly. Shred meat with two forks and return to the slow cooker; heat through. Serve on buns. Cut sandwiches in half. **yield: 16 servings.**

save time & energy

One of the advantages of a slow cooker is that it uses little electricity. Keep in mind that you can save even more energy by not peeking under the lid, which also adds cooking time.

Lisa Stavropoulos, Stouffville, Ontario
Everyone enjoys these yummy burgers. The ground turkey and beef patties are moist,
hearty and seasoned to please. I came up with this recipe as a more nutritious alternative
to store-bought hamburger patties. My husband often requests them for dinner, and
they're great for big get-togethers.

garlic-onion turkey burgers

3	small onions, quartered
1	small carrot, cut into chunks
3	garlic cloves, peeled
1/2	cup dry bread crumbs
1/3	cup fat-free milk
1	egg, lightly beaten
1	teaspoon salt
1/2	teaspoon dried basil
1/2	teaspoon dried thyme
1	teaspoon Worcestershire sauce
2	pounds lean ground turkey
1	pound lean ground beef (90% lean)
12	hamburger buns, split

In a food processor, combine the onions, carrot and garlic; cover and process until finely chopped. Transfer mixture to a large bowl. Add the bread crumbs, milk, egg, salt, basil, thyme and Worcestershire sauce. Crumble turkey and beef over mixture and mix well. Shape into 12 patties.

Using long-handled tongs, moisten a paper towel with cooking oil and lightly coat the grill rack. Grill, covered, over medium-hot heat or broil 4 in. from the heat for 5-7 minutes on each side or until a meat thermometer reads 165° and juices run clear. Serve on buns. **yield: 12 servings.**

boston subs

Sue Erdos
Meriden, Connecticut
My mother has been making these wonderful sandwiches since she left her hometown of Boston many years ago. They're quick to prepare and travel well if tightly wrapped in plastic wrap. The recipe is great for parties if you use a loaf of French or Italian bread instead of the individual rolls.

- 1/2 cup mayonnaise
- 12 submarine sandwich buns, split
- 1/2 cup Italian salad dressing, *divided*
- 1/4 pound *each* thinly sliced bologna, deli ham, hard salami, pepperoni and olive loaf
- 1/4 pound thinly sliced provolone cheese
- 1 medium onion, diced
- 1 medium tomato, diced
- 1/2 cup diced dill pickles
- 1 cup shredded lettuce
- 1 teaspoon dried oregano

Spread mayonnaise on inside of buns. Brush with half of the salad dressing. Layer deli meats and cheese on bun bottoms. Top with onion, tomato, pickles and lettuce. Sprinkle with oregano and drizzle with remaining dressing. Replace bun tops. **yield: 12 servings.**

bacon-wrapped beef patties

- 1 cup (4 ounces) shredded cheddar cheese
- 2/3 cup chopped onion
- 1/4 cup ketchup
- 2 eggs, lightly beaten
- 3 tablespoons Worcestershire sauce
- 2 tablespoons grated Parmesan cheese
- 1 teaspoon seasoned salt
- 1/4 teaspoon pepper
- 2 pounds ground beef
- 10 bacon strips
- 10 hamburger buns, split, optional

In a large bowl, combine the first eight ingredients. Crumble beef over mixture and mix well. Shape into ten 3/4-in.-thick patties. Wrap each patty with a bacon strip; secure with wooden toothpicks.

Grill patties, uncovered, over medium heat for 5-6 minutes on each side or until juices run clear and a meat thermometer reads 160°. Discard toothpicks. Serve on buns if desired. **yield: 10 servings.**

Jody Bahler
Wolcott, Indiana
My whole family loves these spruced-up hamburgers all year long. Bacon flavors the meat and adds a tasty twist. These pleasing patties can also be enjoyed off the bun.

spicy pork chili

1-1/2	pounds pork tenderloin, cubed
2	large onions, diced
4	celery ribs, diced
2	tablespoons butter
6	cans (15-1/2 ounces *each*) great northern beans, rinsed and drained
4	cans (14-1/2 ounces *each*) chicken broth
2	cups water
2	jalapeno peppers, seeded and chopped
2	teaspoons chili powder
1/2	teaspoon *each* white pepper, cayenne pepper, ground cumin and pepper
2	garlic cloves, minced
1/2	teaspoon salt
1/4	teaspoon dried parsley flakes
1/4	teaspoon hot pepper sauce, optional
1	cup (4 ounces) shredded Monterey Jack cheese

Larry Laatsch
Saginaw, Michigan
This chili, loaded with white beans and cubes of pork, has plenty of bite. But if it's not spicy enough for you, top it with shredded jalapeno Jack cheese and finely diced onions.

In a Dutch oven, cook the pork, onions and celery in butter over medium heat until meat is no longer pink. Stir in the beans, broth, water, jalapenos, spices, garlic, salt, parsley and hot pepper sauce if desired. Bring to a boil. Reduce the heat; cover and simmer for 1-1/2 hours.

Uncover; simmer 30-40 minutes longer or until chili reaches desired consistency. Sprinkle with cheese. **yield: 15 servings.**

editor's note: When cutting hot peppers, disposable gloves are recommended. Avoid touching your face.

italian beef

1	beef top round roast (4 pounds)
2	cups water
2	tablespoons Italian seasoning
1	teaspoon *each* salt, dried oregano, dried basil, garlic powder, dried parsley flakes and pepper
1	bay leaf
14	French rolls (5 inches long)

Cut roast in half; place in a 5-qt. slow cooker. Combine the water and seasonings; pour over roast. Cover and cook on low for 10-12 hours or until meat is very tender. Discard bay leaf. Remove meat and shred with a fork. Skim fat from cooking juices; return meat to slow cooker. Serve on rolls. **yield: 14 servings.**

Lori Hayes
Venice, Florida
I make this beef in the slow cooker when I'm having a party so I don't have to spend the whole time in the kitchen. Try the shredded beef on a roll spread with horseradish sauce.

Teresa Dastrup, Meridian, Idaho
I came across a chowder recipe I liked several years ago and have made just enough changes to give it a unique flavor…and feed a pretty large crowd. People always go back for seconds, then ask for the recipe.

rich clam chowder

6	cups diced peeled red potatoes
3	large onions, finely chopped
6	celery ribs, finely chopped
3	cups water
6	cans (6-1/2 ounces *each*) minced clams
1-1/2	cups butter, cubed
1-1/2	cups all-purpose flour
8	cups half-and-half cream
1/4	cup red wine vinegar
2	tablespoons minced fresh parsley
3	teaspoons salt
1/4	teaspoon pepper

In a stockpot, combine the potatoes, onions, celery and water. Drain clams, reserving juice; set clams aside. Add juice to potato mixture. Bring to a boil Reduce heat; cover and simmer for 10 minutes or until potatoes are tender.

Meanwhile, in a large saucepan, melt butter over medium heat. Whisk in flour. Cook and stir for 5 minutes or until lightly browned. Gradually stir in cream. Bring to a boil; cook and stir for 2 minutes or until thickened. Gradually stir into potato mixture.

Add the vinegar, parsley, salt, pepper and clams. Cook 5-10 minutes longer or until heated through. **yield: 22 servings (1 cup each).**

Mary Tallman, Arbor Vitae, Wisconsin
You'll love this delicious vegetarian soup brimming with veggies and barley. The great news is that it's good for you, too!

vegetable barley soup

1	large sweet potato, peeled and cubed
1-1/2	cups fresh baby carrots, halved
1-1/2	cups frozen cut green beans
1-1/2	cups frozen corn
3	celery ribs, thinly sliced
1	small onion, chopped
1/2	cup chopped green pepper
2	garlic cloves, minced
6	cups water
2	cans (14-1/2 ounces *each*) vegetable broth
1	cup medium pearl barley
1	bay leaf
1-3/4	teaspoons salt
1/2	teaspoon fennel seed, crushed
1/4	teaspoon pepper
1	can (14-1/2 ounces) Italian diced tomatoes, undrained

In a 5-qt. slow cooker, combine the first eight ingredients. Stir in the water, broth, barley, bay leaf and seasonings. Cover and cook on low for 8-9 hours or until barley and vegetables are tender.

Stir in tomatoes; cover and cook on high for 10-20 minutes or until heated through. Discard bay leaf. **yield: 12 servings (about 3-1/2 quarts).**

special sandwich loaves

- 2 loaves (1 pound *each*) French bread
- 10 slices deli smoked turkey, halved
- 10 slices deli roast beef, halved
- 20 small lettuce leaves
- 10 slices Colby-Monterey Jack cheese, halved
- 10 slices cheddar cheese, halved
- 2 cups roasted sweet red peppers, drained and patted dry
- 3/4 cup mild pickled pepper rings

GARLIC-LIME MAYONNAISE:

- 1 cup mayonnaise
- 1/2 cup sour cream
- 1 teaspoon lime juice
- 1/2 teaspoon minced garlic
- 1/4 teaspoon chili powder
- 1 bottle (5 ounces) submarine sandwich dressing

Cut each loaf into 22 slices, leaving slices attached at the bottom (cut off and discard end pieces). Between every other slice of bread, place a piece of turkey and beef, a lettuce leaf, a piece of each kind of cheese, red peppers and banana peppers.

In a small bowl, whisk the mayonnaise, sour cream, lime juice, garlic and chili powder. To serve, cut completely through the bread between the plain slices. Serve with mayonnaise mixture and submarine dressing. **yield: 20 sandwiches.**

Taste of Home Test Kitchen
These satisfying sub sandwiches are a study in simplicity. Offering the seasoned mayonnaise and submarine sandwich dressing on the side makes it easy for guests to personalize their helpings and serve themselves.

seeking salad dressing

Look for bottles of submarine salad dressing in the deli section of your grocery store.

Or, use your favorite bottled Italian dressing as an easy alternative.

hickory-smoked cheeseburgers

Michelle Miller
Abbeville, South Carolina
Every time I make this recipe, my guests compliment me on how great the burgers taste. The secret is a little bit of Liquid Smoke and a few sprinkles of seasonings.

3	eggs, lightly beaten
2	tablespoons Liquid Smoke
1	medium onion, finely chopped
1/2	cup crushed saltines (about 15 crackers)
1	teaspoon salt
1/2	teaspoon seasoned salt
1/2	teaspoon seasoning blend
1/2	teaspoon pepper
3	pounds ground beef
12	slices process American cheese
12	sesame seed hamburger buns, split

Mayonnaise, lettuce leaves, tomato slices and pickle slices

In a large bowl, combine the first eight ingredients. Crumble beef over mixture and mix well. Shape into 12 patties.

Grill, covered, over medium heat for 5 minutes on each side or until a meat thermometer reads 160° and juices run clear.

Top each burger with a cheese slice. Grill 1-2 minutes longer or until the cheese begins to melt. Serve on buns with mayonnaise, lettuce, tomato and pickles. **yield: 12 servings.**

editor's note: This recipe was tested with Morton's Nature's Seasons Seasoning Blend.

reuben sandwiches

3/4	cup mayonnaise
3	tablespoons chili sauce
1	can (14 ounces) sauerkraut, rinsed and well drained
12	ounces shredded deli corned beef
2	cups (8 ounces) shredded Swiss cheese
30	slices rye bread
1/2	cup butter, softened

Thousand Island salad dressing, optional

In a large bowl, combine the mayonnaise, chili sauce, sauerkraut, corned beef and Swiss cheese. Spread over 15 slices of bread, about 1/3 cup on each; top with remaining bread. Lightly butter the outside of sandwiches. Toast on a hot griddle for 4-5 minutes on each side or until golden brown. Serve with Thousand Island dressing if desired. **yield: 15 servings.**

Kathryn Binder
Pickett, Wisconsin
My daughter shared this recipe with me. It's become a favorite of our entire family.

turkey sloppy joes

2 pounds lean ground turkey
1 medium onion, finely chopped
1 small green pepper, chopped
2 cans (8 ounces *each*) no-salt-added tomato sauce
1 cup water
2 envelopes sloppy joe mix
1 tablespoon brown sugar
10 hamburger buns, split

Lisa Ann Panzino DiNunzio
Vineland, New Jersey
Letting all the flavors combine in the slow cooker is the key to these mildly sweet sloppy joes. This recipe is sure to be a keeper, and since it calls for turkey, you can feel good about serving it to your gang.

In a large nonstick skillet coated with cooking spray, cook the turkey, onion and pepper over medium heat until meat is no longer pink; drain. Transfer to a 3-qt. slow cooker.

Stir in the tomato sauce, water, sloppy joe mix and brown sugar. Cover and cook on low for 4-5 hours or until flavors are blended. Spoon 1/2 cup onto each bun. **yield: 10 servings.**

hamburger vegetable soup

1 pound ground beef
1 medium onion, chopped
1/2 large green pepper, diced
4 garlic cloves, minced
8 cups beef broth
2 cans (14-1/2 ounces *each*) Italian stewed tomatoes
1 package (9 ounces) frozen cut green beans
1 can (8 ounces) tomato sauce
1 cup ditalini *or* other small pasta
1 tablespoon Worcestershire sauce
2 teaspoons dried oregano
1 teaspoon dried basil
1/2 teaspoon pepper

Traci Wynne
Denver, Pennsylvania
Oregano really shines in this hearty soup. It smells delicious while it's cooking and makes a great lunch or dinner. You could use lima beans instead of the green beans, too.

In a Dutch oven, cook the beef, onion and green pepper over medium heat until meat is no longer pink. Add garlic; cook 1 minute longer. Drain.

Stir in the remaining ingredients. Bring to a boil. Reduce heat; cover and simmer for 30 minutes or until vegetables and pasta are tender. **yield: 10 servings (3-3/4 quarts).**

italian wedding soup

2	eggs, lightly beaten
1/2	cup seasoned bread crumbs
1	pound ground beef
1	pound bulk Italian sausage
3	medium carrots, sliced
3	celery ribs, diced
1	large onion, chopped
4-1/2	teaspoons olive oil
3	garlic cloves, minced
4	cans (14-1/2 ounces *each*) reduced-sodium chicken broth
2	cans (14-1/2 ounces *each*) beef broth
1	package (10 ounces) frozen chopped spinach, thawed and squeezed dry
1/4	cup minced fresh basil
1	envelope onion soup mix
4-1/2	teaspoons ketchup
1/2	teaspoon dried thyme
3	bay leaves
1-1/2	cups uncooked penne pasta

Noelle Myers
Grand Forks, North Dakota
I enjoyed a similar soup for lunch at work one day and decided to re-create it at home. I love the combination of meatballs, vegetables and pasta.

In a large bowl, combine eggs and bread crumbs. Crumble beef and sausage over mixture and mix well. Shape into 3/4-in. balls.

Place meatballs on a greased rack in a foil-lined 15-in. x 10-in. x 1-in. baking pan. Bake at 350° for 15-18 minutes or until no longer pink. Meanwhile, in a Dutch oven, saute the carrots, celery and onion in oil until tender. Add garlic; cook 1 minute longer. Stir in the broth, spinach, basil, soup mix, ketchup, thyme and bay leaves.

Drain meatballs on paper towels. Bring soup to a boil; add meatballs. Reduce heat; simmer, uncovered, for 30 minutes. Add pasta; cook 13-15 minutes longer or until tender, stirring occasionally. Discard bay leaves. **yield: 10 servings (2-1/2 quarts).**

kitchen secret

To quickly chop an onion, peel and cut in half from the root to the top. Leaving root attached, place flat side down on work surface. Cut vertically through the onion, leaving the root end uncut. Cut across the onion, discarding root end.

Bunny Palmertree, Carrollton, Mississippi
I like to serve these mouthwatering sandwiches with a side of coleslaw. The homemade barbecue sauce is exceptional...and it's wonderful for dipping.

shredded beef sandwiches

1	can (10-1/2 ounces) condensed beef broth, undiluted
1	cup ketchup
1/2	cup packed brown sugar
1/2	cup lemon juice
3	tablespoons steak sauce
2	garlic cloves, minced
1	teaspoon pepper
1	teaspoon Worcestershire sauce
1	beef eye round roast (3-1/2 pounds), cut in half
1	teaspoon salt
16	sandwich buns, split

Dill pickle slices, optional

In a small bowl, whisk the first eight ingredients. Pour half of mixture into a 5-qt. slow cooker. Sprinkle beef with salt; add to slow cooker and top with remaining broth mixture.

Cover and cook on low for 10-12 hours or until meat is tender. Shred meat with two forks and return to slow cooker. Using a slotted spoon, place 1/2 cup beef mixture on each bun. Top with pickles if desired. **yield: 16 servings.**

amish chicken corn soup

12	cups water
2	pounds boneless skinless chicken breasts, cubed
1	cup chopped onion
1	cup chopped celery
1	cup shredded carrots
3	chicken bouillon cubes
2	cans (14-3/4 ounces *each*) cream-style corn
2	cups uncooked egg noodles
1/4	cup butter
1	teaspoon salt
1/4	teaspoon pepper

Beverly Hoffman
Sandy Lake, Pennsylvania
Creamed corn and butter add richness to this homey chicken noodle soup. It makes a big batch, but it freezes well for future meals…that is one reason why soups are my preferred thing to make.

In a Dutch oven, combine the water, chicken, onion, celery, carrots and bouillon. Bring to a boil. Reduce heat; simmer, uncovered, for 30 minutes or until chicken is no longer pink and the vegetables are tender.

Stir in the corn, noodles and butter; cook 10 minutes longer or until noodles are tender. Season with salt and pepper. **yield: 16 servings (about 4 quarts).**

turkey pasta soup

1	cup uncooked small pasta shells
1	pound lean ground turkey
2	medium onions, chopped
2	garlic cloves, minced
3	cans (14-1/2 ounces *each*) reduced-sodium chicken broth
2	cans (15 ounces *each*) white kidney *or* cannellini beans, rinsed and drained
2	cans (14-1/2 ounces *each*) Italian stewed tomatoes
2	teaspoons dried oregano
2	teaspoons dried basil
1	teaspoon fennel seed, crushed
1	teaspoon pepper
1/2	teaspoon salt
1/4	teaspoon crushed red pepper flakes

Marie Ewert
Richmond, Michigan
This quick soup has such a great flavor that everyone I've shared it with has added the recipe to their list of favorites. It also simmers up well in a slow cooker.

Cook pasta according to package directions. Meanwhile, in a large stockpot, cook turkey and onions over medium heat until meat is no longer pink. Add garlic; cook 1 minute longer. Drain. Stir in the broth, beans, tomatoes and seasonings. Bring to a boil. Reduce heat; simmer, uncovered, for 10 minutes.

Drain pasta and add to the soup. Cook 5 minutes longer or until heated through. **yield: 10 servings.**

sausage pepper calzones

1 pound Italian turkey sausage links, casings removed
1 cup chopped onion
3/4 cup *each* chopped green, sweet red and yellow peppers
5 teaspoons olive oil, *divided*
2 garlic cloves, minced
2 tablespoons sherry *or* chicken broth
1 teaspoon balsamic vinegar
1 teaspoon salt
1/2 teaspoon pepper
3 teaspoons minced fresh oregano, *divided*
3 teaspoons minced fresh rosemary, *divided*
2 loaves (1 pound *each*) frozen bread dough, thawed
1 can (15 ounces) pizza sauce, *divided*
3 teaspoons cornmeal

Crumble sausage into a large nonstick skillet, add the onion, peppers and 2 teaspoons oil. Cook over medium heat until meat is no longer pink. Add garlic; cook 1 minute longer. Drain.

Stir in the sherry, vinegar, salt, pepper and 1 teaspoon each oregano and rosemary; heat through.

Divide each loaf of dough into six portions. On a floured surface, roll each portion into a 6-in. circle. Brush with remaining oil; sprinkle with remaining oregano and rosemary.

Spread 1 tablespoon pizza sauce over each circle. Spoon about 1/4 cup sausage mixture on half of each circle to within 1/2 in. of edges; fold dough over the filling and seal the edges. Cut a small slit in the top.

Sprinkle cornmeal over greased baking sheets. Place calzones on baking sheets. Cover and let rise in a warm place for 30 minutes.

Bake at 400° for 12-15 minutes or until golden brown. Warm remaining pizza sauce; serve with calzones. **yield: 12 servings.**

Marion Lowery
Medford, Oregon
These tasty Italian sandwiches are chock-full of savory turkey sausage, sweet peppers and herbs, enhanced by zesty pizza sauce. Made from convenient frozen bread dough, the baked calzones should be cooled before they are packed in lunches or stored in the freezer.

Peggy Woodward, East Troy, Wisconsin
Slices of this pretty sandwich are great for any casual get-together. Add or change ingredients to your taste.

focaccia sandwich

1/3	cup mayonnaise
1	can (4-1/4 ounces) chopped ripe olives, drained
1	focaccia bread (about 12 ounces), halved lengthwise
4	romaine leaves
1/4	pound shaved deli ham
1	medium sweet red pepper, thinly sliced into rings
1/4	pound shaved deli turkey
1	large tomato, thinly sliced
1/4	pound thinly sliced hard salami
1	jar (7 ounces) roasted sweet red peppers, drained
4	to 6 slices provolone cheese

In a small bowl, combine mayonnaise and olives; spread over the bottom half of bread. Layer with remaining ingredients; replace bread top. Cut into wedges; secure with toothpicks. **yield: 24 servings.**

minestrone with italian sausage

1 pound bulk Italian sausage
1 large onion, chopped
2 large carrots, chopped
2 celery ribs, chopped
1 medium leek (white portion only), chopped
1 medium zucchini, cut into 1/2-inch pieces
1/4 pound fresh green beans, trimmed and cut into 1/2-inch pieces
3 garlic cloves, minced
6 cups beef broth
2 cans (14-1/2 ounces *each*) diced tomatoes with basil, oregano and garlic
3 cups shredded cabbage
1 teaspoon dried basil
1 teaspoon dried oregano
1/4 teaspoon pepper
1 can (15 ounces) garbanzo beans *or* chickpeas, rinsed and drained
1/2 cup uncooked small pasta shells
3 tablespoons minced fresh parsley
1/3 cup grated Parmesan cheese

In a Dutch oven, cook sausage and onion over medium heat until meat is no longer pink; drain. Stir in the carrots, celery and leek, cook for 3 minutes. Add the zucchini, green beans and garlic; cook 1 minute longer.

Stir in the broth, tomatoes, cabbage, basil, oregano and pepper. Bring to a boil. Reduce heat; cover and simmer for 45 minutes.

Return to a boil. Stir in the garbanzo beans, pasta and parsley. Cook for 6-9 minutes or until pasta is tender. Serve with cheese. **yield: 11 servings (about 3 quarts).**

Linda Reis
Salem, Oregon
I make this zippy, satisfying soup all the time, and it's my dad's favorite. The recipe makes a lot, and I have found that it freezes well and tastes just as great reheated.

sausage and kale soup

3	medium Yukon Gold *or* red potatoes, chopped
2	medium onions, chopped
2	tablespoons olive oil
1	bunch kale, trimmed and torn
4	garlic cloves, minced
1/4	teaspoon pepper
1/4	teaspoon salt
2	bay leaves
1	can (14-1/2 ounces) diced tomatoes, undrained
1	can (15 ounces) garbanzo beans *or* chickpeas, rinsed and drained
1	pound smoked kielbasa *or* Polish sausage, cut into 1/4-inch slices
1	carton (32 ounces) chicken broth

In a Dutch oven over medium-low heat, cook potatoes and onions in oil for 5 minutes, stirring occasionally. Add kale and garlic; cover and cook for 2-3 minutes or until kale is wilted.

Add the remaining ingredients. Bring to a boil. Reduce heat; cover and simmer for 9-12 minutes or until potatoes are tender. Discard bay leaves. **yield: 14 servings (3-1/2 quarts).**

Dawn Rohn
Riverton, Wyoming
This is my family's absolute favorite soup, and I can have it on the table in 30 minutes. I usually double the recipe, as the flavors blend and make the soup even better the next day.

freezer pleaser

When making Sausage and Kale Soup for a potluck, why not double the batch? It freezes well in small containers. This way, you'll have some to take to the covered-dish event, and some kept at home for last-minute dinners.

Taste of Home Test Kitchen
Folks will enjoy a change from the traditional when they spoon into this flavorful combination of tender chunks of chicken, white beans and spices.

white chicken chili

- 1 medium onion, chopped
- 1 tablespoon olive oil
- 2 cloves garlic, minced
- 4 boneless skinless chicken breast halves (4 ounces *each*), chopped
- 2 cans (14 ounces *each*) chicken broth
- 1 can (4 ounces) chopped green chilies
- 2 teaspoons ground cumin
- 2 teaspoons dried oregano
- 1-1/2 teaspoons cayenne pepper
- 3 cans (14-1/2 ounces *each*) great northern beans, drained, *divided*
- 1 cup (4 ounces) shredded Monterey Jack cheese

Chopped jalapeno pepper, optional

In a large saucepan over medium heat, cook onion in oil for 10 minutes or until tender. Add garlic; cook 1 minute longer. Add the chicken, chicken broth, green chilies, cumin, oregano and cayenne pepper; bring to a boil.

Reduce heat to low. With a potato masher, mash one can of beans until smooth. Add to saucepan. Add remaining beans to saucepan. Simmer for 20-30 minutes or until heated through.

Top each serving with cheese and jalapeno pepper if desired. **yield: 10 servings (2-1/2 quarts).**

Darlene Weise-Appleby, Creston, Ohio
Looking for a filling, meatless meal in a bowl? Ladle up this delicious soup! It's a treasured favorite with my husband, five kids and one grandchild.

mushroom barley soup

- 1 medium leek (white portion only), halved and thinly sliced
- 1 cup chopped celery
- 2 teaspoons olive oil
- 4 garlic cloves, minced
- 3/4 pound sliced fresh mushrooms
- 1-1/2 cups chopped peeled turnips
- 1-1/2 cups chopped carrots
- 4 cans (14-1/2 ounces *each*) reduced-sodium beef broth *or* vegetable broth
- 1 can (14-1/2 ounces) diced tomatoes, undrained
- 1 bay leaf
- 1/2 teaspoon salt
- 1/2 teaspoon dried thyme
- 1/4 teaspoon pepper
- 1/4 teaspoon caraway seeds
- 1 cup quick-cooking barley
- 4 cups fresh baby spinach, cut into thin strips

In a large saucepan coated with cooking spray, cook leek and celery in oil for 2 minutes. Add garlic; cook 1 minute longer. Add the mushrooms, turnips and carrots; cook 4-5 minutes longer or until mushrooms are tender.

Stir in the broth, tomatoes and seasonings. Bring to a boil. Reduce heat; cover and simmer for 10-15 minutes or until turnips are tender. Add barley; simmer 10 minutes. Stir in spinach; cook 5 minutes or until spinach and barley are tender. Discard bay leaf. **yield: 10 servings (about 3 quarts).**

ham and bean soup

- 1 pound dried navy beans
- 2 medium onions, chopped
- 2 teaspoons canola oil
- 2 celery ribs, chopped
- 10 cups water
- 4 cups cubed fully cooked ham
- 1 cup mashed potatoes (without added milk and butter)
- 1/2 cup shredded carrot
- 2 tablespoons Worcestershire sauce
- 1 teaspoon salt
- 1/2 teaspoon dried thyme
- 1/2 teaspoon pepper
- 2 bay leaves
- 1 meaty ham bone *or* 2 smoked ham hocks
- 1/4 cup minced fresh parsley

Place beans in a Dutch oven; add water to cover by 2 in. Bring to a boil; boil for 2 minutes. Remove from the heat; cover and let stand for 1 to 4 hours or until beans are softened. Drain and rinse beans, discarding liquid.

In the same pan, saute onions in oil for 2 minutes. Add celery; cook until tender. Stir in the beans, water, ham, potatoes, carrot, Worcestershire sauce, salt, thyme, pepper and bay leaves. Add ham bone. Bring to a boil. Reduce heat; cover and simmer for 1-1/4 to 1-1/2 hours or until beans are tender. Discard bay leaves.

Remove ham bone; and set aside until cool enough to handle. Remove ham from bone and cut into cubes. Discard bone. Return ham to soup. Garnish soup with parsley. **yield: 15 servings (3-3/4 quarts).**

Amanda Reed
Milford, Delaware
I learned to make this soup when we lived in Pennsylvania near several Amish families. It's a great way to use up ham and mashed potatoes. It freezes well, too.

keep parsley fresh

To keep parsley fresh, wash the bunch in warm water, shake off the excess moisture, wrap in paper towel and seal in a plastic bag. To freeze, remove the paper towel and place the sealed bag in the freezer. Then, break off the amount you need.

zesty sloppy joes

2 pounds lean ground beef (90% lean)
1 large green pepper, chopped
2 cans (14-1/2 ounces *each*) diced tomatoes, undrained
2 cans (8 ounces *each*) tomato sauce
1 can (6 ounces) tomato paste
2 tablespoons Worcestershire sauce
1 tablespoon sugar
2 teaspoons celery salt *or* celery seed
2 teaspoons onion salt *or* onion powder
1 teaspoon paprika
1/4 to 1/2 teaspoon cayenne pepper
3 bay leaves
16 hamburger buns, split

Sharon McKee
Denton, Texas
My mother-in-law created this recipe in the early 1950s. Our family likes this classic main dish best served with pickles and potato chips.

In a Dutch oven, cook beef and green pepper over medium heat until meat is no longer pink; drain. Stir in the tomatoes, tomato sauce, tomato paste and seasonings. Bring to a boil. Reduce heat; cover and cook over low heat for 30 minutes.

Cook, uncovered, 30-40 minutes longer or until thickened. Discard bay leaves. Serve 1/2 cup of meat mixture on each bun. **yield: 16 servings.**

firehouse chili

4 pounds lean ground beef (90% lean)
2 medium onions, chopped
1 medium green pepper, chopped
3 cans (14-1/2 ounces *each*) stewed tomatoes, cut up
4 cans (16 ounces *each*) kidney beans, rinsed and drained
1 can (14-1/2 ounces) beef broth
3 tablespoons chili powder
2 tablespoons ground coriander
2 tablespoons ground cumin
4 garlic cloves, minced
1 teaspoon dried oregano

In a Dutch oven, cook the beef, onions and green pepper over medium heat until meat is no longer pink; drain.

Stir in the remaining ingredients. Bring to a boil. Reduce heat; cover and simmer for 1-1/2 hours or until flavors are blended. **yield: 11 servings.**

Richard Clements
San Dimas, California
As a cook at the firehouse, I used to fix meals for 10 men. This chili was a favorite.

main dishes

sirloin roast with gravy

page 104

Janet Sprute, Lewiston, Idaho
Turkey takes center stage in this dish paired with several interesting flavors.
Garlic, ginger and apricot enhance the old favorite without loading on lots
of calories.

apricot-glazed turkey breast

1   **bone-in turkey breast (5 to 6 pounds)**
2   **garlic cloves, peeled and thinly sliced**
1   **tablespoon sliced fresh gingerroot**
1/2   **cup white wine *or* reduced-sodium chicken broth**
1/3   **cup reduced-sugar apricot preserves**
1   **tablespoon spicy brown mustard**
2   **teaspoons reduced-sodium soy sauce**

With fingers, carefully loosen skin from turkey breast. With a sharp knife, cut ten 2-in.-long slits in meat under the skin; insert a garlic and ginger slice into each slit.

Place turkey in a large bowl; pour 1/4 cup wine under the skin. Secure skin to underside of breast with toothpicks. Pour remaining wine over turkey. Cover and refrigerate for 6 hours or overnight.

In a small bowl, combine the preserves, mustard and soy sauce; set aside. Drain and discard marinade; place turkey on a rack in a foil-lined roasting pan.

Bake at 325° for 2 to 2-1/2 hours or until a meat thermometer reads 170°, basting with apricot mixture every 30 minutes (cover loosely with foil if turkey browns too quickly). Cover and let stand for 15 minutes before carving. **yield: 12 servings.**

fresh ginger

Fresh gingerroot is found in the produce section. It should have a smooth skin. When stored in a resealable storage bag, unpeeled gingerroot can be frozen for 1 year. When needed, peel and grate.

turkey brats with slaw

- 4 cups beer *or* nonalcoholic beer
- 3 teaspoons celery salt, *divided*
- 2 teaspoons minced garlic
- 2 packages (19-1/2 ounces *each*) turkey bratwurst links
- 6 cups broccoli coleslaw mix
- 2/3 cup chopped red onion
- 4 teaspoons canola oil
- 2/3 cup dried cranberries
- 1/4 cup red wine vinegar
- 2 tablespoons honey
- 10 brat buns, split

In a Dutch oven, bring the beer, 2 teaspoons celery salt and garlic to a boil. Add bratwurst. Reduce heat; simmer, uncovered, for 20-25 minutes or until firm and cooked through.

Meanwhile, in a large skillet, saute coleslaw mix and onion in oil for 7-9 minutes or until tender. Stir in the cranberries, vinegar, honey and remaining celery salt; heat through. Set aside.

Drain bratwurst. Grill, covered, over medium heat or broil 4 in. from the heat for 2 to 2-1/2 minutes on each side or until browned. Serve on buns with coleslaw mixture. **yield: 10 servings.**

Christy Hinrichs
Parkville, Missouri
The cooked coleslaw-and-cranberry topping on these beer-boiled brats can be served either warm or cold. It makes a very tasty and colorful change from kraut or more conventional condiments.

louisiana shrimp

- 1 pound butter, cubed
- 3 medium lemons, sliced
- 2 tablespoons plus 1-1/2 teaspoons coarsely ground pepper
- 2 tablespoons Worcestershire sauce
- 2 garlic cloves, minced
- 1/2 teaspoon salt
- 1/2 teaspoon hot pepper sauce
- 2-1/2 pounds uncooked shell-on medium shrimp

In a large saucepan, combine the first seven ingredients. Bring to a boil. Reduce heat; cover and simmer for 30 minutes, stirring occasionally.

Place shrimp in a large roasting pan; pour butter mixture over top. Bake, uncovered, at 375° for 20-25 minutes or until shrimp turn pink. Serve warm with a slotted spoon. **yield: 10 servings.**

Sundra Hauck
Bogalusa, Louisiana
This is a Lenten favorite at our home. I serve it right out of the roaster with corn on the cob and boiled potatoes.

italian pasta bake

- 2 pounds ground beef
- 1 large onion, chopped
- 2 garlic cloves, minced
- 1 jar (24 ounces) spaghetti sauce
- 1 can (14-1/2 ounces) diced tomatoes, undrained
- 1 can (4 ounces) mushroom stems and pieces, drained
- 1 teaspoon Italian seasoning
- 3 cups uncooked medium pasta shells
- 3 plum tomatoes, sliced
- 3/4 cup shredded provolone cheese
- 3/4 cup shredded part-skim mozzarella cheese

In a large skillet, cook beef and onion over medium heat until no longer pink. Add garlic; cook 1 minute longer. Drain. Stir in the spaghetti sauce, diced tomatoes, mushrooms and Italian seasoning. Bring to a boil. Reduce the heat; simmer, uncovered, for 20 minutes.

Meanwhile, cook pasta according to package directions; drain. Add to beef mixture and gently stir in tomatoes.

Transfer to an ungreased 13-in. x 9-in. baking dish. Sprinkle with cheeses. Cover and bake at 350° for 25-30 minutes or until bubbly and heated through. **yield: 8 servings.**

Karla Johnson
East Helena, Montana
I love to make this pasta whenever I need to bring a dish to pass. Fresh tomatoes add a nice touch that's missing from most other meat, pasta and tomato casseroles.

rosemary turkey breast

- 8 to 10 garlic cloves
- 3 tablespoons chopped fresh rosemary *or* 3 teaspoons dried rosemary, crushed
- 2 tablespoons olive oil
- 1 teaspoon salt
- 1 teaspoon paprika
- 1/2 teaspoon coarsely ground pepper
- 1 bone-in turkey breast (4 pounds)

Dorothy Pritchett
Wills Point, Texas
I season turkey with a blend of rosemary, garlic and paprika. Because I rub that mixture directly on the meat under the skin, I can remove the skin before serving and not lose any of the flavor. The result is lower-in-fat yet delicious. It's the perfect addition to large holiday gatherings.

In a food processor, combine the garlic, rosemary, oil, salt, paprika and pepper; cover and process until garlic is coarsely chopped.

With your fingers, carefully loosen the skin from both sides of turkey breast. Spread half of the garlic mixture over the meat under the skin. Smooth skin over meat and secure to underside of breast with toothpicks. Spread remaining garlic mixture over turkey skin.

Place turkey breast on a rack in a shallow roasting pan. Bake, uncovered, at 325° for 1-1/2 to 2 hours or until a meat thermometer reads 170°. Let stand for 10-15 minutes. Discard toothpicks. **yield: 11 servings.**

new orleans jambalaya

- 1/2 teaspoon mustard seed
- 1/2 teaspoon coriander seeds
- 1/2 teaspoon whole peppercorns
- 1/2 teaspoon dill seed
- 1/2 teaspoon whole allspice
- 2 pounds boneless skinless chicken breasts, cut into 1-inch cubes
- 1 pound boneless skinless chicken thighs, cut into 1-inch cubes
- 1/2 pound boneless pork, cut into 1-inch cubes
- 1 medium onion, chopped
- 1 large green pepper, chopped
- 1 celery rib, chopped
- 2 tablespoons butter
- 1 tablespoon canola oil
- 2 garlic cloves, minced
- 1 pound smoked kielbasa or Polish sausage, cut into 1-inch slices
- 1 cup diced fully cooked ham
- 1 can (14-1/2 ounces) diced tomatoes, undrained
- 1 to 2 cups water, divided
- 1/2 cup tomato puree
- 2 tablespoons minced fresh parsley
- 2 teaspoons salt
- 3/4 teaspoon pepper
- 1/2 teaspoon dried thyme
- 1/2 teaspoon cayenne pepper
- 1/2 teaspoon chili powder
- 1/8 teaspoon apple pie spice
- 2 bay leaves
- 1/2 pound uncooked small shrimp, peeled and deveined

Hot cooked rice

Place the first five ingredients on a double thickness of cheesecloth; bring up corners of cloth and tie with kitchen string to form a bag. Set aside.

In a stockpot, saute the chicken, pork, onion, green pepper and celery in butter and oil until meat is browned. Add garlic; cook 1 minute longer. Stir in the sausage, ham, tomatoes, 1 cup water, tomato puree, parsley, salt, pepper, thyme, cayenne, chili powder, apple pie spice, bay leaves and spice bag.

Bring to a boil. Reduce heat; cover and simmer for 1 hour, stirring occasionally. During the last 3 minutes, add shrimp and remaining water if necessary. Discard bay leaves and spice bag. Serve with rice. **yield: 16 servings.**

Sabrina Hickey
Columbus, Ohio
Jambalaya is a catchall for meat and seafood, making it a favorite of my husband! It's sure to warm everyone up on a chilly night.

turkey pecan enchiladas

- 1 medium onion, chopped
- 4 ounces reduced-fat cream cheese
- 1 tablespoon water
- 1 teaspoon ground cumin
- 1/4 teaspoon pepper
- 1/8 teaspoon salt
- 4 cups cubed cooked turkey breast
- 1/4 cup chopped pecans, toasted
- 12 flour tortillas (6 inches), warmed
- 1 can (10-3/4 ounces) reduced-fat reduced-sodium condensed cream of chicken soup, undiluted
- 1 cup (8 ounces) reduced-fat sour cream
- 1 cup fat-free milk
- 2 tablespoons canned chopped green chilies
- 1/2 cup shredded reduced-fat cheddar cheese
- 2 tablespoons minced fresh cilantro

In a small nonstick skillet coated with cooking spray, cook and stir onion over medium heat until tender. Set aside. In a large bowl, beat the cream cheese, water, cumin, pepper and salt until smooth. Stir in the onion, turkey and pecans.

Spoon 1/3 cup turkey mixture down the center of each tortilla. Roll up and place seam side down in a 13-in. x 9-in. baking dish coated with cooking spray. Combine the soup, sour cream, milk and chilies; pour over enchiladas.

Cover and bake at 350° for 40 minutes. Uncover; sprinkle with cheese. Bake 5 minutes longer or until heated through and cheese is melted. Sprinkle with cilantro. **yield: 12 servings.**

Cathy Huppe
Georgetown, Massachusetts
I got this recipe from a friend, and I've often served it at church potlucks. I always go home with an empty dish! It's nice because it's creamy, just a little spicy and unique.

a toast to good health

Toasting nuts is a quick and easy way to unleash their earthy flavors. This means you can use fewer of them in your recipe, cutting calories but keeping all the taste.

spicy goulash

1	pound lean ground beef (90% lean)
4	cans (14-1/2 ounces *each*) Mexican diced tomatoes, undrained
2	cans (16 ounces *each*) kidney beans, rinsed and drained
2	cups water
1	medium onion, chopped
1	medium green pepper, chopped
1/4	cup red wine vinegar
2	tablespoons chili powder
1	tablespoon Worcestershire sauce
2	teaspoons beef bouillon granules
1	teaspoon dried basil
1	teaspoon dried parsley flakes
1	teaspoon ground cumin
1/4	teaspoon pepper
2	cups uncooked elbow macaroni

In a large skillet, cook beef over medium heat until no longer pink; drain. Transfer to a 5-qt. slow cooker. Stir in the tomatoes, beans, water, onion, green pepper, vinegar, chili powder, Worcestershire sauce, bouillon and seasonings.

Cover and cook on low for 5-6 hours or until heated through. Stir in macaroni; cover and cook 30 minutes longer or until macaroni is tender. **yield: 12 servings.**

Melissa Polk
West Lafayette, Indiana
Ground cumin, chili powder and a can of Mexican diced tomatoes easily jazz up my goulash recipe. You can even prepare the elbow macaroni in the slow cooker.

big-yield chicken salad

Sister Judith LaBrozzi
Canton, Ohio
Crisp apples lend autumn appeal to my chunky chicken salad. I sometimes serve it on a bed of lettuce with a sliced tomato on top...or mounded inside melon slices. You can dice the ingredients smaller and use as a sandwich filling.

4-1/2	cups diced cooked chicken
1-1/2	cups diced apples
3/4	cup halved green grapes
6	tablespoons sweet pickle relish
6	tablespoons mayonnaise
6	tablespoons prepared ranch salad dressing
3/4	teaspoon onion salt
3/4	teaspoon garlic salt
	Lettuce leaves

In a large bowl, combine the chicken, apples and grapes. In a small bowl, combine the pickle relish, mayonnaise, ranch dressing, onion salt and garlic salt. Pour over chicken mixture and toss to coat. Serve in a lettuce-lined bowl. **yield 18 servings.**

irish beef stew

8	bacon strips, diced
1/3	cup all-purpose flour
1	teaspoon salt
1/2	teaspoon pepper
3	pounds beef stew meat, cut into 1-inch cubes
1	pound whole fresh mushrooms, quartered
3	medium leeks (white portion only), chopped
2	medium carrots, chopped
1/4	cup chopped celery
1	tablespoon canola oil
4	garlic cloves, minced
1	tablespoon tomato paste
4	cups reduced-sodium beef broth
1	cup dark stout beer *or* additional reduced-sodium beef broth
2	bay leaves
1	teaspoon dried thyme
1	teaspoon dried parsley flakes
1	teaspoon dried rosemary, crushed
2	pounds Yukon Gold potatoes, cut into 1-inch cubes
2	tablespoons cornstarch
2	tablespoons cold water
1	cup frozen peas

Carrie Karleen
St. Nicolas, Quebec
Rich and hearty, this stew is my husband's favorite because the beef is incredibly tender. Served with crusty bread, it's an ideal cool-weather meal and perfect for any large Irish get-together.

In a stockpot, cook bacon over medium heat until crisp. Using a slotted spoon, remove to paper towels. In a large resealable plastic bag, combine the flour, salt and pepper. Add beef, a few pieces at a time, and shake to coat. Brown beef in the bacon drippings. Remove and set aside.

In the same pan, saute the mushrooms, leeks, carrots and celery in oil until tender. Add garlic; cook 1 minute longer. Stir in tomato paste until blended. Add the broth, beer, bay leaves, thyme, parsley and rosemary. Return beef and bacon to pan. Bring to a boil. Reduce the heat; cover and simmer for 2 hours or until the beef is tender.

Add potatoes. Return to a boil. Reduce heat; cover and simmer 1 hour longer or until potatoes are tender. Combine cornstarch and water until smooth; stir into stew. Bring to a boil; cook and stir for 2 minutes or until thickened. Add peas; heat through. Discard bay leaves. **yield: 15 servings (3-3/4 quarts).**

beef brisket with mop sauce

1/2	cup water
1/4	cup cider vinegar
1/4	cup Worcestershire sauce
1/4	cup ketchup
1/4	cup dark corn syrup
2	tablespoons canola oil
2	tablespoons prepared mustard
1	fresh beef brisket (3 pounds)

In a large saucepan, combine the first seven ingredients. Bring to a boil, stirring constantly. Reduce heat; simmer for 5 minutes, stirring occasionally. Remove from the heat.

Place the brisket in a shallow roasting pan; pour sauce over the top. Cover and bake at 350° for 2 to 2-1/2 hours or until meat is tender. Let stand for 5 minutes. Thinly slice meat across the grain. **yield: 10-12 servings.**

editor's note: This is a fresh beef brisket, not corned beef.

Darlis Wilfer
West Bend, Wisconsin
This brisket roasts in a sauce that adds great flavor. When one of our sons lived in the South, I learned that "mop sauce" is traditionally prepared for Texas ranch-style barbecues in batches so large it is brushed on the meat with a mop! You won't need that much for my recipe, but you will still get the big-time taste.

honey-glazed ham

1	boneless fully cooked ham (4 pounds)
1-1/2	cups ginger ale
1/4	cup honey
1/2	teaspoon ground mustard
1/2	teaspoon ground cloves
1/4	teaspoon ground cinnamon

Sour cream, optional

Cut ham in half; place in a 5-qt. slow cooker. Pour ginger ale over ham. Cover and cook on low for 4-5 hours or until the ham is heated through.

Combine the honey, mustard, cloves and cinnamon; stir until smooth. Spread over ham; cook 30 minutes longer. Garnish with sour cream if desired. **yield: 14 servings.**

Jacquie Stolz
Little Sioux, Iowa
Here's an easy solution for feeding a large group. The simple ham is perfect for family dinners where time in the kitchen is as valuable as space in the oven.

mushroom-blue cheese tenderloin

1-1/2 cups soy sauce
3/4 cup Worcestershire sauce
1 beef tenderloin roast (3-1/2 to 4 pounds)
4 garlic cloves, minced
1 tablespoon coarsely ground pepper
1 can (10-1/2 ounces) condensed beef broth, undiluted

SAUCE:
1/2 pound sliced fresh mushrooms
1/2 cup butter, cubed
2 garlic cloves, minced
1 cup (4 ounces) crumbled blue cheese
1 tablespoon Worcestershire sauce
1/4 teaspoon caraway seeds
4 green onions, chopped

In a large resealable plastic bag, combine soy sauce and Worcestershire sauce. Add the beef; seal bag and turn to coat. Refrigerate for 2 hours, turning occasionally.

Drain and discard marinade. Rub the beef with garlic and pepper; place in a shallow roasting pan. Add broth to the pan. Bake, uncovered, at 425° for 45-55 minutes or until meat reaches desired doneness (for medium-rare, a meat thermometer should read 145°; medium, 160°; well-done, 170°). Let stand for 10 minutes before slicing.

Meanwhile, in a small saucepan, saute mushrooms in butter until tender. Add garlic; cook 1 minute longer. Add the cheese, Worcestershire sauce and caraway seeds; cook and stir over low heat until cheese is melted. Stir in onions; heat through. Serve sauce with beef. **yield: 10 servings (1-1/2 cups sauce).**

Eric Schoen
Lincoln, Nebraska
This is a simple entree that tastes fabulous. I usually double the mushroom-blue cheese sauce, because it always disappears very fast. Enjoy the lovely tenderloin!

Edie DeSpain, Logan, Utah
I got the recipe for this tender pork roast from an aunt who made it all the time. What a delicious taste sensation with sauerkraut, carrots, onions and even apples.

bavarian pork loin

1	boneless whole pork loin roast (3 to 4 pounds)
1	can (14 ounces) Bavarian sauerkraut, rinsed and drained
1-3/4	cups chopped carrots
1	large onion, finely chopped
1/2	cup unsweetened apple juice
2	teaspoons dried parsley flakes
3	large tart apples, peeled and quartered

Cut roast in half; place in a 5-qt. slow cooker. In a small bowl, combine the sauerkraut, carrots, onion, apple juice and parsley; spoon over roast. Cover and cook on low for 4 hours.

Add apples to slow cooker. Cover and cook 2 to 2-1/2 hours longer or until meat is tender.

Remove roast; let stand for 5 minutes before slicing. Serve with sauerkraut mixture. **yield: 10 servings.**

save space in the fridge

When purchasing apple juice to prepare the Bavarian Pork Loin, consider buying individual juice boxes. This way, you can use what you need without opening a large bottle.

Paula Young, Tiffin, Ohio
Beautifully glazed with a mouthwatering marinade, this entree is relatively low in fat but still juicy, flavorful and tender.

marinated pork loin

1	cup orange juice
3/4	cup apricot preserves
2	tablespoons plus 1/4 cup sherry *or* vegetable broth, *divided*
3	tablespoons lemon juice
2	tablespoons olive oil
1	tablespoon curry powder
1	tablespoon Worcestershire sauce
1	teaspoon dried thyme
1/2	teaspoon pepper
1	boneless whole pork loin roast (3 pounds)
1	tablespoon cornstarch

In a small bowl, combine the orange juice, preserves, 2 tablespoons sherry, lemon juice, oil, curry, Worcestershire sauce, thyme and pepper. Pour 3/4 cup marinade into a large resealable plastic bag; add the pork. Seal bag and turn to coat; refrigerate overnight, turning occasionally. Set aside 1 cup remaining marinade for sauce; cover and refrigerate. Cover and refrigerate the rest of the marinade for basting.

Drain and discard marinade; place pork on a rack in a shallow roasting pan. Bake, uncovered, at 350° for 1-1/2 to 1-3/4 hours or until a meat thermometer reads 160°, basting occasionally with the reserved marinade.

Transfer to a serving platter. Let stand for 10 minutes before slicing.

Meanwhile, in a small saucepan, combine cornstarch with the remaining sherry and 1 cup marinade. Bring to a boil; cook and stir for 2 minutes or until thickened. Serve with roast. **yield: 12 servings.**

chicago-style deep-dish pizza

3-1/2 cups all-purpose flour
1/4 cup cornmeal
1 package (1/4 ounce) quick-rise yeast
1-1/2 teaspoons sugar
1/2 teaspoon salt
1 cup water
1/3 cup olive oil

TOPPINGS:

6 cups (24 ounces) shredded part-skim mozzarella cheese, *divided*
1 can (28 ounces) diced tomatoes, well drained
1 can (8 ounces) tomato sauce
1 can (6 ounces) tomato paste
1/2 teaspoon salt
1/4 teaspoon *each* garlic powder, dried oregano, dried basil and pepper
48 slices pepperoni
1 pound bulk Italian sausage, cooked and crumbled
1/2 pound sliced fresh mushrooms
1/4 cup grated Parmesan cheese

Lynn Hamilton
Naperville, Illinois
My husband and I tried to duplicate the pizza from a popular Chicago restaurant, and I think our recipe turned out even better. The secret is baking it in a cast-iron skillet.

In a large bowl, combine 1-1/2 cups flour, cornmeal, yeast, sugar and salt. In a saucepan, heat water and oil to 120°-130°. Add to dry ingredients; beat just until moistened. Add remaining flour to form a stiff dough.

Turn onto a floured surface; knead until smooth and elastic, about 6-8 minutes. Place in a greased bowl, turning once to grease top. Cover and let rise in warm place until doubled, roughly 30 minutes.

Punch dough down; divide in half. Roll each portion into an 11-in. circle. Press dough onto the bottom and up the sides of two greased 10-in. ovenproof skillets. Sprinkle each with 2 cups mozzarella cheese.

In a large bowl, combine the tomatoes, tomato sauce, tomato paste and seasonings. Spoon 1-1/2 cups over each pizza. Layer each with half of the pepperoni, sausage, mushrooms, 1 cup mozzarella and 2 tablespoons Parmesan cheese.

Cover and bake at 450° for 35 minutes. Uncover; bake 5 minutes longer or until lightly browned. **yield: 2 pizzas (8 slices each).**

editor's note: Two 9-in. springform pans may be used in place of the skillet. Place pans on baking sheets. Run knife around edge of pan to loosen crust before removing sides.

taco-filled pasta shells

2	pounds ground beef
2	envelopes taco seasoning
1	package (8 ounces) cream cheese, cubed
24	uncooked jumbo pasta shells
1/4	cup butter, melted

ADDITIONAL INGREDIENTS (for each casserole):

1	cup salsa
1	cup taco sauce
1	cup (4 ounces) shredded cheddar cheese
1	cup (4 ounces) shredded Monterey Jack cheese
1-1/2	cups crushed tortilla chips
1	cup (8 ounces) sour cream
3	green onions, chopped

Marge Hodel
Roanoke, Illinois
I've been stuffing pasta shells with different fillings for years, but my family enjoys this version with taco-seasoned meat the most. The frozen shells are convenient, because you can take both casseroles to a potluck, or you can take out only the number of shells you need for a single-serving lunch or fast family dinner.

In a Dutch oven, cook beef over medium heat until no longer pink; drain. Add taco seasoning; prepare according to package directions. Add cream cheese; cook and stir for 5-10 minutes or until melted. Transfer to a bowl; chill for 1 hour.

Cook pasta according to package directions; drain. Gently toss with butter. Fill each shell with about 3 tablespoons of meat mixture. Place 12 shells in a freezer container. Cover and freeze for up to 3 months.

To prepare remaining shells, spoon salsa into a greased 9-in. square baking dish. Top with stuffed shells and taco sauce. Cover and bake at 350° for 30 minutes. Uncover; sprinkle with cheeses and chips. Bake 15 minutes longer or until heated through. Serve with sour cream and onions.

To use frozen shells: Thaw in the refrigerator for 24 hours (shells will be partially frozen). Spoon salsa into a greased 9-in. square baking dish; top with shells and taco sauce. Cover and bake at 350° for 40 minutes. Uncover and continue as above. **yield: 2 casseroles (6 servings each).**

potluck pointer

When organizing a buffet, most people stack the eating utensils at the front of the table with the plates. However, moving them to the end of the buffet frees up your guests' hands as they make their way through the buffet line.

angel hair pasta with tuna

4 garlic cloves, minced
2 tablespoons olive oil
2 cans (29 ounces *each*) tomato puree
1/2 cup dry red wine *or* chicken broth
2 tablespoons minced fresh basil
1 to 1-1/2 teaspoons crushed red pepper flakes
1 teaspoon salt
2 to 2-1/2 pounds tuna steaks
2 packages (16 ounces *each*) angel hair pasta
1/2 cup grated Parmesan cheese

Weda Mosellie
Phillipsburg, New Jersey
When my summer garden is in full bloom, I like to make this dish with a homemade puree of fresh tomatoes. Feel free to use two 10-ounce cans of chunk white tuna instead of the fillets if you'd like.

In a large saucepan, saute garlic in oil for 1-2 minutes or until tender. Stir in the tomato puree, wine, basil, pepper flakes and salt. Bring to a boil. Reduce heat; simmer, uncovered, for 35-45 minutes or until flavors are blended.

In a large skillet coated with cooking spray, cook tuna over medium-high heat for 6-8 minutes on each side for medium-rare or until slightly pink in the center.

Flake tuna into large chunks; add to sauce. Cook pasta according to package directions; drain. Top with sauce; sprinkle with cheese. **yield: 12 servings.**

fake steak

2 cups milk, *divided*
1-3/4 cups dry bread crumbs
2 medium onions, finely chopped
4 teaspoons salt
3/4 teaspoon pepper
5 pounds ground beef
2 cans (26 ounces *each*) condensed cream of mushroom soup, undiluted

Fran Wolfley
St. Mary, Indiana
My husband and I are hosts at a mission house and cook for 30 to 60 people each week. This simple but tasty beef entree is one we can always rely on.

In a large bowl, combine 1-3/4 cups milk, bread crumbs, onions, salt and pepper. Crumble beef over mixture and mix well. Shape into 24 oval patties, about 4 in. x 2-1/2 in. Place in two greased 15-in. x 10-in. x 1-in. baking pans. Cover and refrigerate for 8 hours or overnight.

Bake, uncovered, at 350° for 15 minutes; drain. Combine soup and remaining milk; pour over patties. Cover and bake 20-30 minutes longer or until meat is no longer pink and a meat thermometer reads 160°. **yield: 24 servings.**

cuban pork roast

1 cup lime juice
1 cup orange juice
10 garlic cloves, minced
4 teaspoons ground cumin
2 tablespoons minced fresh thyme *or* 2 teaspoons dried thyme
2 tablespoons minced fresh cilantro
4 bay leaves
1 boneless pork top loin roast (3 pounds)
1/2 teaspoon salt
1/4 teaspoon pepper

Virginia Cronk
Little Torch Key, Florida
A citrus and spice marinade seasons this moist, succulent roast. The pork is flavorful but mild, so everyone likes it. You can serve it Cuban-style with black beans and rice, or make a traditional Cuban sandwich of pork, ham, Swiss cheese, tomatoes, lettuce, mustard, mayonnaise and dill pickle.

In a large bowl, combine the first seven ingredients. Pour half of the marinade into a large resealable plastic bag; add the pork roast. Seal bag and turn to coat; refrigerate for 2 hours. Refrigerate remaining marinade.

Drain and discard marinade from pork. Place roast in an ungreased 13-in. x 9-in. baking dish. Pour reserved marinade over the roast. Sprinkle with salt and pepper.

Cover and bake at 350° for 1 hour. Uncover; baste with pan drippings. Bake 15 minutes longer or until a meat thermometer reads 160°. Discard bay leaves. Let roast stand for 15 minutes before slicing. **yield: 12 servings.**

kentucky grilled chicken

1 cup cider vinegar
1/2 cup canola oil
5 teaspoons Worcestershire sauce
4 teaspoons hot pepper sauce
2 teaspoons salt
10 bone-in chicken breast halves (10 ounces *each*)

In a small bowl, combine the first five ingredients. Pour 1 cup marinade into a large resealable plastic bag; add the chicken. Seal bag and turn to coat; refrigerate for at least 4 hours. Cover and refrigerate the remaining marinade for basting.

Drain and discard marinade from chicken. Using long-handled tongs, moisten a paper towel with cooking oil and lightly coat the grill rack. Prepare grill for indirect heat, using a drip pan.

Place chicken breast bone side down and grill, covered, over indirect medium heat for 20 minutes on each side or until a meat thermometer reads 170°, basting occasionally with reserved marinade. **yield: 10 servings.**

Jill Evely
Wilmore, Kentucky
This chicken is perfect for an outdoor summer meal, and my family thinks it's fantastic. It takes about an hour on the grill but is worth the wait. I use a new paintbrush to "mop" on the basting sauce.

Laurel Leslie, Sonora, California
This tender, Texas-style brisket, paired nicely with a savory sauce, is a superb contribution at cool weather events.

panhandle beef brisket

2-1/4	cups ketchup
1-1/2	cups beef broth
1	large onion, chopped
1/2	cup packed brown sugar
1/2	cup white wine vinegar
2	tablespoons chili powder
2	tablespoons Worcestershire sauce
3	garlic cloves, minced
1/4	teaspoon cayenne pepper
1	fresh beef brisket (5 to 7 pounds), trimmed
2	tablespoons Liquid Smoke, optional

In a large saucepan, combine the first nine ingredients. Bring to a boil, stirring constantly. Reduce heat; simmer, uncovered, for 30 minutes, stirring occasionally. Remove from the heat. Remove 2 cups sauce to a bowl; cover and refrigerate for serving.

Place brisket in a shallow roasting pan; brush with Liquid Smoke if desired. Pour remaining sauce over meat. Cover and bake at 325° for 3 hours or until meat is tender.

Let stand for 5 minutes. Heat reserved sauce. Thinly slice meat across the grain. Serve sauce with meat. **yield: 16 servings (2 cups sauce).**

editor's note: This is a fresh beef brisket, not corned beef.

Taste of Home Test Kitchen
An Italian flair is given to this lightened-up meat loaf by adding tangy sun-dried tomatoes to the mixture.

sun-dried tomato meat loaf

1-1/4	cups sun-dried tomatoes (not packed in oil)
3	cups boiling water
1/2	cup chopped onion
1/2	cup chopped green pepper
2	teaspoons canola oil
1/2	cup milk
1	egg, lightly beaten
1	cup soft bread crumbs
2	teaspoons dried basil
1	teaspoon dried oregano
1	teaspoon salt
1	teaspoon pepper
1/2	teaspoon dried thyme
1-1/2	pounds ground beef
1/4	cup ketchup

In a large bowl, combine tomatoes and water; let stand for 15 minutes or until softened. Meanwhile, in a small skillet, saute onion and green pepper in oil for 3 minutes or until tender. In a large bowl, combine milk, egg and bread crumbs.

Drain and chop the tomatoes; set aside 1/4 cup for topping. Add onion mixture, basil, oregano, salt, pepper, thyme and remaining chopped tomatoes to the crumb mixture. Crumble beef over mixture and mix well. Shape into a loaf in an ungreased 13-in. x 9-in. baking dish.

In a small bowl, combine ketchup and reserved tomatoes. Spread over loaf. Bake, uncovered, at 350° for 55-60 minutes or until no pink remains and a meat thermometer reads 160°. Drain; let stand for 10 minutes before slicing. **yield: 10 servings.**

spinach cheese enchiladas

1 carton (15 ounces) reduced-fat ricotta cheese
1 package (10 ounces) frozen chopped spinach, thawed and drained
2 cups frozen corn, thawed and drained
2 cups (8 ounces) shredded part-skim mozzarella cheese, *divided*
1/4 cup egg substitute
10 fat-free flour tortillas (8 inches)
1 can (14-1/2 ounces) Italian diced tomatoes, undrained
1 can (8 ounces) tomato sauce
1 teaspoon dried basil
1/4 cup grated Parmesan cheese

In a large bowl, combine the ricotta, spinach, corn, 1 cup mozzarella and egg substitute. Spoon about 1/2 cup on each tortilla; roll up tightly. Place, seam side down, in 13-in. x 9-in. baking dish coated with cooking spray.

In a small bowl, combine the tomatoes, tomato sauce and basil; spoon over tortillas. Sprinkle with Parmesan cheese and remaining mozzarella cheese.

Bake, uncovered, at 375° for 35 minutes or until heated through **yield: 10 servings.**

Carol Jackson
Eden Prairie, Minnesota
This tasty meatless dish is great because it's easy to prepare and low in fat. Plus, it travels well to potlucks and often prompts recipe requests.

Kat Thompson
Prineville, Oregon
A taco shell makes a good holder for a hot dog dressed up with a tasty combination of baked beans and cheese. When our children were young, they asked for this meal at least once a week.

taco dogs

1 package (1 pound) hot dogs
10 slices process American cheese
10 hard taco shells, warmed
1 can (16 ounces) baked beans, warmed

Prepare hot dogs according to package directions. Place a cheese slice and hot dog in each taco shell; top with beans. **yield: 10 tacos.**

sloppy joe pizza

- 2 tubes (13.8 ounces *each*) refrigerated pizza crust
- 1 pound ground beef
- 1 can (15-1/2 ounces) sloppy joe sauce
- 2 cups (8 ounces) shredded part-skim mozzarella cheese
- 1 cup (4 ounces) shredded cheddar cheese
- 1/2 cup grated Parmesan cheese

Unroll pizza dough; place on two greased 12-in. pizza pans. Bake at 425° for 6-7 minutes or until golden brown.

In a large skillet, cook beef over medium heat until no longer pink; drain. Add sloppy joe sauce. Spread over crusts. Sprinkle with cheeses. Bake at 425° for 6-8 minutes or until cheese is melted. **yield: 2 pizzas (8 slices each).**

Brenda Rohlman
Kingman, Kansas
If your children like sloppy joes, they're sure to enjoy this change-of-pace pizza. The six-ingredient recipe has lots of kid-pleasing flavor and goes together in a flash.

pinwheel pizza loaf

- 2 eggs

Salt and pepper to taste
- 3 pounds lean ground beef (90% lean)
- 6 thin slices deli ham
- 2 cups (8 ounces) shredded part-skim mozzarella cheese
- 1 jar (14 ounces) pizza sauce

In a large bowl, beat the eggs, salt and pepper. Crumble beef over eggs and mix well. On a piece of heavy-duty foil, pat beef mixture into a 12-in. x 10-in. rectangle. Cover with ham and cheese to within 1/2 in. of edges. Roll up jelly-roll style, starting with a short side and peeling away foil while rolling. Seal seam and ends.

Place the loaf seam side down in a greased 13-in. x 9-in. baking dish. Top with pizza sauce. Bake, uncovered, at 350° for 1-1/4 hours or until meat is no longer pink and a meat thermometer reads 160°. Let stand for 10 minutes before slicing. **yield: 12 servings.**

Rhonda Touchet
Jennings, Louisiana
This fun, pizza-flavored loaf is popular with folks of all ages. Many neighbors have called me to get the recipe after their kids tried it at my house.

home-style chicken potpie

3/4   cup cold butter, cubed
2   cups all-purpose flour
1   cup (4 ounces) shredded cheddar cheese
1/4   cup cold water

FILLING:

2-1/2   cups halved baby carrots
3   celery ribs, sliced
6   tablespoons butter, cubed
7   tablespoons all-purpose flour
1   teaspoon salt
1/4   teaspoon coarsely ground pepper
2-1/2   cups chicken broth
1   cup heavy whipping cream
4   cups cubed cooked chicken
1   cup frozen pearl onions, thawed
1   cup frozen peas, thawed
3   tablespoons minced chives
3   tablespoons minced fresh parsley
2   teaspoons minced fresh thyme
1   egg, lightly beaten

In a large bowl, cut butter into flour until crumbly. Stir in cheese. Gradually add water, tossing with a fork until dough forms a ball. Cover and refrigerate for at least 1 hour.

In a large saucepan, cook carrots and celery in a small amount of water until crisp-tender; drain and set aside.

In another saucepan, melt butter. Whisk in the flour, salt and pepper until smooth. Gradually whisk in broth and cream. Bring to a boil; cook and stir for 2 minutes or until thickened. Stir in the carrot mixture, chicken, onions, peas, chives, parsley and thyme; heat through. Transfer to a greased 13-in. x 9-in. baking dish.

On a floured surface, roll out dough to fit top of dish; cut out vents. Place dough over filling; trim and flute edges. Brush with egg. Bake at 400° for 25-30 minutes or until bubbly and crust is golden brown. Let stand for 10 minutes before serving. **yield: 10-12 servings.**

Darlene Claxton
Brighton, Michigan
I served this potpie along with chili for a bowl game. No one ate the chili. In fact, one of my husband's single friends called the next day and asked for the leftover pie.

hearty beef enchiladas

- 4 pounds ground beef
- 4 medium onions, chopped
- 4 cans (16 ounces *each*) chili beans, undrained
- 4 cans (10 ounces *each*) enchilada sauce, *divided*
- 1 jar (16 ounces) salsa, *divided*

Canola oil

- 28 corn *or* flour tortillas (8 inches)
- 4 cups (16 ounces) shredded cheddar cheese
- 2 cans (2-1/4 ounces *each*) sliced ripe olives, drained

In a stockpot, cook beef and onions over medium heat until meat is no longer pink; drain. Stir in the beans, two cans of enchilada sauce and 1 cup salsa; set aside.

In a small skillet, heat 1/4 in. of oil. Dip each tortilla in hot oil for 3 seconds on each side or just until limp; drain on paper towels.

Top each tortilla with 2/3 cup beef mixture. Roll up and place seam side down in four greased 13-in. x 9-in. baking dishes. Drizzle with remaining enchilada sauce and salsa. Sprinkle with cheese and olives.

Bake, uncovered, at 350° for 20-25 minutes or until bubbly. **yield: 28 servings.**

Richard Clements
San Dimas, California
I set out small bowls of shredded cheese, diced onions and diced tomatoes so folks can feel free to add their own toppings. Since this recipe fills four 13-inch x 9-inch baking dishes, it's ideal for feeding a gang.

lemon-herb leg of lamb

Patricia Crandall
Inchelium, Washington
This lamb dish would be perfect for Easter or any other festive gathering. I created the recipe from a combination of several others. It's the only lamb my daughter would eat when she was young.

- 2 teaspoons lemon juice
- 1-1/2 teaspoons grated lemon peel
- 1 teaspoon garlic salt
- 1 teaspoon dried oregano
- 1 teaspoon dried thyme
- 1 teaspoon dried rosemary, crushed
- 1 teaspoon ground mustard
- 1 boneless leg of lamb (4 pounds), rolled and tied

In a small bowl, combine the first seven ingredients. Rub over leg of lamb. Cover and refrigerate overnight.

Place lamb on a rack in a shallow roasting pan. Bake, uncovered, at 325° for 1-3/4 to 2-1/4 hours or until meat reaches desired doneness (for medium-rare, a meat thermometer should read 145°; medium, 160°; well-done, 170°). Let stand for 15 minutes before slicing. **yield: 12 servings.**

turkey potpies

- 2 medium potatoes, peeled and cut into 1-inch pieces
- 3 medium carrots, cut into 1-inch slices
- 1 medium onion, chopped
- 1 celery rib, diced
- 2 tablespoons butter
- 1 tablespoon olive oil
- 6 tablespoons all-purpose flour
- 3 cups chicken broth
- 4 cups cubed cooked turkey
- 2/3 cup frozen peas
- 1/2 cup plus 1 tablespoon heavy whipping cream, *divided*
- 1 tablespoon minced fresh parsley
- 1 teaspoon garlic salt
- 1/4 teaspoon pepper
- 1 package (15 ounces) refrigerated pie pastry
- 1 egg

In a Dutch oven, saute the potatoes, carrots, onion and celery in butter and oil until tender. Stir in flour until blended; gradually add broth. Bring to a boil; cook and stir for 2 minutes or until thickened. Stir in the turkey, peas, 1/2 cup cream, parsley, garlic salt and pepper.

Spoon into two ungreased 9-in. pie plates. Roll out pastry to fit top of each pie; place over filling. Trim, seal and flute edges. Cut out a decorative center or cut slits in pastry. In a small bowl, whisk egg and remaining cream; brush over pastry.

Cover and freeze one potpie for up to 3 months. Bake the remaining potpie at 375° for 40-45 minutes or until golden brown. Let stand for 10 minutes before cutting.

To use frozen potpie: Remove from the freezer 30 minutes before baking. Cover edges of crust loosely with foil; place on a baking sheet. Bake at 425° for 30 minutes. Reduce heat to 350°; remove foil. Bake 55-60 minutes longer or until golden brown. **yield: 2 pies (6 servings each).**

Laurie Jensen
Cadillac, Michigan
With its golden-brown crust and scrumptious filling, these comforting potpies will warm you down to your toes. Because the recipe makes two, you can take one to the potluck and freeze the other for a busy weeknight at home.

odds and ends

When attending a potluck, don't forget to bring along the necessary utensils needed to serve your contribution. When bringing a dish in a slow cooker, you might want to bring a short extension cord as well.

pepper-lime pork kabobs

3/4 cup olive oil
1/4 cup lime juice
1/4 cup minced fresh parsley
2 tablespoons cider vinegar
2 jalapeno peppers, seeded and chopped
1/2 teaspoon *each* salt, garlic powder and ground cumin
3 pounds pork tenderloin, thinly sliced

Donna Godfrey
Cumming, Georgia
This is my family's favorite treatment for pork. The slices of tenderloin get a flavorful zip from a Mexican-inspired marinade. I often fix the skewers for company, because much of the prep work can be done ahead of time.

In a large resealable plastic bag, combine the oil, lime juice, parsley, vinegar, jalapenos and seasonings; add pork and turn to coat. Seal and refrigerate for 24 hours, turning occasionally.

Drain and discard marinade. Loosely thread the pork slices onto metal or soaked wood skewers. Using long-handled tongs, moisten a paper towel with cooking oil and lightly coat the grill rack. Grill kabobs, covered, over medium heat for 14-16 minutes or until the meat juices run clear, turning occasionally. **yield: 10-12 servings.**

editor's note: When cutting hot peppers, disposable gloves are recommended. Avoid touching your face.

italian pot roast

1 beef rump roast *or* bottom round roast (3 pounds)
1-1/2 cups water
6 garlic cloves, minced
2 bay leaves
2 tablespoons dried basil
4-1/2 teaspoons dried oregano
1-1/2 teaspoons salt
1/2 teaspoon crushed red pepper flakes
1/2 teaspoon garlic powder
1 tablespoon cornstarch
3 tablespoons cold water

In a Dutch oven coated with cooking spray, brown roast on all sides; drain. Combine the water, garlic and seasonings; pour over roast. Bring to a boil. Reduce heat; cover and simmer for 2-3/4 to 3-1/4 hours or until meat is tender.

Discard bay leaves. Remove roast to a serving platter; let stand for 10 minutes. Meanwhile, for gravy, pour pan drippings and loosened browned bits into a measuring cup; skim and discard fat. Transfer to a small saucepan. Combine cornstarch and cold water until smooth; gradually stir into drippings. Bring to a boil; cook and stir for 2 minutes or until thickened. Slice beef; serve with gravy. **yield: 12 servings.**

Karen Schultz Breda
Needham, Massachusetts
This tender roast with its rich, savory gravy fills the entire house with a wonderful aroma as it cooks and will have the gang waiting at the table for dinner. Serve it with a crusty loaf of bread and tossed salad.

Allan Stackhouse Jr., Jennings, Louisiana
My friends have asked me to bottle my barbecue sauce, rub and marinades. My favorite saying is, "You cook it, and they will come," and they sure will with these succulent ribs on the menu!

sweet 'n' spicy country ribs

3/4	cup unsweetened apple juice
1/2	cup canola oil
1/2	cup cola
1/4	cup packed brown sugar
1/4	cup honey
1	tablespoon minced garlic
1	tablespoon Worcestershire sauce
2	teaspoons Liquid Smoke, optional
1	teaspoon salt
1	teaspoon dried thyme
1	teaspoon pepper
1/2	teaspoon cayenne pepper
1/2	teaspoon ground nutmeg
3	to 4 pounds boneless country-style pork ribs

In a small bowl, combine the apple juice, oil, cola, brown sugar, honey, garlic, Worcestershire sauce, Liquid Smoke if desired and seasonings.

Pour 1-1/2 cups marinade into a large resealable plastic bag; add ribs. Seal bag and turn to coat; refrigerate for 5 hours or overnight, turning once. Cover and refrigerate remaining marinade for basting.

Drain and discard marinade. Using long-handled tongs, moisten a paper towel with cooking oil and lightly coat the grill rack. Prepare grill for indirect heat, using a drip pan. Place ribs over drip pan and grill, covered, over indirect medium heat for 10 minutes on each side, basting occasionally.

Grill 20-25 minutes longer or until meat is tender, turning and basting occasionally with remaining marinade. **yield: 12 servings.**

paella

3	pounds uncooked skinless turkey breast, cubed
4	pounds uncooked chorizo, cut into 1-1/2-inch pieces *or* bulk spicy pork sausage
3	tablespoons olive oil
2	medium onions, chopped
1	medium sweet red pepper, chopped
4	garlic cloves, minced
1/2	teaspoon cayenne pepper
2	cups tomato puree
1	cup white wine *or* chicken broth
5	cups water
4	cups uncooked long grain rice
3-1/2	cups chicken broth
2	teaspoons salt
1	teaspoon dried thyme
3/4	teaspoon saffron threads *or* 2 teaspoons ground turmeric
1	bay leaf
2	pounds uncooked medium shrimp, peeled and deveined
3/4	cup pitted Greek olives
1/2	cup minced fresh parsley

In a large skillet, cook turkey and chorizo in oil in batches until browned. Remove with a slotted spoon and keep warm.

In the same skillet, saute onions and red pepper until tender. Add garlic and cayenne; cook 1 minute longer. Stir in tomato puree and wine. Bring to a boil; cook and stir for 2 minutes or until thickened.

Transfer to a stockpot. Stir in the water, rice, broth, salt, thyme, saffron, bay leaf, turkey and chorizo. Bring to a boil. Reduce heat; cover and simmer for 20 minutes or until rice is tender.

Add shrimp; cook for 2-3 minutes or until shrimp turn pink. Remove from the heat; discard bay leaf. Stir in olives and parsley. **yield: 24 servings (1 cup each).**

Jane Montgomery
Hilliard, Ohio
A big pan of paella is the perfect choice when cooking for a crowd. All you need to round out the meal is fresh bread and a green salad.

golden baked chicken

- 2 cups mashed potato flakes
- 3/4 cup grated Parmesan cheese
- 2 tablespoons dried parsley flakes
- 1 tablespoon paprika
- 3/4 teaspoon garlic salt
- 3/4 teaspoon onion powder
- 1/2 teaspoon pepper
- 1 cup butter, melted
- 3 broiler/fryer chicken (3 to 4 pounds *each*), cut up and skin removed

In a shallow bowl, combine the potato flakes, cheese, parsley, paprika, garlic salt, onion powder and pepper. In another shallow bowl, add butter. Dip chicken into butter, then into potato flake mixture

Place on two greased 15-in. x 10-in. x 1-in. baking pans. Bake at 375° for 50-60 minutes or until the chicken juices run clear. **yield: 12 servings.**

Harriet Stichter
Milford, Indiana
This recipe makes a delicious crispy chicken without frying, and the paprika gives the chicken pieces a pleasant punch, plus pretty color.

creole black beans 'n' sausage

Cheryl Landers
LaTour, Missouri
I can make this dish easily and get it to the table in no time. I brown the meat, cut up veggies and measure spices the night before, and then assemble and start it cooking the next morning. When I get home, I make the rice...and dinner is served!

- 2 pounds smoked sausage, cut into 1-inch slices
- 3 cans (15 ounces *each*) black beans, rinsed and drained
- 1-1/2 cups *each* chopped onion, celery and green pepper
- 1 cup water
- 1 can (8 ounces) tomato sauce
- 4 garlic cloves, minced
- 2 teaspoons dried thyme
- 1 teaspoon chicken bouillon granules
- 1 teaspoon white pepper
- 1/4 teaspoon cayenne pepper
- 2 bay leaves

Hot cooked rice

In a large skillet, brown sausage over medium heat; drain. Transfer to a 5-qt. slow cooker.

In a large bowl, combine the beans, onion, celery, green pepper, water, tomato sauce, garlic, thyme, bouillon, white pepper, cayenne and bay leaves; pour over sausage. Cover and cook on low for 6 hours or until vegetables are tender. Discard bay leaves. Serve with rice. **yield: 10 servings.**

fiesta lasagna

1	pound ground beef
1/4	cup chopped onion
1	can (16 ounces) refried beans
1	can (16 ounces) mild chili beans, undrained
1	can (14-1/2 ounces) Mexican stewed tomatoes, drained
1	cup salsa
1	can (4 ounces) chopped green chilies
1	envelope reduced-sodium taco seasoning
1	teaspoon dried oregano
1	teaspoon ground cumin
1/4	teaspoon garlic powder
1-1/4	cups shredded Monterey Jack cheese
1-1/4	cups shredded part-skim mozzarella cheese
3/4	cup 4% cottage cheese
1-1/4	cups sour cream, *divided*
9	lasagna noodles, cooked, rinsed and drained

Karen Ann Bland
Gove, Kansas
Loaded with Mexican-style ingredients, this filling lasagna is sure to please the whole gang, whether you make it for your family or take it to a potluck. Every bite is tasty.

In a Dutch oven, cook beef and onion over medium heat until meat is no longer pink; drain. Stir in the beans, tomatoes, salsa, chilies and seasonings.

In a large bowl, combine Monterey Jack and mozzarella cheeses; set aside 1 cup. Stir cottage cheese and 3/4 cup sour cream into remaining cheese mixture.

Spread 1 cup meat sauce into a greased 13-in. x 9-in. baking dish. Layer with three noodles, and a third of the cottage cheese mixture and meat sauce. Repeat layers twice (dish will be full).

Cover and bake at 350° for 1 hour. Uncover; spread with remaining sour cream. Sprinkle with reserved cheeses. Bake 10-12 minutes longer or until cheese is melted. Let stand for 10 minutes before serving. **yield: 12 servings.**

making a tasty transport

When taking a cheesy casserole, such as Fiesta Lasagna, to a covered-dish dinner, keep the cheesy topping from sticking to the foil covering by spraying the foil with cooking spray.

Taste of Home Test Kitchen
Ground turkey in this recipe lowers the fat while spinach gives the meat loaf even more nutritional value. The spinach also helps keep the texture moist...and the green flecks add such pretty color to the slices.

turkey meat loaf

1	medium onion, finely chopped
1	tablepoon canola oil
2	eggs
1/2	cup 2% milk
2	teaspoons lemon juice
1	teaspoon salt
1	teaspoon dried basil
1/2	teaspoon dried oregano
1/2	teaspoon pepper
2	cups soft whole wheat bread crumbs (about 5 slices)
1	package (10 ounces) frozen chopped spinach, thawed and squeezed dry
2-1/2	pounds lean ground turkey
1/2	cup salsa
1	tablespoon butter, melted

In a small skillet, saute onion in oil until tender; set aside. In a small bowl, combine the eggs, milk, lemon juice, salt, basil, oregano and pepper. Stir in the bread crumbs, spinach and reserved onion. Crumble turkey over mixture and mix well.

Shape into a 12-in. x 5-in. loaf; place in a 13-in. x 9-in. baking dish coated with cooking spray. Spoon salsa over top.

Bake, uncovered, at 350° for 30 minutes. Drizzle with butter; bake 30-35 minutes longer or until no pink remains and a meat thermometer reads 165°. **yield: 10 slices.**

Phyllis Minter, Wakefield, Kansas
I came up with this recipe years ago by combining a couple of family favorites. Easy and versatile, it's great for potlucks. I can make the sauce ahead and use all wings or leg quarters when they're on sale. I've found this to be a welcomed entree at senior citizen fellowship dinners.

pineapple pepper chicken

4	cups unsweetened pineapple juice
2-1/2	cups sugar
2	cups white vinegar
1-1/2	cups water
1	cup packed brown sugar
2/3	cup cornstarch
1/2	cup ketchup
6	tablespoons soy sauce
2	teaspoons chicken bouillon granules
3/4	teaspoon ground ginger
3	tablespoons canola oil
2	broiler/fryer chickens (3 to 3-1/2 pounds *each*), cut up
1	can (8 ounces) pineapple chunks, drained
1	medium green pepper, julienned

In a large saucepan, combine the first 11 ingredients; stir until smooth. Bring to a boil; cook and stir for 2 minutes or until thickened. Set aside. In a large skillet over medium-high heat, brown the chicken on all sides.

Place chicken in two greased 13-in. x 9-in. baking dishes. Pour reserved sauce over chicken. Bake, uncovered, at 350° for 45 minutes or until chicken juices run clear. Add pineapple and green pepper. Bake 15 minutes longer or until heated through. **yield: 12 servings.**

turkey stir-fry supper

2-1/4 pounds boneless skinless turkey breast
2 tablespoons canola oil
3/4 cup uncooked long grain rice
2 cans (14-1/2 ounces *each*) chicken broth, *divided*
5 tablespoons soy sauce
2 garlic cloves, minced
1/2 teaspoon ground ginger
1/4 teaspoon pepper
1 package (10 ounces) frozen broccoli spears, thawed
1 pound carrots, thinly sliced
3 bunches green onions, sliced
3 tablespoons cornstarch
1 can (14 ounces) bean sprouts, drained

Cut turkey into 2-in. strips. In a Dutch oven or wok, stir-fry turkey in batches in oil for 5-7 minutes or until the juices run clear. Set turkey aside.

Add rice, 3-1/2 cups broth, soy sauce, garlic, ginger and pepper to pan; bring to a boil. Reduce heat; cover and simmer for 15 minutes or until rice is tender.

Cut broccoli into 3-in. pieces. Add the broccoli, carrots and onions to rice mixture; simmer for 3-5 minutes. Combine cornstarch and remaining broth; add to pan. Bring to a boil; cook and stir for 2 minutes or until thickened. Stir in turkey and bean sprouts; heat through. **yield: 14 servings.**

Mavis Diment
Marcus, Iowa
Tempting turkey is combined with rice, colorful vegetables and a mild sauce in this delightful meal-in-one entree. I share it at many gatherings and always get compliments in return.

stir-fry substitute

When preparing the Turkey Stir-Fry Supper, feel free to replace the turkey with chicken if you'd like. In addition, add whatever frozen veggies you like best. Toss in some sliced mushrooms or water chestnuts or stir in sweet red pepper strips.

three-meat spaghetti sauce

- 1 pound ground beef
- 1 pound bulk Italian sausage
- 1 cup chopped onion
- 1 can (28 ounces) crushed tomatoes
- 3 cups water
- 2 cans (6 ounces *each*) tomato paste
- 2 jars (4-1/2 ounces *each*) sliced mushrooms, drained
- 1 cup chopped pepperoni
- 2 tablespoons grated Parmesan cheese
- 2 tablespoons Italian seasoning
- 1 tablespoon sugar
- 2 teaspoons garlic salt
- 1 teaspoon pepper
- 1 teaspoon dried parsley flakes

Hot cooked spaghetti

Ellen Stringer
Bourbonnais, Illinois
I experimented with a recipe until I came up with the perfect sauce. Others think it's perfect, too, since I've received many compliments on it. I like to simmer the sauce in large batches, freeze it and use it for spaghetti, lasagna, mostaccioli and pizza.

In a Dutch oven, cook the beef, sausage and onion over medium heat until meat is no longer pink; drain. Stir in the tomatoes, water, tomato paste, mushrooms, pepperoni, cheese and seasonings. Bring to a boil. Reduce heat; cover and simmer for 30 minutes. Serve desired amount. Cool remaining sauce.

Freeze in serving-size portions in freezer containers. May be frozen for up to 3 months.

To use frozen spaghetti sauce: Thaw in the refrigerator overnight. Place in a saucepan; heat through. Serve over spaghetti. **yield: 11-1/2 cups.**

friendly combo

Because it makes a large batch, this sauce is perfect for sharing. Ask a friend to provide the cooked pasta and find another to toss up a large salad, and you've got a meal that feeds a crowd. A few loaves of bread round out the dinner perfectly.

Karen Haen, Sturgeon Bay, Wisconsin
Everyone loves these warm tortillas wrapped around delicious fillings, such as veggies and cheese. The recipe is my original, and I found you cannot make an error with it!

mixed grill fajitas

1	*each* medium green, sweet red and yellow pepper, julienned
2	medium red onions, sliced
3	tablespoons olive oil
1	cup (8 ounces) sour cream
2	teaspoons ground cumin
2	garlic cloves, minced
1/2	teaspoon salt
1/2	teaspoon pepper
1/2	teaspoon chili powder
6	boneless skinless chicken breast halves (4 ounces *each*)
3	Italian sausage links
2	beef cubed steaks (4 ounces *each*)
24	flour tortillas (8 inches), warmed
6	cups (24 ounces) shredded cheddar cheese

In a large skillet, saute peppers and onions in oil until tender; keep warm. In a small bowl, combine the sour cream, cumin and garlic; cover and refrigerate until serving.

Combine the salt, pepper and chili powder; sprinkle over chicken, sausages and steaks. Grill chicken and sausages, covered, over medium heat for 5-8 minutes on each side or until a meat thermometer inserted in the chicken reads 170° and the sausage is no longer pink. Slice and keep warm.

Grill steaks, covered, over medium heat for 2-3 minutes on each side or until meat reaches desired doneness (for medium-rare, a meat thermometer should read 145°; medium, 160°; well-done, 170°). Slice and keep warm.

Divide meats and vegetables among tortillas; sprinkle with cheese. Roll up; serve with sour cream mixture. **yield: 12 servings.**

Rita Clark, Monument, Colorado
This recipe is perfect for my husband, who is a meat-and-potatoes kind of guy. The peppery, fork-tender roast combined with the rich gravy creates a delicious centerpiece for any buffet.

serve with a slow cooker

Before heading off to the potluck, consider slicing the beef roast first. Combine the slices with the gravy, and keep everything warm in a slow cooker.

sirloin roast with gravy

1	beef sirloin tip roast (3 pounds)
1	to 2 tablespoons coarsely ground pepper
1-1/2	teaspoons minced garlic
1/4	cup reduced-sodium soy sauce
3	tablespoons balsamic vinegar
1	tablespoon Worcestershire sauce
2	teaspoons ground mustard
2	tablespoons cornstarch
1/4	cup cold water

Rub roast with pepper and garlic; cut in half and place in a 3-qt. slow cooker. Combine the soy sauce, vinegar, Worcestershire sauce and mustard; pour over beef. Cover and cook on low for 5-1/2 to 6 hours or until the meat is tender.

Remove roast and keep warm. Strain cooking juices into a small saucepan; skim fat. Combine cornstarch and water until smooth; gradually stir into cooking juices. Bring to a boil; cook and stir for 2 minutes or until thickened. Serve with beef. **yield: 10 servings.**

sausage ham loaves

12	eggs, lightly beaten
6	cups milk
6	cups soft bread crumbs
1-1/2	teaspoons pepper
4	pounds ground fully cooked ham
8	pounds bulk pork sausage

GLAZE:

6	tablespoons ground mustard
4	cups packed brown sugar
1-1/2	cups white vinegar

Esther Martin
Goshen, Indiana
This savory ham loaf was requested often when I served on our church's hostess committee. When our pastor got married, he wanted the ham loaf for his rehearsal dinner, with triple the glaze. The ham and pork sausage add mouthwatering flavor, and the glaze is nice and tangy.

In a several large bowls, combine the eggs, milk, bread crumbs and pepper. Crumble ham and pork over mixture and mix well.

Shape into four loaves; place each in a greased 13-in. x 9-in. baking dish. Bake, uncovered, at 350° for 45 minutes.

In a large saucepan, combine the glaze ingredients. Bring to a boil; cook and stir until sugar is dissolved. Pour 1/2 cup over each ham loaf; bake for 30 minutes.

Pour remaining glaze over loaves; bake 5-10 minutes longer or until a meat thermometer reads 160°. Let stand for 5 minutes before slicing. **yield: 4 loaves (12 servings each).**

honey-lime roasted chicken

1	whole roasting chicken (5 to 6 pounds)
1/2	cup lime juice
1/4	cup honey
1	tablespoon stone-ground mustard *or* spicy brown mustard
1	teaspoon ground cumin

Carefully loosen the skin from the entire chicken. Place breast side up on a rack in a roasting pan. In a small bowl, whisk the lime juice, honey, mustard and cumin. Using a turkey baster, baste under the chicken skin with 1/3 cup lime juice mixture. Tie drumsticks together. Pour remaining lime juice mixture over chicken.

Bake, uncovered, at 350° for 2-1/2 to 3 hours or until a meat thermometer reads 180°, basting every 30 minutes with drippings (cover loosely with foil after 1 to 1-1/2 hours or when golden brown). Let stand for 10 minutes before carving. Remove and discard skin before serving. **yield: 10 servings.**

Lori Carbonell
Springfield, Vermont
It's hard to believe this finger-licking main course starts with only five ingredients. The chicken is easy, light and so good. It's just as tasty prepared outside on the grill.

fruit-glazed spiral ham

Joan Hallford
North Richland Hills, Texas
The combo of zesty horseradish and tangy mustard creates a delicious glaze perfect for pork. I've used this recipe for years and always receive compliments.

1   bone-in fully cooked spiral-sliced ham (8 to 10 pounds)
1   can (8 ounces) unsweetened crushed pineapple, drained
1/2   cup apricot jam
1   tablespoon spicy brown mustard
2   teaspoons prepared horseradish

Place ham on a rack in a large roasting pan. Cover and bake at 325° for 1-1/2 hours.

Combine the pineapple, jam, mustard and horseradish; spread over ham. Bake, uncovered, for 30-45 minutes or until a meat thermometer reads 140°. **yield: 16-20 servings.**

roasted garlic pork supper

2   whole garlic bulbs
2   teaspoons olive oil
1/2   teaspoon dried basil
1/2   teaspoon dried oregano
2   tablespoons lemon juice
1   boneless pork loin roast (4 to 5 pounds)
6   medium red potatoes, quartered
3   cups baby carrots
1   large sweet onion, thinly sliced
1-1/2   cups water
1   teaspoon salt
1/2   teaspoon pepper

Remove papery outer skin from garlic (do not peel or separate cloves). Cut top off garlic heads, leaving root end intact. Brush with oil; sprinkle with basil and oregano. Wrap each bulb in heavy-duty foil. Bake at 425° for 30-35 minutes or until softened. Cool for 10-15 minutes. Squeeze softened garlic into a small bowl. Add lemon juice; mix well. Rub over the roast.

Place roast in a shallow roasting pan. Arrange potatoes, carrots and onion around roast. Pour water into the pan. Sprinkle meat and vegetables with salt and pepper. Cover and bake at 350° for 1-1/2 hours. Uncover; bake 1-1/2 hours longer or until a meat thermometer reads 160°, basting often. Cover and let stand for 10 minutes before slicing. **yield: 10-12 servings.**

Joseph Obbie
Webster, New York
I grow sweet onions and garlic, so they're always on hand when I want to make this roast. I first fixed the recipe for a church retreat, and it was a big hit. Since then, I've prepared it often for large groups and family dinners over the years.

Darlene Brenden, Salem, Oregon
I first tasted this dish at an office potluck, and now I like to serve it whenever company comes. I set out an array of toppings and let everyone fix their own taco salad.

pork and pinto beans

1	pound dried pinto beans
1	boneless pork loin roast (3 to 4 pounds), halved
1	can (14-1/2 ounces) stewed tomatoes
5	medium carrots, chopped
4	celery ribs, chopped
1-1/2	cups water
2	cans (4 ounces *each*) chopped green chilies
2	tablespoons chili powder
4	garlic cloves, minced
2	teaspoons ground cumin
1	teaspoon dried oregano

Dash pepper

2	packages (10-1/2 ounces *each*) corn tortilla chips *or* 30 flour tortillas (10 inches)

Chopped green onions, sliced ripe olives, chopped tomatoes, shredded cheddar cheese, sour cream *and/or* shredded lettuce

Sort beans and rinse with cold water. Place beans in a Dutch oven; add water to cover by 2 in. Bring to a boil; boil for 2 minutes. Remove from the heat; cover and let stand for 1 to 4 hours or until beans are softened.

Drain and rinse beans, discarding liquid. Place roast in a 5-qt. slow cooker. In a bowl, combine the beans, tomatoes, carrots, celery, water, chilies, chili powder, garlic, cumin, oregano and pepper. Pour over roast. Cover and cook on high for 3 hours. Reduce heat to low; cook 5 hours longer or until beans are tender.

Remove meat, shred with two forks and return to slow cooker. With a slotted spoon, serve meat mixture over corn chips or in tortillas; serve with toppings of your choice. **yield: 10 servings.**

Juline Goelzer, Arroyo Grande, California
I often whip up this easy stew on days when I am juggling a lot of the kids' sports schedules.
Add a green salad and some corn bread or homemade rolls for a perfect meal.

tender beef 'n' bean stew

1   pound beef stew meat, cut into 1-inch cubes
2   cans (16 ounces *each*) kidney beans, rinsed and drained
1   can (14-1/2 ounces) diced tomatoes, undrained
1-1/2   cups frozen corn
1   cup hot water
1   cup chopped onion
2   celery ribs, chopped
1   can (4 ounces) chopped green chilies
1   can (2-1/4 ounces) sliced ripe olives, drained
2   tablespoons uncooked long grain rice
1   to 2 tablespoons chili powder
2   teaspoons beef bouillon granules
1/4   teaspoon salt
1   can (8 ounces) tomato sauce
Shredded cheddar cheese and sour cream, optional

In a 5-qt. slow cooker, combine the first 13 ingredients. Cover and cook on low for 8-9 hours or until the beef is tender. Stir in the tomato sauce; cover and cook for 30 minutes or until heated through. Garnish with the cheese and sour cream if desired. **yield: 10 servings.**

french canadian meat pie

- 1 pound ground beef
- 3/4 pound ground pork
- 3/4 cup chopped onion
- 2 celery ribs, chopped
- 2 garlic cloves, minced
- 6 cups hot mashed potatoes (prepared without milk and butter)
- 1/4 cup chicken broth
- 1/2 teaspoon dried rosemary, crushed
- 1/2 teaspoon rubbed sage
- 1/2 teaspoon dried thyme
- 1/4 teaspoon dried marjoram

Salt and pepper to taste
Pastry for two double-crust pies (9 inches)
Milk, optional

In a large skillet, cook the beef, pork, onion and celery over medium heat until meat is no longer pink. Add garlic; cook 1 minute longer. Drain. Remove from the heat. Stir in the potatoes, broth and seasonings.

Line two 9-in. pie plates with pastry. Divide meat mixture between crusts. Top with remaining pastry; trim, seal and flute edges.

Cut slits in top. Brush with milk if desired. Bake at 375° for 30-35 minutes or until golden brown. **yield: 2 pies (6-8 servings each).**

Diane Davies
Indian Trail, North Carolina
This hearty meat pie was traditionally served on Christmas Eve by my mother's family in Quebec. The recipe has been passed down through at least four generations and has been translated from my grandmother's original recipe in French.

dressed-up dish

Jazz up your meat pies by lining the bottom crust with a few slices of cheese. Top the cheese with the filling and add another layer of cheese over the top. Then add the top crust as instructed. Get creative with different types of cheese.

hearty chicken lasagna

12	uncooked lasagna noodles
2	cans (14-1/2 ounces *each*) diced tomatoes, drained
3	cans (6 ounces *each*) tomato paste
2	cups sliced fresh mushrooms
1/3	cup chopped onion
4-1/2	teaspoons dried basil
1-3/4	teaspoons salt, *divided*
1/8	teaspoon garlic powder
4	cups shredded cooked chicken
2	eggs, lightly beaten
4	cups (24 ounces) 2% cottage cheese
3/4	cup grated Parmesan cheese
1/2	cup minced fresh parsley
3/4	teaspoon pepper
3	cups (12 ounces) shredded part-skim mozzarella cheese

Sharon Skildum
Maple Grove, Minnesota
This is the perfect dish to take to a potluck or charity dinner because no one can believe how comforting and hearty it is! Chicken makes a nice change of pace from the ground beef versions that most people are used to eating.

Cook noodles according to package directions. Meanwhile, in a large saucepan, combine tomatoes, tomato paste, mushrooms, onion, basil, 3/4 teaspoon salt and garlic powder. Bring to a boil. Reduce heat; cover and simmer for 25 minutes. Add the chicken; heat through.

In a large bowl, combine the eggs, cottage cheese, Parmesan cheese, parsley, pepper and remaining salt.

Drain noodles. Place four noodles in a 13-in. x 9-in. baking dish coated with cooking spray. Layer with a third of the cheese mixture, chicken mixture and mozzarella. Repeat layers twice.

Cover and bake at 375° for 30 minutes. Uncover; bake 10-15 minutes longer or until bubbly and top is lightly browned. Let stand for 15 minutes before cutting. **yield: 12 servings.**

cut kitchen time

Save time on preparing your potluck contribution by doing some of the work ahead of time. With Hearty Chicken Lasagna, for instance, you can prepare the chicken mixture a day early. Then just cook the noodles and assemble before your event.

Taste of Home Test Kitchen
For a melt-in-your-mouth delicious main course at your next event, try these super-tender boneless ribs. They're treated to a sweet apple juice, brown sugar and an herb combination that's sure to have folks asking for seconds.

apple country ribs

3/4 cup unsweetened apple juice
1/2 cup beer *or* nonalcoholic beer
1/2 cup canola oil
1/4 cup packed brown sugar
1 tablespoon Worcestershire sauce
1 tablespoon minced garlic
1 teaspoon salt
1 teaspoon dried thyme
1 teaspoon pepper
1/2 teaspoon cayenne pepper
3 pounds boneless country-style pork ribs

In a small bowl, combine the first 10 ingredients. Pour 1-1/2 cups marinade into a large resealable plastic bag; add the ribs. Seal bag and turn to coat; refrigerate for 5 hours or overnight, turning once. Cover and refrigerate remaining marinade for basting.

Prepare grill for indirect heat. Drain and discard marinade. Grill ribs, covered, over indirect medium heat for 10 minutes on each side. Baste with some of the reserved marinade. Grill 20-25 minutes longer or until ribs are tender, turning and basting occasionally. **yield: 12 servings.**

corn-stuffed crown roast

      1 pork crown roast (about 7 pounds and 12 ribs)
    1/2 teaspoon pepper, *divided*
      1 cup chopped celery
      1 cup chopped onion
      1 cup butter, cubed
      6 cups crushed corn bread stuffing
      2 cups frozen corn, thawed
      2 jars (4-1/2 ounces *each*) sliced mushrooms, undrained
      1 teaspoon salt
      1 teaspoon poultry seasoning

Place roast on a rack in a large roasting pan. Sprinkle with 1/4 teaspoon pepper. Cover rib ends with small pieces of foil. Bake, uncovered, at 350° for 2 hours.

In a Dutch oven, saute celery and onion in butter until tender. Stir in the stuffing, corn, mushrooms, salt, poultry seasoning and remaining pepper. Loosely spoon 1-3 cups into center of roast. Place remaining stuffing in a greased 2-qt. baking dish.

Bake roast 30-60 minutes or until a meat thermometer reads 160° and juices run clear.

Cover and bake extra stuffing for 30-40 minutes. Transfer roast to serving platter. Let stand for 10 minutes. Remove foil; cut between ribs to serve. **yield: 12 servings.**

Dorothy Swanson
St. Louis, Missouri
My mother always made this elegant entree for company dinners and our large family get-togethers.

special touch

Corn-Stuffed Crown Roast may be too extravagant for potlucks, but it's the perfect way to feed a group when hosting holidays and other special occasions. Some family cooks double the dressing portion of the recipe to be sure there's extra on hand.

turkey stew with dumplings

8 medium carrots, cut into 1-inch chunks
4 celery ribs, cut into 1-inch chunks
1 cup chopped onion
1/2 cup butter, cubed
2 cans (10-1/2 ounces *each*) condensed beef consomme, undiluted
4-2/3 cups water, *divided*
2 teaspoons salt
1/4 teaspoon pepper
3 cups cubed cooked turkey
2 cups frozen cut green beans
1/2 cup all-purpose flour
2 teaspoons Worcestershire sauce

DUMPLINGS:
1-1/2 cups all-purpose flour
2 teaspoons baking powder
1 teaspoon salt
2 tablespoons minced parsley
1/8 teaspoon poultry seasoning
3/4 cup milk
1 egg

In a Dutch oven, saute the carrots, celery and onion in butter for 10 minutes. Add the consomme, 4 cups water, salt and pepper. Cover and cook over low heat for 15 minutes or until vegetables are tender. Add turkey and beans; cook for 5 minutes. Combine the flour, Worcestershire sauce and remaining water until smooth; stir into turkey mixture. Bring to a boil. Reduce heat; cover and simmer for 5 minutes.

For dumplings, combine the flour, baking powder and salt in a bowl. Stir in parsley and poultry seasoning. Combine milk and egg; stir into flour mixture just until moistened. Drop by tablespoonfuls onto simmering stew. Cover and simmer for 10 minutes. Uncover and simmer 10 minutes longer. **yield: 10-12 servings.**

Rita Taylor
St. Cloud, Minnesota
My husband and I love dumplings. This mild-tasting, homey dish has flavorful ones floating on a tasty turkey and vegetable stew. It really hits the spot on chilly fall and winter days.

Darlene King, Steven, Saskatchewan
After purchasing a steer at a local 4-H fair, we were looking for tasty new beef recipes.
A blend of seasonings makes this tender cut of meat even more succulent.

southwest rib roast with salsa

2	tablespoons chili powder
2	teaspoons salt
2	teaspoons ground cumin
1	teaspoon cayenne pepper
1	bone-in beef rib roast (8 to 10 pounds)
2	cans (15 ounces *each*) black beans, rinsed and drained
2	medium tomatoes, seeded and chopped
1	medium red onion, chopped
1/3	cup minced fresh cilantro

In a small bowl, combine the chili powder, salt, cumin and cayenne. Set aside 2 teaspoons for salsa. Rub the remaining seasoning mixture over roast. Place roast fat side up in a shallow roasting pan.

Bake, uncovered, at 325° for 2-1/2 to 3 hours or until meat reaches desired doneness (for medium-rare, a meat thermometer should read 145°; medium, 160°; well-done, 170°). Transfer to serving platter. Let stand for 15 minutes before carving.

For salsa, combine the beans, tomatoes, onion, cilantro and reserved seasoning mixture in a bowl. Serve with roast. **yield: 12-16 servings.**

casseroles

hamburger noodle
casserole
page 119

broccoli chicken lasagna

1/2	pound sliced fresh mushrooms
1	large onion, chopped
1/4	cup butter, cubed
1/2	cup all-purpose flour
1/2	teaspoon salt
1/4	teaspoon pepper
1/8	teaspoon ground nutmeg
1	can (14-1/2 ounces) chicken broth
1-3/4	cups milk
2/3	cup grated Parmesan cheese
1	package (16 ounces) frozen broccoli cuts, thawed
9	lasagna noodles, cooked and drained
1-1/3	cups julienned fully cooked ham, *divided*
2	cups (8 ounces) shredded Monterey Jack cheese, *divided*
2	cups cubed cooked chicken

In a large skillet, saute mushrooms and onion in butter until tender. Stir in the flour, salt, pepper and nutmeg until blended. Gradually stir in broth and milk. Bring to a boil; cook and stir for 2 minutes or until thickened. Stir in Parmesan cheese and broccoli; heat mixture through.

Spread 1/2 cup broccoli mixture in a greased 13-in. x 9-in. baking dish. Layer with three noodles, a third of the remaining broccoli mixture, 1 cup ham and 1 cup Monterey Jack cheese. Top with three noodles, half of the remaining broccoli mixture, all of the chicken and 1/2 cup Monterey Jack cheese. Top with remaining noodles, broccoli mixture and ham.

Cover and bake at 350° for 45-50 minutes or until bubbly. Sprinkle with remaining Monterey Jack cheese. Bake 5 minutes longer or until cheese is melted. Let stand for 15 minutes before cutting. **yield: 12 servings.**

Dawn Owens
Palatka, Florida
As a working mother with four children, I often prepare meal-in-one dishes. This recipe is different from the traditional lasagnas since it doesn't have tomato sauce.

choice cuts

When a recipe calls for something to be "julienned," such as the cooked ham in Broccoli Chicken Lasagna, it means to slice the foods into long, thin matchstick-like shapes about 2 inches long and 1/8 inch thick.

creamy turkey casserole

     1   can (10-3/4 ounces) condensed cream of celery
         soup, undiluted
     1   can (10-3/4 ounces) condensed cream of mushroom
         soup, undiluted
     1   can (10-3/4 ounces) condensed cream of onion
         soup, undiluted
     5   ounces process cheese (Velveeta), cubed
   1/3   cup mayonnaise
     4   cups cubed cooked turkey
     1   package (16 ounces) frozen broccoli cuts, thawed
 1-1/2   cups cooked white rice
 1-1/2   cups cooked wild rice
     1   can (8 ounces) sliced water chestnuts, drained
     1   jar (4 ounces) sliced mushrooms, drained
 1-1/2   to 2 cups salad croutons

In a large bowl, combine the soups, cheese and mayonnaise. Stir
in the turkey, broccoli, rice, water chestnuts and mushrooms.

Transfer to a greased 13-in. x 9-in. baking dish. Bake, uncovered,
at 350° for 30 minutes; stir. Sprinkle with croutons. Bake 8-12
minutes longer or until bubbly. **yield: 12 servings.**

Mary Jo O'Brien
Hastings, Minnesota
This satisfying supper idea
puts Thanksgiving leftovers to
terrific use. I sometimes make
turkey just so I have the extras
for the casserole.

deep-dish beef bake

     1   pound ground beef
     2   cups biscuit/baking mix
   1/2   cup cold water
     3   medium tomatoes, thinly sliced
     1   medium green pepper, chopped
     2   large onions, chopped
     1   cup (4 ounces) shredded cheddar cheese, *divided*
     1   cup (8 ounces) sour cream
   2/3   cup mayonnaise

Karen Owen
Rising Sun, Indiana
You'll need just 15 minutes to
assemble this before popping it
in the oven. The golden crust
is topped with beef, tomatoes
and a creamy cheese layer.

In a skillet, cook beef over medium heat until no longer pink; drain.

Meanwhile, in a large bowl, combine the biscuit mix and water
until a soft dough forms. Spread into a greased 13-in. x 9-in. baking
dish. Layer with the beef, tomatoes and green pepper.

In a large bowl, combine the onions, 1/2 cup cheese, sour cream
and mayonnaise; spread over top.

Bake, uncovered, at 375° for 30-35 minutes or until edges are
browned. Sprinkle with remaining cheese. Bake 5 minutes longer
or until the cheese is melted. **yield: 12 servings.**

Fran Huettner, Beaver Dam, Wisconsin
All five of our children and six grandchildren expect me to serve this hot bake when they visit. It makes just the right amount for a big group.

casserole for a crowd

- 2 pounds ground beef
- 1 large onion, chopped
- 8 ounces wide egg noodles, cooked and drained
- 1 can (15-1/4 ounces) whole kernel corn, drained
- 1 can (15-1/4 ounces) peas, drained
- 1 can (8 ounces) mushroom stems and pieces, drained
- 4 cups (16 ounces) shredded cheddar cheese, *divided*
- 1 can (10-3/4 ounces) condensed cream of celery soup, undiluted
- 1-1/4 cups milk
- 1 tablespoon chili powder
- 1 tablespoon Worcestershire sauce
- 2 teaspoons salt
- 1/4 teaspoon pepper
- 1/4 teaspoon garlic powder

In a large skillet, cook beef and onion over medium heat until meat is no longer pink; drain. Transfer to a greased roasting pan. Stir in the noodles, corn, peas and mushrooms.

In a large saucepan, combine 2-1/2 cups cheese with the remaining ingredients. Cook and stir over low heat until cheese is melted. Pour over noodle mixture and mix well. Sprinkle with remaining cheese.

Bake, uncovered, at 350° for 30 minutes or until casserole is heated through. **yield: 12-14 servings.**

hamburger noodle casserole

- 5 cups uncooked egg noodles
- 1-1/2 pounds lean ground beef (90% lean)
- 2 garlic cloves, minced
- 3 cans (8 ounces *each*) tomato sauce
- 1/2 teaspoon sugar
- 1/2 teaspoon salt
- 1/8 teaspoon pepper
- 1 package (8 ounces) reduced-fat cream cheese
- 1 cup reduced-fat ricotta cheese
- 1/4 cup reduced-fat sour cream
- 3 green onions, thinly sliced, *divided*
- 2/3 cup shredded reduced-fat cheddar cheese

Cook noodles according to package directions. Meanwhile, in a large nonstick skillet over medium heat, cook beef until meat is no longer pink. Add garlic; cook 1 minute longer. Drain. Stir in the tomato sauce, sugar, salt and pepper; heat through. Drain noodles; stir into beef mixture.

In a small bowl, beat the cream cheese, ricotta cheese and sour cream until blended. Stir in half of the onions.

Spoon half of the noodle mixture into a 13-in. x 9-in. baking dish coated with cooking spray. Top with cheese mixture and remaining noodle mixture

Cover and bake at 350° for 30 minutes. Uncover; sprinkle with cheddar cheese. Bake 5-10 minutes longer or until heated through and cheese is melted. Sprinkle with remaining onions. **yield: 10 servings.**

Martha Henson
Winnsboro, Texas
People have a hard time believing this homey and hearty casserole uses lighter ingredients. The taste is so rich and creamy...a great entree for any occasion!

kitchen staple

Fresh garlic always perks up a dish, but the convenience of the jarred minced garlic is ideal for busy family cooks who are tight on time. When using jarred garlic, remember that 1/2 teaspoon of minced garlic equals 1 fresh garlic clove, minced.

chicken noodle casserole

- 1 package (16 ounces) egg noodles
- 1 medium sweet red pepper, chopped
- 1 large onion, chopped
- 1 celery rib, chopped
- 1/4 cup butter, cubed
- 2 garlic cloves, minced
- 1-1/2 cups sliced fresh mushrooms
- 3 tablespoons all-purpose flour
- 3 cups chicken broth
- 3 cups half-and-half cream
- 2 packages (8 ounces *each*) cream cheese, cubed
- 12 cups cubed cooked chicken
- 1 to 1-1/2 teaspoons salt

TOPPING:
- 1 cup finely crushed cornflakes
- 2 tablespoons butter, melted
- 1 tablespoon canola oil
- 3 tablespoons minced fresh parsley
- 1/2 teaspoon paprika

Cook noodles according to package directions; drain. In a large skillet, saute the red pepper, onion and celery in butter until tender. Add garlic; cook 1 minute longer. Add mushrooms; cook 2-3 minutes or until tender. Remove vegetables with a slotted spoon; set aside.

Add flour to the skillet; stir until blended. Gradually add broth. Bring to a boil; cook and stir for 2 minutes or until thickened. Reduce heat. Gradually stir in cream. Add the cream cheese; cook and stir until cheese is melted. Remove from the heat.

In a large bowl, combine the chicken, salt, noodles, vegetables and cheese sauce. Transfer to two ungreased shallow 3-qt. baking dishes.

Combine topping ingredients. Sprinkle over top. Cover and bake at 350° for 20 minutes. Uncover; bake 15-20 minutes longer or until bubbly. **yield: 2 casseroles (8-10 servings each).**

Cheryl Watts
Natural Bridge, Virginia
This tasty dish gets even better after it's been refrigerated a day or two, so the leftovers are always great. We like to eat it hot in the winter and cold in the summer.

make-ahead chicken bake

- 5 cups cubed cooked chicken
- 2 cups chopped celery
- 5 hard-cooked eggs, sliced
- 1 can (10-3/4 ounces) condensed cream of chicken soup, undiluted
- 3/4 cup mayonnaise
- 2 tablespoons lemon juice
- 1 tablespoon pimientos, optional
- 1 teaspoon finely chopped onion
- 1 cup (4 ounces) shredded cheddar cheese
- 1 can (3 ounces) chow mein noodles
- 1/2 cup slivered almonds, toasted

In a large bowl, combine the first eight ingredients. Transfer to a greased 3-qt. baking dish; sprinkle with cheese, chow mein noodles and almonds. Cover and refrigerate overnight.

Remove from the refrigerator 30 minutes before baking. Bake, uncovered, at 350° for 30-35 minutes until lightly browned and cheese is bubbly. **yield: 12 servings.**

Joyce Wilson
Omaha, Nebraska
This crunchy, saucy hot dish is potluck-perfect! It's so convenient because you can make the casserole the day before and bake it the day of the event. It's good made with turkey, too.

Faythe Anderson
Racine, Wisconsin
Here's a spin on pizza everyone is sure to enjoy.

pizza hot dish

- 2 eggs
- 1/2 cup milk
- 1 package (7 ounces) elbow macaroni, cooked and drained
- 1 pound ground beef
- 1 medium onion, chopped
- 1 can (10-3/4 ounces) condensed tomato soup, undiluted
- 1 teaspoon salt
- 1/2 teaspoon dried basil
- 1/2 teaspoon dried oregano
- 1/4 teaspoon pepper
- 2 cups (8 ounces) shredded cheddar cheese

In a small bowl, beat eggs. Add milk and macaroni. Pour into a greased 13-in. x 9-in. baking dish; set aside.

In a large skillet, cook beef and onion over medium heat until meat is no longer pink; drain. Stir in the soup and seasonings.

Spoon over macaroni. Sprinkle with cheese. Bake, uncovered, at 350° for 20-25 minutes or until heated through. **yield: 12-16 servings.**

baked rice with sausage

2 pounds bulk Italian sausage
4 celery ribs, thinly sliced
1 large onion, chopped
1 large green pepper, chopped
4-1/2 cups water
3/4 cup dry chicken noodle soup mix
1 can (10-3/4 ounces) condensed cream of chicken soup, undiluted
1 cup uncooked long grain rice
1/4 cup dry bread crumbs
2 tablespoons butter, melted

Naomi Flood
Emporia, Kansas
This recipe is perfect for potlucks or church suppers since it produces a big batch and has flavors with broad appeal. Most folks can't guess that the secret ingredient is chicken noodle soup mix.

In a large skillet, cook the sausage, celery, onion and green pepper over medium heat until meat is no longer pink and vegetables are tender; drain. In a large saucepan, bring water to a boil; add dry soup mix. Reduce heat; simmer uncovered, for 5 minutes or until the noodles are tender. Stir in canned soup, rice and sausage mixture; mix well.

Transfer to a greased 13-in. x 9-in. baking dish. Cover and bake at 350° for 40 minutes. Toss bread crumbs and butter; sprinkle over rice mixture. Bake, uncovered, for 10-15 minutes or until rice is tender. Let stand for 10 minutes before serving. **yield: 12-14 servings.**

angel hair shrimp bake

1 package (9 ounces) refrigerated angel hair pasta
1-1/2 pounds uncooked medium shrimp, peeled and deveined
3/4 cup crumbled feta cheese
1/2 cup shredded Swiss cheese
1 jar (16 ounces) chunky salsa
1/2 cup shredded Monterey Jack cheese
3/4 cup minced fresh parsley
1 teaspoon dried basil
1 teaspoon dried oregano
2 eggs
1 cup half-and-half cream
1 cup (8 ounces) plain yogurt

In a greased 13-in. x 9-in. baking dish, layer half of the pasta, shrimp, feta cheese, Swiss cheese and salsa. Repeat layers. Sprinkle with the Monterey Jack cheese, parsley, basil and oregano.

In a small bowl, whisk the eggs, cream and yogurt; pour over casserole. Bake, uncovered, at 350° for 25-30 minutes or until a knife inserted near the center comes out clean. Let stand for 5 minutes before serving. **yield: 12 servings.**

Susan Davidson
Elm Grove, Wisconsin
Shrimp and pasta blend beautifully with the herb, salsa and three kinds of cheese in this layered casserole. The shrimp make this dish special enough at events, but your family is sure to enjoy it, too.

Nancy Foust, Stoneboro, Pennsylvania
Pepperoni tops these ooey-gooey casseroles. They're truly like serving pizza in a dish!

supreme pizza casserole

- 8 ounces uncooked fettuccine
- 2 pounds ground beef
- 1 medium onion, chopped
- 2 cans (8 ounces *each*) mushroom stems and pieces, drained
- 1 can (15 ounces) tomato sauce
- 1 jar (14 ounces) pizza sauce
- 1 can (6 ounces) tomato paste
- 1/2 teaspoon sugar
- 1/2 teaspoon garlic powder
- 1/2 teaspoon onion powder
- 1/2 teaspoon dried oregano
- 4 cups (16 ounces) shredded part-skim mozzarella cheese, *divided*
- 1 package (3-1/2 ounces) sliced pepperoni
- 1/2 cup grated Parmesan cheese

Cook fettuccine according to package directions. Meanwhile, in a Dutch oven, cook beef and onion over medium heat until meat is no longer pink; drain. Stir in the mushrooms, tomato sauce, pizza sauce, tomato paste, sugar and seasonings. Drain pasta; stir into meat sauce.

Divide half of the mixture between two greased 2-qt. baking dishes; sprinkle each with 1 cup mozzarella cheese. Repeat layers. Top each with pepperoni and Parmesan cheese.

Cover and bake at 350° for 20 minutes. Uncover, bake 10-15 minutes longer or until heated through. **yield: 2 casseroles (8 servings each).**

ham & shells casserole

1	package (16 ounces) medium pasta shells
3	large onions, halved and sliced
1	tablespoon olive oil
1	package (9 ounces) fresh spinach, torn
1	tablespoon minced fresh rosemary *or* 1 teaspoon dried rosemary, crushed
1/4	cup butter, cubed
1/3	cup all-purpose flour
1/4	teaspoon pepper
3-1/2	cups fat-free milk
1	cup part-skim ricotta cheese
1	cup crumbled goat cheese
2	cups cubed fully cooked ham
1/3	cup grated Parmesan cheese

Cook pasta according to package directions. Meanwhile, in a large skillet over medium heat, cook and stir onions in oil for 15-20 minutes or until golden brown. Add spinach and rosemary; cook 1-2 minutes longer or until spinach is wilted.

In a large saucepan, melt butter. Stir in flour and pepper until smooth. Gradually add milk. Bring to a boil; cook and stir for 2 minutes or until thickened. Remove from the heat. Stir in ricotta and goat cheeses until blended.

Drain pasta; place in a large bowl. Add the ham, onion mixture and sauce; toss to coat.

Transfer to a greased 13-in. x 9-in. baking dish; sprinkle with Parmesan cheese. Bake, uncovered, at 350° for 25-30 minutes or until bubbly. **yield: 12 servings (1 cup each).**

Genise Krause
Sturgeon Bay, Wisconsin
I altered this recipe to include ham and spinach, and I think it created a well-rounded meal guaranteed to win you rave reviews at your next party!

get fresh

If you enjoy the flavor of rosemary, try growing some in a pot on your kitchen windowsill...or freeze fresh rosemary from the supermarket. Simply wrap sprigs of fresh rosemary in foil and place in a freezer bag. Freeze for up to 3 months.

cheesy sausage penne

- 1 pound bulk Italian sausage
- 1 garlic clove, minced
- 1 jar (26 ounces) spaghetti sauce
- 1 package (16 ounces) uncooked penne pasta
- 1 package (8 ounces) cream cheese, softened
- 1 cup (8 ounces) sour cream
- 4 green onions, sliced
- 2 cups (8 ounces) shredded cheddar cheese

In a large skillet, cook the sausage over medium heat until meat is no longer pink. Add garlic; cook 1 minute longer. Drain. Stir in spaghetti sauce; bring to a boil. Reduce heat; cover and simmer for 20 minutes. Cook pasta according to package directions; drain. Meanwhile, in a small bowl, combine the cream cheese, sour cream and onions.

In a greased shallow 3-qt. baking dish, layer half of the pasta and sausage mixture. Dollop with half the cream cheese mixture; sprinkle with half the cheddar cheese. Repeat layers.

Bake, uncovered, at 350° for 30-35 minutes or until bubbly. **yield: 12 servings.**

Dallas McCord
Reno, Nevada
This lasagna-like entree takes me back to my childhood. I got the recipe from a friend's mother, who fixed it for us when we were kids. It's still quick and delicious.

Martha St. Clair
Salem, Illinois
I got this recipe from a ladies' circle years ago, and I have had many requests for it. It's a real crowd-pleaser, because my large family is a crowd!

chicken macaroni casserole

- 3 cups cubed cooked chicken
- 2 cups uncooked elbow macaroni
- 2 cups (8 ounces) shredded cheddar cheese
- 2 cans (14-1/2 ounces *each*) chicken broth
- 2 cans (10-3/4 ounces *each*) condensed cream of mushroom soup, undiluted
- 1/3 cup finely chopped onion
- 1 can (8 ounces) sliced water chestnuts, drained
- 1 jar (6 ounces) sliced mushrooms
- 1/4 cup chopped green pepper
- 1 jar (2 ounces) sliced pimientos, drained
- 1 tablespoon soy sauce
- 4 cups herb-flavored stuffing mix
- 1/2 cup butter, melted

In a large bowl, combine the first 11 ingredients. Transfer to a greased 13-in. x 9-in. baking dish. Refrigerate overnight.

Remove from the refrigerator 30 minutes before baking. Toss the stuffing mix with butter; sprinkle over casserole. Bake, uncovered, at 350° for 50-55 minutes or until heated through. **yield: 10 servings.**

Rose Enns, Abbotsford, British Columbia
I've been making this recipe since I discovered it a while ago. Over the years, I've
tweaked it to better suit my family's taste. You can substitute chopped salami, pepperoni
or cooked ground beef for the ham. Or, add olives and red peppers.

hawaiian pizza pasta

1/2	pound sliced fresh mushrooms
1	medium onion, chopped
1	medium green pepper, chopped
3	tablespoons canola oil
2	garlic cloves, minced
1	can (15 ounces) tomato sauce
2	bay leaves
1	teaspoon dried oregano
1	teaspoon dried basil
1/2	teaspoon sugar
3-1/2	cups uncooked spiral pasta
6	cups (24 ounces) shredded part-skim mozzarella cheese, *divided*
1	can (20 ounces) pineapple chunks, drained
1	cup cubed fully cooked ham

In a large saucepan, saute the mushrooms, onion and pepper in oil for 5 minutes or until tender. Add garlic; cook 1 minute longer. Add the tomato sauce, bay leaves, oregano, basil and sugar. Bring to a boil. Reduce the heat; simmer, uncovered, for 20-30 minutes or until thickened, stirring the mixture frequently.

Meanwhile, cook pasta according to package directions; drain. Discard bay leaves from sauce. Stir in the pasta, 5 cups of mozzarella cheese, pineapple and ham.

Transfer to a greased shallow 3-qt. baking dish. Sprinkle with remaining cheese. Bake, uncovered, at 350° for 30-35 minutes or until heated through. **yield: 12 servings.**

cheesy rigatoni bake

1 package (16 ounces) rigatoni *or* large tube pasta
2 tablespoons butter
1/4 cup all-purpose flour
1/2 teaspoon salt
2 cups milk
1/4 cup water
4 eggs, lightly beaten
2 cans (8 ounces *each*) tomato sauce
2 cups (8 ounces) shredded part-skim mozzarella cheese, *divided*
1/4 cup grated Parmesan cheese, *divided*

Cook pasta according to package directions. Meanwhile, in a small saucepan, melt butter. Stir in flour and salt until smooth; gradually add milk and water. Bring to a boil; cook and stir for 2 minutes or until thickened.

Drain pasta, place in a large bowl. Add eggs. Spoon into two greased 8-in. square baking dishes. Layer each with one can of tomato sauce, half the mozzarella cheese and half the white sauce. Sprinkle each with half the Parmesan cheese.

Cover and freeze one casserole for up to 3 months. Bake second casserole, uncovered, at 375° for 30-35 minutes or until a meat thermometer reads 160°.

To use frozen casserole: Thaw in the refrigerator overnight. Cover and bake at 375° for 40 minutes. Uncover; bake 7-10 minutes longer or until a meat thermometer reads 160°. **yield: 2 casseroles (6-8 servings each).**

Nancy Urbine
Lancaster, Ohio
This all-time favorite makes two casseroles, one for home and one for a potluck. My kids adore it!

cheese please

Before shredding soft cheeses such as mozzarella, it can help to put the cheese in the freezer for about 30 minutes. This makes it easier to shred, and the cheese doesn't stick to the grater as easily.

polish reuben casserole

1 package (8 ounces) egg noodles
2 cans (14 ounces *each*) Bavarian sauerkraut, drained
2 cans (10-3/4 ounces *each*) condensed cream of mushroom soup, undiluted
1-1/3 cups milk
1 medium onion, chopped
1 tablespoon prepared mustard
1-1/2 pounds Polish sausage *or* kielbasa, halved and cut into 1/2-inch slices
2 cups (8 ounces) shredded Swiss cheese
1/2 cup soft rye bread crumbs
2 tablespoons butter, melted

Imogene Peterson
Ontario, Oregon
People are always asking me for this change-of-pace recipe. It's easy to assemble, and it is great to take to covered-dish events, which we have a lot of in our farming community.

Cook noodles according to package directions; drain. Spread sauerkraut in a greased shallow 4-qt. baking dish. Top with noodles. In a large bowl, combine the soup, milk, onion and mustard; pour over the noodles. Top with sausage; sprinkle with cheese.

Combine bread crumbs and butter; sprinkle over the top. Cover and bake at 350° for 30-35 minutes or until golden brown and bubbly. **yield: 12-14 servings.**

texas style lasagna

1-1/2 pounds ground beef
1 teaspoon seasoned salt
1 package (1-1/4 ounces) taco seasoning mix
1 can (14-1/2 ounces) diced tomatoes, undrained
1 can (15 ounces) tomato sauce
1 can (4 ounces) chopped green chilies
2 cups (16 ounces) 4% cottage cheese
2 eggs, lightly beaten
12 corn tortillas (6 inches), torn
3-1/2 to 4 cups shredded Monterey Jack cheese

In a skillet, cook beef over medium heat until no longer pink; drain. Add the seasoned salt, taco seasoning mix, tomatoes, tomato sauce and chilies. Reduce heat, simmer, uncovered, for 15-20 minutes. In a small bowl, combine cottage cheese and eggs.

In a greased 13-in. x 9-in. baking dish, layer half of the meat sauce, half of the tortillas, half the cottage cheese mixture and half of the Monterey Jack cheese. Repeat layers.

Bake, uncovered, at 350° for 30 minutes or until bubbly. Let stand 10 minutes before serving. **yield: 10-12 servings.**

Effie Gish
Fort Worth, Texas
With its spicy flavor, this entree is a crowd-pleaser...I make it often. It goes great with side servings of picante sauce, guacamole, corn chips, olives and fresh fruit.

Shirley Unger, Bluffton, Ohio
Talk about a potluck pleaser! This comforting, creamy casserole is bursting with tender chunks of chicken. Even the pickiest eater will gobble up this tasty bake.

creamy chicken noodle bake

4	cups uncooked egg noodles
1/2	cup butter, *divided*
1/4	cup all-purpose flour
1/2	teaspoon salt
1/8	teaspoon white pepper
3-1/2	cups milk
4	cups cubed cooked chicken
2	jars (12 ounces *each*) chicken gravy
1	jar (2 ounces) diced pimientos, drained
1/2	cup cubed process cheese (Velveeta)
1/2	cup dry bread crumbs
4	teaspoons butter, melted

Cook noodles according to package directions. Meanwhile, in a Dutch oven, melt 6 tablespoons butter. Stir in the flour, salt and pepper until smooth. Gradually add milk. Bring to a boil; cook and stir for 1-2 minutes or until thickened. Remove from the heat. Stir in the chicken, gravy and pimientos.

Drain noodles; toss with remaining butter. Stir into chicken mixture. Transfer to a greased 13-in. x 9-in. baking dish.

Cover and bake at 350° for 30-35 minutes or until bubbly. Combine the cheese, bread crumbs and melted butter. Sprinkle around edges of casserole. Bake, uncovered, for 10 minutes longer or until golden brown. Let stand for 10 minutes before serving. **yield: 12 servings (1 cup each).**

Debra Martin, Belleville, Michigan
Every time I make this nice take on enchiladas for guests, I'm asked for my recipe!

turkey enchilada casserole

 1 **pound lean ground turkey**
 1 **medium green pepper, chopped**
 1 **medium onion, chopped**
 3 **garlic cloves, minced**
 2 **cans (15 ounces *each*) black beans, rinsed and drained**
 1 **jar (16 ounces) salsa**
 1 **can (15 ounces) tomato sauce**
 1 **can (14-1/2 ounces) Mexican stewed tomatoes**
 1 **teaspoon *each* onion powder, garlic powder and ground cumin**
12 **corn tortillas (6 inches)**
 2 **cups (8 ounces) shredded reduced-fat cheddar cheese, *divided***

In a large nonstick saucepan coated with cooking spray, cook the turkey, green pepper and onion over medium heat until meat is no longer pink. Add garlic; cook 1 minute longer. Drain. Stir in the beans, salsa, tomato sauce, tomatoes, onion powder, garlic powder and cumin. Bring to a boil. Reduce heat; simmer, uncovered, for 10 minutes.

Spread 1 cup meat sauce into a 13-in. x 9-in. baking dish coated with cooking spray. Top with six tortillas. Spread with half of the remaining meat sauce; sprinkle with 1 cup cheese. Layer with remaining tortillas and meat sauce.

Cover and bake at 350° for 20 minutes. Uncover; sprinkle with the remaining cheese. Bake 5-10 minutes longer or until bubbly and the cheese is melted. **yield: 10 servings.**

ground beef spiral bake

1 package (16 ounces) spiral pasta
2 pounds ground beef
2/3 cup chopped onion
1 teaspoon minced garlic
2 jars (28 ounces *each*) spaghetti sauce
2 tablespoons tomato paste
1 teaspoon dried basil
1 teaspoon dried oregano
4 cups (16 ounces) shredded part-skim mozzarella cheese

Cook pasta according to package directions; drain. Meanwhile, in a Dutch oven, cook beef and onion over medium heat until meat is no longer pink. Add garlic; cook 1 minute longer. Drain. Stir in the spaghetti sauce, tomato paste, basil and oregano. Bring to a boil. Reduce heat; simmer, uncovered, for 5-10 minutes.

Stir pasta into meat mixture. Transfer to two greased 13-in. x 9-in. baking dishes. Sprinkle each with 2 cups cheese. Cover and freeze one casserole for up to 3 months.

Bake the second casserole, uncovered, at 350° for 25-30 minutes or until heated through.

To use frozen casserole: Thaw in the refrigerator overnight. Bake, uncovered, at 350° for 35-40 minutes or until heated through. **yield: 2 casseroles (8-10 servings each).**

Monika Rahn
Dillsburg, Pennsylvania
We got this recipe from a restaurant cook who lived in the duplex beside my mother-in-law. It was one of his favorites. It's easy to make, tastes great and freezes well.

baked ziti casserole

1 package (16 ounces) ziti *or* small tube pasta
1 egg, lightly beaten
1 carton (15 ounces) part-skim ricotta cheese
1/2 cup grated Parmesan cheese, *divided*
1 jar (28 ounces) meatless spaghetti sauce
2 cups (8 ounces) shredded part-skim mozzarella cheese

Paula Zsiray
Logan, Utah
With its rich Italian flavor and generous combination of cheeses, my six-ingredient specialty hardly seems light. It's perfect when you take something to an event but would like to bring something a bit lighter than the average potluck contribution.

Cook pasta according to package directions. Drain pasta; set aside. In a small bowl, combine the egg, ricotta and 1/4 cup Parmesan cheese.

Spread 1 cup spaghetti sauce in a 13-in. x 9-in. baking dish coated with cooking spray. Top with a third of the pasta, half of the ricotta mixture, 2/3 cup mozzarella cheese, 1 tablespoon Parmesan cheese and 1 cup sauce. Repeat layers of pasta, ricotta mixture and mozzarella cheese. Sprinkle with 2 tablespoons Parmesan cheese. Top with remaining pasta, sauce, mozzarella cheese and Parmesan cheese. Cover and bake at 375° for 45-50 minutes or until heated through. **yield: 12 servings.**

firefighter's chicken spaghetti

12	ounces uncooked spaghetti, broken in half
1	can (10-3/4 ounces) condensed cream of chicken soup, undiluted
1	can (10-3/4 ounces) condensed cream of mushroom soup, undiluted
1	cup (8 ounces) sour cream
1/2	cup milk
1/4	cup butter, melted, *divided*
2	tablespoons dried parsley flakes
1/2	teaspoon garlic powder
1/2	teaspoon salt
1/4	teaspoon pepper
2	cups (8 ounces) shredded part-skim mozzarella cheese
1	cup grated Parmesan cheese
2	to 3 celery ribs, chopped
1	medium onion, chopped
1	can (4 ounces) mushroom stems and pieces, drained
5	cups cubed cooked chicken
1-1/2	cups crushed cornflakes

Krista Davis-Keith
New Castle, Indiana
I'm usually in the kitchen most of the day making some kind of dish for my family, neighbors or the local fire department to pass around and sample. My husband is a firefighter in our town, and this casserole is a favorite with his coworkers.

Cook spaghetti according to package directions; drain. In a large bowl, combine the soups, sour cream, milk, 2 tablespoons butter and seasonings. Add the cheeses, celery, onion and mushrooms. Stir in the chicken and spaghetti.

Transfer to a greased 3-qt. baking dish (dish will be full). Combine cornflakes and remaining butter; sprinkle over the top.

Bake, uncovered, at 350° for 45-50 minutes or until bubbly. **yield: 12-14 servings.**

time to measure up

To properly measure sour cream, yogurt and other wet ingredients, first spoon the ingredient into a dry measuring cup. Then level the top by sweeping a metal spatula or flat side of a knife across the top of the cup.

Edna Coburn, Tucson, Arizona
Peas, pecans and pimientos complement the salmon in this potluck-perfect dish, which is topped with crushed potato chips to give it a little added crunch. It's great for family dinners as well!

pecan salmon casserole

1	package (16 ounces) small shell pasta
2	medium onions, finely chopped
1/2	pound sliced fresh mushrooms
1/4	cup butter, cubed
2	cans (10-3/4 ounces *each*) condensed cream of mushroom soup, undiluted
1-1/2	cups milk
2	teaspoons Worcestershire sauce
1	teaspoon salt
1/2	teaspoon pepper
2	cans (14-3/4 ounces *each*) salmon, drained, bones and skin removed
2	cups frozen peas
1	cup chopped pecans, toasted
1	jar (2 ounces) diced pimientos, drained
1/2	cup crushed potato chips

Cook pasta according to package directions. Meanwhile in a large skillet, saute the onions and mushrooms in butter until tender. Stir in the soup, milk, Worcestershire sauce, salt and pepper until blended; bring to a boil. Remove from the heat.

Drain pasta. Add the pasta, salmon, peas, pecans and pimientos to the skillet. Transfer to a greased shallow 3-qt. baking dish.

Cover and bake at 350° for 30-35 minutes or until heated through. Sprinkle with potato chips. **yield: 12 servings.**

Hope LaShier, Amarillo, Texas
This colorful casserole is named after the West Coast, but it always brings appreciative oohs and aahs when I serve it to fellow Texans. It's compatible with a large variety of side dishes, so it's great on a buffet.

california casserole

2	pounds ground beef
1	medium green pepper, chopped
3/4	cup chopped onion
1	can (14-3/4 ounces) cream-style corn
1	can (10-3/4 ounces) condensed tomato soup, undiluted
1	can (10 ounces) tomatoes with green chilies, undrained
1	can (8 ounces) tomato sauce
1	jar (4-1/2 ounces) whole mushrooms, drained
1	jar (4 ounces) chopped pimientos, drained
1	can (2-1/4 ounces) sliced ripe olives, drained
1-1/2	teaspoons celery salt
1/2	teaspoon ground mustard
1/2	teaspoon chili powder
1/4	teaspoon pepper
8	ounces wide egg noodles, cooked and drained
2	cups (8 ounces) shredded cheddar cheese

In a large skillet, cook the beef, green pepper and onion over medium heat until meat is no longer pink and vegetables are tender; drain. Stir in the next 11 ingredients. Add noodles.

Pour into a greased 13-in. x 9-in. baking dish. Cover and bake at 350° for 50 minutes. Sprinkle with cheese; bake 10 minutes longer or until the cheese is melted. **yield: 12-16 servings.**

eggplant sausage casserole

1 package (16 ounces) penne pasta
2 pounds bulk Italian sausage
1 medium eggplant, peeled and cubed
1 large onion, chopped
2 tablespoons olive oil
2 garlic cloves, minced
1 can (28 ounces) diced tomatoes, undrained
1 can (6 ounces) tomato paste
1 teaspoon salt
1 teaspoon dried basil
1 teaspoon paprika
1 carton (15 ounces) ricotta cheese
4 cups (16 ounces) shredded part-skim mozzarella cheese, *divided*

Cook pasta according to package directions. Meanwhile, in a large skillet, cook sausage over medium heat until no longer pink; drain. Set sausage aside.

In the same skillet, saute eggplant and onion in oil. Add garlic; cook 1 minute longer. Stir in the tomatoes, tomato paste, salt, basil and paprika; simmer, partially covered, for 15 minutes. Remove from heat. Drain pasta; stir into eggplant mixture. Add sausage.

Spread half of the sausage mixture in a greased 13-in. x 9-in. baking dish. Spread with ricotta. Top with half of the cheese and remaining sausage mixture.

Cover and bake at 350° for 40 minutes. Uncover; sprinkle with remaining cheese. Bake 5 minutes longer or until cheese is melted. Let stand for 10 minutes before serving. **yield: 12 servings.**

Carol Mieske
Red Bluff, California
If you want your kids to happily eat their eggplant, serve it in this lovely layered casserole. Our whole family enjoys it. Always a popular potluck item, it's a great company dish, as well.

pasta pointer

To cook pasta more evenly, prevent it from sticking together and avoid boil-overs, always cook pasta in a large kettle or Dutch oven. Unless you have a very large kettle, don't prepare more than 2 pounds of pasta at a time.

biscuit-topped lemon chicken

2 large onions, finely chopped
4 celery ribs, finely chopped
1 cup butter, cubed
2 garlic cloves, minced
8 green onions, thinly sliced
2/3 cup all-purpose flour
8 cups 2% milk
12 cups cubed cooked chicken
2 cans (10-3/4 ounces *each*) condensed cream of chicken soup, undiluted
1/2 cup lemon juice
2 tablespoons grated lemon peel
2 teaspoons pepper
1 teaspoon salt

CHEDDAR BISCUITS:

5 cups self-rising flour
2 cups 2% milk
2 cups (8 ounces) shredded cheddar cheese
1/4 cup butter, melted

In a Dutch oven, saute onions and celery in butter. Add garlic; cook 1 minute longer. Add green onions. Stir in flour until blended; gradually add milk. Bring to a boil; cook and stir for 2 minutes or until thickened.

Stir in the chicken, soup, lemon juice and peel, pepper and salt; heat through. Pour into two greased 13-in. x 9-in. baking dishes; set aside.

In a large bowl, combine the biscuit ingredients just until moistened. Turn onto a lightly floured surface; knead 8-10 times. Pat or roll out to 3/4-in. thickness. With a floured 2-1/2-in. biscuit cutter, cut out 30 biscuits.

Place over chicken mixture. Bake, uncovered, at 350° for 35-40 minutes or until golden brown. **yield: 15 servings (30 biscuits).**

Pattie Ishee
Stringer, Mississippi
This homey recipe is great at large get-togethers.

Doreen Martin, Kitimat, British Columbia
I layer cabbage and a ground beef filling lasagna-style in this hearty casserole that cabbage-roll lovers will savor.

cabbage roll casserole

- 2 pounds ground beef
- 1 large onion, chopped
- 3 garlic cloves, minced
- 2 cans (15 ounces *each*) tomato sauce, *divided*
- 1 teaspoon dried thyme
- 1/2 teaspoon dill weed
- 1/2 teaspoon rubbed sage
- 1/4 teaspoon salt
- 1/4 teaspoon pepper
- 1/4 teaspoon cayenne pepper
- 2 cups cooked rice
- 4 bacon strips, cooked and crumbled
- 1 medium head cabbage (2 pounds), shredded
- 1 cup (4 ounces) shredded part-skim mozzarella cheese

In a large skillet, cook beef and onion over medium heat until meat is no longer pink. Add garlic; cook 1 minute longer. Drain. Stir in one can of tomato sauce and seasonings. Bring to a boil. Reduce heat; cover and simmer for 5 minutes. Stir in rice and bacon; heat through. Remove from the heat.

Layer a third of the cabbage in a greased 13-in. x 9-in. baking dish. Top with half of the meat mixture. Repeat layers; top with remaining cabbage. Pour remaining tomato sauce over top.

Cover and bake at 375° for 45 minutes. Uncover; sprinkle with cheese. Bake 10 minutes longer or until cheese is melted. Let stand for 5 minutes before serving. **yield: 12 servings.**

Shannon Weddle, Berryville, Virginia
This casserole is so easy to make and works well with either leftover turkey or fresh turkey cutlets. You can also substitute flavored bread crumbs for the plain ones and a jarred, roasted red pepper for the fresh variety.

classic turkey tetrazzini

1	package (16 ounces) spaghetti
2	medium onions, chopped
9	tablespoons butter, *divided*
1	pound sliced fresh mushrooms
1	large sweet red pepper, chopped
1/2	cup all-purpose flour
1	teaspoon salt
6	cups 2% milk
1	tablespoon chicken bouillon granules
6	cups cubed cooked turkey breast
1	cup grated Parmesan cheese
1-1/2	cups dry bread crumbs
4	teaspoons minced fresh parsley

Cook spaghetti according to package directions. Meanwhile, in a Dutch oven, saute onions in 6 tablespoons butter until tender. Add mushrooms and red pepper; saute 4-5 minutes longer.

Stir in flour and salt until blended. Gradually whisk in milk and bouillon. Bring to a boil; cook and stir for 2 minutes or until thickened. Stir in turkey and cheese; heat through. Remove from the heat.

Drain spaghetti; add to turkey mixture and mix well. Transfer to one greased 13-in. x 9-in. baking dish and one greased 11-in. x 7-in. baking dish.

Melt remaining butter; toss with bread crumbs. Sprinkle over casseroles. Bake, uncovered, at 350° for 30-35 minutes or until heated through. Sprinkle with parsley. **yield: 12 servings.**

pecan chicken casserole

- 1 cup all-purpose flour
- 1 cup (4 ounces) finely shredded cheddar cheese
- 3/4 cup finely chopped pecans
- 1/2 teaspoon salt
- 1/4 teaspoon paprika
- 1/3 cup canola oil

FILLING:
- 4 eggs, lightly beaten
- 1 cup (8 ounces) sour cream
- 1 cup chicken broth
- 4 cups diced cooked chicken
- 1/2 cup finely shredded cheddar cheese
- 1/4 cup finely chopped onion
- 1/4 cup mayonnaise
- 1/4 teaspoon dill seed
- 1/8 teaspoon hot pepper sauce

In a large bowl, combine the first six ingredients. Set aside 1/2 cup of crumb mixture for topping. Press remaining crumb mixture onto the bottom of a greased 13-in. x 9-in. baking dish. (Crust will be crumbly.) Bake at 350° for 10 minutes or until mixture is lightly browned.

In a large bowl, combine the remaining ingredients. Pour over crust. Sprinkle with reserved crumb mixture.

Bake at 350° for 25-30 minutes or until a knife inserted near the center comes out clean. Let stand for 10 minutes before cutting. **yield: 12 servings.**

Jackie Heyer, Cushing, Iowa
I got this recipe from a radio show years ago, and it's one of my favorites. The tasty pecan-and-cheddar-cheese crust holds a zippy filling that is flavored with chicken, cheddar cheese, dill, onion and even a splash of hot pepper sauce.

happy trails

When taking a casserole to a potluck, try setting the dish inside a clear plastic oven bag. The bag traps any spills, it doesn't melt and organizers can see what's inside. It's so easy to slide the dish in and seal it with a simple twist tie.

eggplant parmigiana

- 2 medium eggplant, peeled and cut into 1/2-inch slices
- 2 teaspoons salt
- 2 large onions, chopped
- 2 tablespoons minced fresh basil *or* 2 teaspoons dried basil
- 2 bay leaves
- 1 tablespoon minced fresh oregano *or* 1 teaspoon dried oregano
- 1 tablespoon minced fresh thyme *or* 1 teaspoon dried thyme
- 3 tablespoons olive oil
- 1 can (14-1/2 ounces) diced tomatoes, undrained
- 1 can (12 ounces) tomato paste
- 1 tablespoon honey
- 1-1/2 teaspoons lemon-pepper seasoning
- 4 garlic cloves, minced
- 2 eggs, lightly beaten
- 1/2 teaspoon pepper
- 1-1/2 cups dry bread crumbs
- 1/4 cup butter, *divided*
- 8 cups (32 ounces) shredded part-skim mozzarella cheese
- 1 cup grated Parmesan cheese

Valerie Belley
St. Louis, Missouri
My delicious eggplant casserole is ideal for serving a large crowd of friends and family.

Place eggplant in a colander; sprinkle with salt. Let stand for 30 minutes. Meanwhile, in a large skillet, saute the onions, basil, bay leaves, oregano and thyme in oil until onions are tender.

Add the tomatoes, tomato paste honey and lemon-pepper. Bring to a boil. Reduce heat; cover and simmer for 30 minutes. Add garlic; simmer 10 minutes longer. Discard bay leaves.

Rinse eggplant slices; pat dry with paper towels. In a shallow bowl, combine eggs and pepper; place bread crumbs in another shallow bowl. Dip eggplant into eggs, then coat with crumbs. Let stand for 5 minutes.

In a large skillet, cook half of the eggplant in 2 tablespoons butter for 3 minutes on each side or until lightly browned. Repeat with remaining eggplant and butter.

In each of two greased 11-in. x 7-in. baking dishes, layer half of each of the eggplant, tomato sauce and mozzarella cheese. Repeat layers. Sprinkle with Parmesan cheese. Bake, uncovered, at 375° for 35 minutes or until bubbly. **yield: 10-12 servings.**

quick &
easy

honey-mustard
glazed salmon

page 157

Suzette Jury, Keene, California
We love casseroles we can just pop in the oven and enjoy. This one comes from our family cookbook that's filled with recipes from generations of women.

bow tie ham bake

- 4 cups uncooked bow tie pasta
- 6 cups frozen broccoli florets
- 4 cups cubed fully cooked ham
- 2 cartons (10 ounces *each*) refrigerated Alfredo sauce
- 2 cups (8 ounces) shredded Swiss cheese
- 1 can (8 ounces) mushroom stems and pieces, drained

Cook pasta according to package directions, adding the broccoli during the last 5 minutes of cooking.

Meanwhile, in a large bowl, combine the ham, Alfredo sauce, cheese and mushrooms. Drain pasta mixture; add to ham mixture and toss to coat. Transfer to two greased 11-in. x 7-in. baking dishes. Cover and freeze one casserole for up to 3 months. Cover and bake remaining casserole at 375° for 20 minutes. Uncover; bake 5-10 minutes longer or until bubbly.

To use frozen casserole: Thaw in the refrigerator overnight. Remove from the refrigerator 30 minutes before heating. Cover and microwave on high for 8-10 minutes or until heated through, stirring once. **yield: 2 casseroles (6 servings each).**

pepperoni roll-ups

1 package (8 ounces) cream cheese, softened
1 package (3-1/2 ounces) sliced pepperoni, finely chopped
1 cup (4 ounces) shredded provolone cheese
2 tablespoons onion soup mix
2 tablespoons sour cream
1 teaspoon grated Romano cheese
2 tubes (13.8 ounces *each*) refrigerated pizza crust

In a small bowl, combine the first six ingredients. Unroll each tube of pizza dough into a long rectangle; spread each rectangle evenly with 1 cup pepperoni mixture.

Roll up jelly-roll style, starting with a short side; pinch seam to seal. Cut each roll into 16 slices; place cut side down on ungreased baking sheets.

Bake at 400° for 10-14 minutes or until golden brown. Serve warm. Refrigerate leftovers. **yield: 32 appetizers.**

Cynthia Bent
Newark, Delaware
I love to serve these crowd-pleasing appetizers at many celebrations. The pinwheels are easy to prepare, and they always disappear quickly!

Suzy Horvath
Gladstone, Oregon
Here's a terrific coleslaw to include with all the fixings for your holiday meal. Just dice up apples and cabbage, whisk the sauce, and don't forget the pretty red cranberries.

thanksgiving cabbage salad

2 medium apples, chopped
1 tablespoon lemon juice
1 cup heavy whipping cream
2 tablespoons sugar
2 tablespoons cumin seeds
1/2 teaspoon salt
1/4 teaspoon pepper
1 tablespoon red wine vinegar
6 cups shredded green cabbage
2 cups shredded red cabbage
2/3 cup dried cranberries

In a small bowl, combine apples and lemon juice. In another bowl, combine the cream, sugar, cumin seeds, salt and pepper; gradually whisk in vinegar.

In a large bowl, combine the green cabbage, red cabbage, cranberries and apples. Add dressing and gently toss to coat. Cover and refrigerate for at least 1 hour before serving. **yield: 10 servings.**

vegetable beef soup

4   cups cubed peeled potatoes
6   cups water
1   pound ground beef
5   teaspoons beef bouillon granules
1   can (10-3/4 ounces) condensed tomato soup, undiluted
2   cups frozen corn, thawed
2   cups frozen sliced carrots, thawed
2   cups frozen cut green beans, thawed
2   cups frozen sliced okra, thawed
3   tablespoons dried minced onion

Marie Carlisle
Sumrall, Mississippi
Just brimming with veggies, this hearty soup will warm family and friends right to their toes! It's especially good served with corn bread, and we think it's even better the second day.

In a Dutch oven, bring potatoes and water to a boil. Cover and cook for 10-15 minutes or until tender. Meanwhile, in a large skillet, cook beef over medium heat until no longer pink; drain.

Add the bouillon, soup, vegetables, dried minced onion and beef to the undrained potatoes. Bring to a boil. Reduce heat; simmer, uncovered, for 8-10 minutes or until heated through, stirring occasionally. **yield: 14 servings (3-1/2 quarts).**

chocolate peanut butter cake

2   cups miniature marshmallows
1   package (18-1/4 ounces) chocolate cake mix
1-1/4   cups water
3/4   cup peanut butter
1/3   cup canola oil
3   eggs
1   cup (6 ounces) semisweet chocolate chips

Sprinkle marshmallows into a greased 13-in. x 9-in. baking pan. In a large bowl, combine the cake mix, water, peanut butter, oil and eggs; beat on low speed for 30 seconds. Beat on medium for 2 minutes or until smooth. Pour over marshmallows; sprinkle with chocolate chips.

Bake at 350° for 30-35 minutes or until a toothpick inserted near the center comes out clean. Cool on a wire rack. **yield: 12-15 servings.**

Brenda Melancon
Gonzales, Louisiana
The two great flavors of chocolate and peanut butter come together in this moist, delicious cake. Kids of every age will be all over this one!

almond-avocado tossed salad

3 cups torn iceberg lettuce
3 cups torn leaf lettuce
2-1/2 cups fresh baby spinach
2 medium ripe avocados, peeled and chopped
1 can (11 ounces) mandarin oranges, drained
1 small cucumber, halved lengthwise, seeded and sliced
1 small sweet red pepper, chopped
1/2 cup honey-roasted almonds
1/2 cup red wine vinaigrette or vinaigrette of your choice

In a large salad bowl, combine the first seven ingredients. Sprinkle with almonds. Drizzle with vinaigrette and toss to coat. Serve immediately. **yield: 14 servings.**

editor's note: This recipe was tested with Almond Accents honey-roasted almonds.

Suzanne Sager
Dallas, Texas
I received this recipe from a friend, and my guests always let me know how much they've enjoyed it. It's so easy to prepare! I didn't think it could be improved upon, but almonds add a nice crunch. Fresh and colorful, it also travels well.

steak sauce sloppy joes

3 pounds ground beef
4 medium onions, chopped
2 celery ribs, chopped
1 garlic clove, minced
1 can (28 ounces) diced tomatoes, undrained
1/4 cup Worcestershire sauce
1/4 cup A.1. steak sauce
2 tablespoons chili powder
2 tablespoons paprika
1/4 teaspoon pepper
15 hamburger buns, split

In a Dutch oven, cook the beef, onions and celery over medium heat until the meat is no longer pink. Add the garlic; cook 1 minute longer. Drain.

Stir in the tomatoes, Worcestershire sauce, steak sauce, chili powder, paprika and pepper. Bring to a boil. Reduce heat; simmer, uncovered, for 20 minutes or until thickened and heated through. Serve on buns. **yield: 15 servings.**

Patti Basten
DePere, Wisconsin
Everyone in our family loves these flavorful barbecue sandwiches. The recipe makes a big batch, and it freezes nicely, too.

apple cream cheese pie

- 1 package (8 ounces) cream cheese, softened
- 1/2 cup confectioners' sugar
- 1 teaspoon vanilla extract
- 1 carton (8 ounces) frozen whipped topping, thawed
- 1 graham cracker crust (9 inches)
- 1-3/4 cups apple pie filling
- Dash ground cinnamon

In a large bowl, beat cream cheese and confectioners' sugar until smooth. Beat in vanilla. Fold in whipped topping.

Pour into the crust. Top with pie filling; sprinkle with cinnamon. Refrigerate for at least 2 hours before serving. **yield: 6-8 servings.**

Linda Duncan
Junction City, Oregon
With just a handful of ingredients and a topping of apples, this smooth and fluffy cream-cheese pie will put smiles on everyone's faces at the potluck!

crab crescents

- 1 tube (8 ounces) refrigerated crescent rolls
- 3 tablespoons prepared pesto
- 1/2 cup fresh crabmeat

Unroll crescent dough; separate into eight triangles. Cut each triangle in half lengthwise, forming two triangles. Spread 1/2 teaspoon pesto over each triangle; place 1 rounded teaspoonful of crab along the wide end of each triangle.

Roll up triangles from the wide ends and place point side down 1 in. apart on an ungreased baking sheet.

Bake at 375° for 10-12 minutes or until golden brown. Serve warm. **yield: 16 appetizers.**

Stephanie Howard
Oakland, California
This recipe is so good, no one will guess how quickly you put it together. The little bites are so delicious and decadent!

pork burgers deluxe

Peggy Bellar
Howard, Kansas
I found this recipe in a book I received as a wedding present. The flavor of the burgers is fantastic. Ground pork is a nice change from beef, and the pineapple slice on top makes it extra special.

- 1/3 cup vinegar
- 1/4 cup packed brown sugar
- 1 small onion, chopped
- 2 tablespoons soy sauce
- 1 teaspoon salt
- 1 teaspoon garlic salt
- 2 pounds ground pork
- 1 can (20 ounces) sliced pineapple, drained
- 10 bacon strips
- 10 hamburger buns, split

Combine the first six ingredients. Crumble pork over mixture and mix well. Shape into 10 patties. Top each with a pineapple slice; wrap with a bacon strip and secure with a toothpick.

Broil or grill over medium-hot heat for 7-10 minutes on each side or until a meat thermometer reads 160° and juices run clear. Remove toothpicks. Serve on buns. **yield: 10 servings.**

cranberry chili meatballs

- 1 can (14 ounces) jellied cranberry sauce
- 1 bottle (12 ounces) chili sauce
- 3/4 cup packed brown sugar
- 1/2 teaspoon chili powder
- 1/2 teaspoon ground cumin
- 1/4 teaspoon cayenne pepper
- 1 package (32 ounces) frozen fully cooked homestyle meatballs, thawed

In a large saucepan over medium heat, combine the first six ingredients; stir until sugar is dissolved. Add the meatballs; cook for 20-25 minutes or until hot, stirring occasionally. **yield: about 6 dozen.**

Amy Scamerhorn
Indianapolis, Indiana
My friends look forward to enjoying these meatballs at our gatherings, and there are never any leftovers! The sauce is tangy yet sweet, and frozen meatballs make it a snap to throw together, even when you're busy.

spinach bacon tartlets

1 package (8 ounces) reduced-fat cream cheese
1 egg white
1/2 cup frozen chopped spinach, thawed and squeezed dry
3 tablespoons chopped green onions (white part only)
1 teaspoon salt-free seasoning blend
1/4 teaspoon ground nutmeg
2 packages (1.9 ounces *each*) frozen miniature phyllo tart shells
3 turkey bacon strips, diced and cooked

In a small bowl, beat the first six ingredients until blended. Spoon filling into tart shells. Place on an ungreased baking sheet.

Bake at 350° for 10 minutes. Sprinkle with bacon; bake 2-5 minutes longer or until filling is set and shells are lightly browned. Serve warm. **yield: 2-1/2 dozen.**

Linda Evancoe-Coble
Leola, Pennsylvania
These delicious bites make a lovely presentation on a buffet table. Best of all, they come together very easily!

holiday peas

2 packages (16 ounces *each*) frozen peas
2 teaspoons salt
1 cup finely crushed wheat crackers
2 tablespoons grated Parmesan cheese
2 tablespoons butter, melted

Place peas in a large saucepan; add salt. Cover with water. Bring to a boil. Reduce the heat; cover and simmer for 5-6 minutes or until tender.

Meanwhile, toss the cracker crumbs, cheese and butter. Drain peas and place in a serving bowl; top with crumb mixture.

yield: 12 servings.

Sue Gronholz
Beaver Dam, Wisconsin
My mom used to dress up peas with buttered cracker crumbs when I was little, and it remains one of my favorite dishes. Just about any type of savory crackers can be substituted, including herb-flavored varieties.

Mary Relyea, Canastota, New York
Earthy herbs bring a full chorus of tastes to creamy red potatoes, making this side dish anything but ordinary. Save it for special occasions or serve as a dressy accompaniment to a weeknight meal.

flavorful mashed potatoes

4	pounds red potatoes (about 12 medium)
6	garlic cloves, peeled and thinly sliced
1/2	cup fat-free milk
1/2	cup reduced-fat sour cream
2	tablespoons butter, melted
2	tablespoons minced fresh parsley *or* 2 teaspoons dried parsley flakes
2	tablespoons minced fresh thyme *or* 2 teaspoons dried thyme
1	tablespoon minced fresh rosemary *or* 1 teaspoon dried rosemary, crushed
1-1/4	teaspoons salt

Scrub and quarter potatoes; place in a large saucepan and cover with water. Add garlic. Bring to a boil. Reduce heat; cover and cook for 15-20 minutes or until potatoes are tender; drain.

In a large bowl, mash potato mixture. Stir in the remaining ingredients. **yield: 12 servings.**

italian subs

1/3 cup olive oil
4-1/2 teaspoons white wine vinegar
1 tablespoon dried parsley flakes
2 to 3 garlic cloves, minced
1 can (2-1/4 ounces) sliced ripe olives, drained
1/2 cup chopped pimiento-stuffed olives
1 loaf (1 pound, 20 inches) French bread, unsliced
24 thin slices hard salami
24 slices provolone *or* part-skim mozzarella cheese
24 slices fully cooked ham
Lettuce leaves, optional

Delores Christner
Spooner, Wisconsin
Olive lovers are sure to rejoice over this stacked sandwich! Stuffed and ripe olives are marinated in white wine vinegar and garlic before using them to flavor these speedy salami, ham and provolone subs.

In a small bowl, combine the oil, vinegar, parsley and garlic. Stir in olives. Cover and refrigerate for 8 hours or overnight.

Cut bread in half lengthwise. Spread olive mixture on the bottom of the bread. Top with salami, cheese and ham; add lettuce if desired. Replace top. Cut into 2-in. slices. Insert a toothpick in each slice. **yield: 10 servings.**

creamy spinach casserole

2 cans (10-3/4 ounces *each*) reduced-fat reduced-sodium condensed cream of chicken soup, undiluted
1 package (8 ounces) reduced-fat cream cheese, cubed
1/2 cup fat-free milk
1/2 cup grated Parmesan cheese
4 cups herb seasoned stuffing cubes
2 packages (10 ounces *each*) frozen chopped spinach, thawed and squeezed dry

In a large bowl, beat the soup, cream cheese, milk and Parmesan cheese until blended. Stir in stuffing cubes and spinach.

Spoon into a 2-qt. baking dish coated with cooking spray. Bake, uncovered, at 350° for 35-40 minutes or until heated through. **yield: 10 servings.**

Annette Marie Young
West Lafayette, Indiana
Rich and comforting, this savory spinach bake will be a welcome addition to the table. You'll love the short prep time and decadent taste.

fancy bean salad

1 package (16 ounces) frozen gold and white corn, thawed
1 can (16 ounces) kidney beans, rinsed and drained
1 can (15 ounces) garbanzo beans or chickpeas, rinsed and drained
1 can (15 ounces) black beans, rinsed and drained
1 medium cucumber, finely chopped
1 cup finely chopped sweet onion
1 medium sweet red pepper, finely chopped
1 cup fat-free honey Dijon salad dressing

In a large bowl, combine the first seven ingredients. Pour salad dressing over mixture and toss to coat. Cover and refrigerate until serving. **yield: 12 servings (3/4 cup each).**

Iola Egle
Bella Vista, Arkansas
Bursting with color, this pretty bean salad is a snap thanks to canned goods and store-bought salad dressing.

greek tacos

1 pound lean ground beef (90% lean)
1 can (14-1/2 ounces) diced tomatoes, undrained
2 teaspoons Greek seasoning
1/2 teaspoon minced garlic
1/4 teaspoon pepper
2 cups fresh baby spinach
1 can (2-1/4 ounces) sliced ripe olives, drained
1 package (4-1/2 ounces) taco shells
1/2 cup crumbled feta cheese
1/4 cup chopped red onion

In a large skillet, cook beef over medium heat until no longer pink; drain. Stir in the tomatoes, Greek seasoning, garlic and pepper. Bring to a boil. Reduce heat; simmer for 8-10 minutes or until thickened. Add spinach and olives; cook and stir for 2-3 minutes or until spinach is wilted.

Meanwhile, place taco shells on an ungreased baking sheet. Bake at 300° for 3-5 minutes or until heated through. Spoon about 1/4 cup beef mixture into each shell. Top with feta cheese and onion. **yield: 12 tacos.**

editor's note: For a substitute for 1 tablespoon Greek seasoning, use 1/2 teaspoon each dried oregano, dried marjoram, garlic powder, lemon-pepper seasoning, ground mustard and salt. Omit the salt if recipes calls for salt.

Taste of Home Test Kitchen
Try a surprising twist on tacos by using Greek seasoning, spinach and feta instead of taco seasoning, lettuce and cheddar. You'll be impressed.

simple sauteed zucchini

    12   cups thinly sliced zucchini (about 10 medium)
    3/4 teaspoon dried thyme
    3/4 teaspoon dried rosemary, crushed
    1/2 teaspoon dill weed
     3   tablespoons olive oil
Salt and pepper to taste

In a Dutch oven, saute the zucchini, thyme, rosemary and dill in oil until crisp-tender. Reduce heat to medium; cover and cook for 5-7 minutes or until tender, stirring occasionally. Season with salt and pepper. **yield: 10-12 servings.**

Christy Maestri
Ozark, Arkansas
This easy vegetable side dish can be cooked up in just a few minutes and is a compatible addition to many entrees.

lemon berry pie

     4   ounces reduced-fat cream cheese
     1   tablespoon plus 1 cup cold fat-free milk
     1   tablespoon sugar
     1   tablespoon lemon juice
     2   teaspoons grated lemon peel
   2-1/4 cups reduced-fat whipped topping, *divided*
     1   reduced-fat graham cracker crust (8 inches)
     1   pint fresh strawberries
     1   package (3.4 ounces) instant lemon
         pudding mix

In a small bowl, combine the cream cheese, 1 tablespoon milk and sugar until blended. Add lemon juice and lemon peel; mix well. Fold in 1-1/2 cups whipped topping. Carefully spread into crust. Set aside 4 strawberries. Cut remaining strawberries in half and place over cream cheese mixture.

In a bowl, place the remaining milk; whisk in pudding mix for 2 minutes or until thickened. Fold in 1/2 cup whipped topping. Spoon over strawberries. Cover and refrigerate for at least 2 hours. Garnish with remaining whipped topping and reserved strawberries. **yield: 8 servings.**

Ann Flores
Seneca, Kansas
This refreshing dessert makes a beautiful presentation and is so delectable! To cut a few calories, I use Splenda sugar substitute instead of sugar when preparing the cream cheese layer.

raspberry chicken sandwiches

- 1 cup chili sauce
- 3/4 cup raspberry preserves
- 2 tablespoons red wine vinegar
- 1 tablespoon Dijon mustard
- 6 boneless skinless chicken breast halves (4 ounces *each*)
- 2 tablespoons plus 1/2 cup olive oil, *divided*
- 1/2 teaspoon salt
- 1/4 teaspoon pepper
- 24 slices French bread (1/2 inch thick)
- 12 slices Muenster cheese, halved

Shredded lettuce

In a small saucepan, combine the first four ingredients. Bring to a boil. Reduce heat; simmer, uncovered, for 2 minutes. Set aside 1 cup for serving and remaining sauce for basting.

Flatten chicken breasts to 1/4-in. thickness. Cut in half widthwise; place in a large resealable plastic bag. Add 2 tablespoons oil, salt and pepper. Seal bag and turn to coat. Brush remaining oil over both sides of bread.

Using long-handled tongs, moisten a paper towel with cooking oil and lightly coat the grill rack. Grill chicken, uncovered, over medium heat for 5-7 minutes on each side or until no longer pink, basting frequently with raspberry sauce. Remove and keep warm.

Grill bread, uncovered, for 1-2 minutes or until lightly browned on one side. Turn and top each piece of bread with a slice of cheese. Grill 1-2 minutes longer or until bottom of bread is toasted. Place a piece of chicken, lettuce and reserved raspberry sauce on half of bread slices; top with remaining bread. **yield: 12 servings.**

Kelly Williams
Morganville, New Jersey
A raspberry barbecue sauce makes my grilled chicken sandwiches special. I also use this sauce on meatballs, chicken wings and pork chops.

flat and fabulous

A quick way to flatten boneless chicken breasts is to place them in a resealable plastic bag. Starting in the center, work out to the edges by pounding lightly with the flat side of a meat mallet until the chicken is an even thickness.

Amy Voights, Brodhead, Wisconsin
This luscious cheese bread will have guests reaching for more. The cheese, onions and olives make this bread a delicious and flavorful sensation.

olive-onion cheese bread

4 cups (16 ounces) shredded part-skim mozzarella cheese
1 cup butter, softened
1 cup mayonnaise
8 green onions, thinly sliced
1 can (8 ounces) mushroom stems and pieces, drained and chopped
1 can (4-1/4 ounces) chopped ripe olives
1 loaf (1 pound) unsliced French bread

In a large bowl, combine the first six ingredients. Cut bread in half lengthwise; place on an ungreased baking sheet. Spread with cheese mixture.

Bake at 350° for 15-20 minutes or until cheese is melted. Cut each half into eight slices. **yield: 16 servings.**

herbed beef tenderloin

- 1 beef tenderloin roast (3 pounds)
- 2 teaspoons olive oil
- 2 garlic cloves, minced
- 1-1/2 teaspoons dried basil
- 1-1/2 teaspoons dried rosemary, crushed
- 1 teaspoon salt
- 1 teaspoon pepper

Tie tenderloin at 2-in. intervals with kitchen string. Combine oil and garlic; brush over meat. Combine the basil, rosemary, salt and pepper; sprinkle evenly over meat. Place on a rack in a shallow roasting pan.

Bake, uncovered, at 425° for 40-50 minutes or until meat reaches desired doneness (for medium-rare, a meat thermometer should read 145°; medium, 160°; well-done, 170°). Let stand for 10 minutes before slicing. **yield: 12 servings.**

Ruth Andrewson
Leavenworth, Washington
You don't need much seasoning to add flavor to this tender beef roast. The mild blending of rosemary, basil and garlic does the trick in no time!

chili con queso dip

- 1 can (14-1/2 ounces) no-salt-added diced tomatoes
- 1 can (10 ounces) diced tomatoes and green chilies
- 1 small onion, chopped
- 1 teaspoon olive oil
- 2 garlic cloves, minced
- 1 package (8 ounces) fat-free cream cheese, cubed
- 6 ounces reduced-fat process cheese (Velveeta), cubed
- 1 teaspoon chili powder
- 2 tablespoons minced fresh cilantro

Baked tortilla chip scoops

Pour both cans of tomatoes into a colander over a small bowl; drain, reserving 1/3 cup liquid. Discard remaining liquid or save for another use.

In a large skillet, saute onion in oil until tender. Add garlic; cook 1 minute longer. Stir in cream cheese until melted. Add the tomatoes, process cheese, chili powder and reserved liquid. Cook and stir over low heat until cheese is melted. Stir in cilantro.

Keep warm; serve with tortilla chips. **yield: 3 cups.**

Sarah Mohrman, RD, MA
Fort Wayne, Indiana
This cheesy dip never lets on that it has only 2g of fat per serving. Chilies and garlic kick up the flavor, making it a real crowd-pleaser.

flavorful southwestern chili

2	pounds lean ground beef (90% lean)
1-1/2	cups chopped onions
2	cans (14-1/2 ounces *each*) diced tomatoes, undrained
1	can (15 ounces) pinto beans, rinsed and drained
1	can (15 ounces) tomato sauce
1	package (10 ounces) frozen corn, thawed
1	cup salsa
3/4	cup water
1	can (4 ounces) chopped green chilies
1	teaspoon ground cumin
1/2	teaspoon garlic powder

In a Dutch oven, cook beef and onions over medium heat until meat is no longer pink; drain. Stir in the remaining ingredients. Bring to a boil. Reduce heat; simmer, uncovered, for 15 minutes.

Serve desired amount. Cool the remaining chili; transfer to freezer containers. May be frozen for up to 3 months.

To use frozen chili: Thaw in the refrigerator. Place in a saucepan; heat through. **yield: 10 servings (2-1/2 quarts).**

Jenny Greear
Huntington, West Virginia
This filling, hearty recipe comes from my grandmother. It's full of flavor, freezes beautifully and makes a complete last-minute meal. I top it with grated cheddar cheese and chopped black olives and serve tortilla chips on the side. If I'm feeding a crowd, I increase the pinto beans to four cans to make the meat go further.

turkey focaccia sandwich

Tina Miller
Sun Valley, Nevada
My family believes that nothing satisfies hunger like a sandwich, so I make them often for lunch, dinner and late-night snacking. They request this version often.

1	loaf (1 pound) focaccia bread
1/2	cup spinach dip *or* chive and onion cream cheese spread
2	tablespoons Dijon mustard
8	ounces thinly sliced deli smoked turkey
4	slices Swiss cheese (1 ounce *each*)
1	medium tomato, thinly sliced

Cut bread in half horizontally. Spread 1/4 cup spinach dip on each half; spread with mustard. Layer the turkey, cheese and tomato on bottom half; replace top half. Cut into wedges. **yield: 10-12 servings.**

honey-mustard glazed salmon

- 10 salmon fillets (5 ounces *each*)
- 2/3 cup packed brown sugar
- 2 tablespoons Dijon mustard
- 2 tablespoons honey
- 1/2 teaspoon salt

Place fillets, skin side down, on a greased baking sheet. In a small bowl, combine the brown sugar, mustard, honey and salt; spoon over salmon.

Broil 3-4 in. from the heat for 8-12 minutes or until fish flakes easily with a fork. **yield: 10 servings.**

Taste of Home Test Kitchen
You won't need to fish for compliments from dinner guests when you serve this spectacular salmon!

Mary Fox
Forest City, Iowa
A boxed mix is the base for these moist brownies with from-scratch taste. The recipe uses about half a can of frosting. Save the rest, because you'll make them again!

frosted cake brownies

- 1 package fudge brownie mix (13-inch x 9-inch pan size)
- 1 cup (8 ounces) sour cream
- 1 cup milk chocolate chips
- 1/2 cup chopped walnuts
- 1 cup milk chocolate frosting

Prepare brownie mix according to package directions. Fold in the sour cream, chocolate chips and walnuts into batter.

Pour into a greased 13-in x 9-in. baking pan. Bake at 350° for 30-35 minutes or until a toothpick inserted near the center comes out clean. Cool completely on a wire rack. Frost. Cut into bars. **yield: 2-1/2 dozen.**

tortellini spinach casserole

- 2 packages (10 ounces *each*) frozen cheese tortellini
- 1 pound sliced fresh mushrooms
- 1 teaspoon garlic powder
- 1/4 teaspoon onion powder
- 1/4 teaspoon pepper
- 1/2 cup butter, *divided*
- 1 can (12 ounces) evaporated milk
- 1 block (8 ounces) brick cheese, cubed
- 3 packages (10 ounces *each*) frozen chopped spinach, thawed and squeezed dry
- 2 cups (8 ounces) shredded part-skim mozzarella cheese

Cook tortellini according to package directions. Meanwhile, in a large skillet, saute the mushrooms, garlic powder, onion powder and pepper in 1/4 cup butter until mushrooms are tender. Remove and keep warm.

In the same skillet, combine milk and remaining butter. Bring to a gentle boil; stir in brick cheese. Cook and stir until smooth. Drain tortellini; place in a large bowl. Stir in the mushroom mixture and spinach. Add cheese sauce and toss to coat.

Transfer to a greased 3-qt. baking dish; sprinkle with mozzarella cheese. Cover and bake at 350° for 15 minutes. Uncover; bake 5-10 minutes longer or until heated through and cheese is melted. **yield: 12 servings.**

Barbara Kellen
Antioch, Illinois
Spinach gives this popular casserole a fresh taste that will delight even those who say they don't like spinach. In fact, people are often surprised at just how good it is! Whenever I bring it to a gathering, it doesn't sit around long.

brick by brick

If you're not familiar with brick cheese, it is a semisoft, pale-yellow, mild-tasting cheese that looks like a small rectangular block. It is not a processed cheese. You can try to substitute a Monterey Jack cheese for the brick if you'd like.

raspberry lemon torte

- 1 package (18-1/4 ounces) lemon cake mix
- 1 tablespoon poppy seeds
- 1 tablespoon grated lemon peel
- 1 jar (12 ounces) seedless raspberry jam
- 2-3/4 cups vanilla frosting

Fresh raspberries

Grease two 9-in. round baking pans and line with waxed paper; grease and flour the paper. Prepare cake batter according to package directions; stir in poppy seeds and lemon peel.

Pour into prepared pans. Bake at 350° for 21-26 minutes or until a toothpick inserted near the center comes out clean. Cool for 10 minutes before removing from pans to wire racks to cool completely.

Cut each cake horizontally into two layers. Place bottom layer on a serving plate; top with half of the jam. Top with a second layer; spread with 3/4 cup frosting. Top with a third layer and remaining jam. Top with remaining layer; spread remaining frosting over top and sides of cake. Garnish with fresh raspberries. **yield: 12 servings.**

Taste of Home Test Kitchen
A box of lemon cake mix, raspberry jam and canned frosting make it a breeze to assemble this lovely, impressive layered torte.

Cathy Smith
Wyoming, Michigan
This tasty chicken casserole is packed with homey, comforting flavor! It's a great way to use up leftover cooked chicken, plus it's quick to put together using handy pantry items.

chicken stuffing casserole

- 2 packages (6 ounces *each*) chicken stuffing mix
- 2 cans (10-3/4 ounces *each*) condensed cream of mushroom soup, undiluted
- 1 cup 2% milk
- 4 cups cubed cooked chicken
- 2 cups frozen corn
- 2 cans (8 ounces *each*) mushroom stems and pieces, drained
- 4 cups (16 ounces) shredded cheddar cheese

Prepare stuffing mixes according to package directions. Meanwhile, in a large bowl, combine soup and milk; set aside. Spread the stuffing into two greased 8-in. square baking dishes. Layer with chicken, corn, mushrooms, soup mixture and cheese.

Cover and freeze one casserole for up to 3 months. Cover and bake the second casserole at 350° for 30-35 minutes or until cheese is melted.

To use frozen casserole: Remove from the freezer 30 minutes before baking (do not thaw). Bake at 350° for 1-1/2 hours. Uncover; bake 10-15 minutes longer or until heated through. **yield: 2 casseroles (6 servings each).**

almost a candy bar

     1   tube (16-1/2 ounces) refrigerated chocolate chip cookie dough
     4   nutty s'mores trail mix bars (1.23 ounces *each*), chopped
     1   package (10 to 11 ounces) butterscotch chips
 2-1/2   cups miniature marshmallows
     1   cup chopped walnuts
 1-1/2   cups miniature pretzels
     1   package (10 ounces) peanut butter chips
   3/4   cup light corn syrup
   1/4   cup butter, cubed
     1   package (11-1/2 ounces) milk chocolate chips

Let dough stand at room temperature for 5-10 minutes to soften. In a large bowl, combine dough and trail mix bars. Press into an ungreased 13-in. x 9-in. baking pan. Bake, uncovered, at 350° for 10-12 minutes or until golden brown.

Sprinkle with butterscotch chips and marshmallows. Bake 3-4 minutes longer or until marshmallows begin to brown. Sprinkle with walnuts; arrange pretzels over the top. In a small saucepan, melt the peanut butter chips, corn syrup and butter; spoon over bars.

In a microwave, melt chocolate chips; stir until smooth. Spread or drizzle over bars. Refrigerate for 1 hour or until firm before cutting. **yield: 3 dozen.**

Barb Wyman
Hankinson, North Dakota
Because I love candy bars and marshmallows, this recipe was a cinch to invent.

peanut butter chippers

Pat Doerflinger
Centerview, Missouri
The smell of peanut butter and chocolate always brings my cookie-hungry gang running to the kitchen. The recipe is so quick and easy, I often stir up a batch while making dinner.

     6   tablespoons butter, softened
   1/4   cup peanut butter
   1/2   cup sugar
   1/2   cup packed brown sugar
     1   egg
     1   teaspoon vanilla extract
 1-1/4   cups all-purpose flour
   1/2   teaspoon baking soda
   1/4   teaspoon salt
     1   cup milk chocolate chips

In a small bowl, cream the butter, peanut butter and sugars until light and fluffy. Beat in egg and vanilla. Combine the flour, baking soda and salt; gradually add to creamed mixture and mix well. Stir in chocolate chips.

Drop by tablespoonfuls 2 in. apart onto ungreased baking sheets. Bake at 350° for 11-14 minutes or until golden brown. Remove to wire racks. **yield: 3-1/2 dozen.**

seafood cakes

- 1/2 pound uncooked scallops
- 1/4 pound uncooked medium shrimp, peeled and deveined
- 1/2 cup heavy whipping cream
- 1 egg yolk
- 1 tablespoon Dijon mustard
- 1/2 teaspoon salt
- 1/4 teaspoon cayenne pepper
- 5 cans (6 ounces *each*) lump crabmeat, drained
- 2 tablespoons minced chives
- 1/4 cup canola oil

Seafood cocktail sauce, optional

Place scallops and shrimp in a food processor; cover and pulse until chopped. Add the cream, egg yolk, mustard, salt and cayenne; cover and process until pureed. Transfer to a large bowl; fold in crab and chives. Refrigerate for at least 30 minutes.

With floured hands, shape mixture by 2 tablespoonfuls into 1/2-in.-thick patties. In a large skillet over medium-high heat, cook seafood cakes in oil in batches for 3-4 minutes on each side or until golden brown. Serve with seafood sauce if desired. **yield: 3 dozen.**

Kimberlie Scott
Massena, New York
Ordinary crab cakes are fine, but my family prefers this version featuring scallops and shrimp as well as crab.

Wendy Conger
Winfield, Illinois
If you're a fan of baked beans, you'll love this hearty wrap. I mix the beans with beef, corn and cheese, then roll it all up in tortillas.

chuck wagon wraps

- 1 pound lean ground beef (90% lean)
- 1 can (28 ounces) barbecue-flavored baked beans
- 2 cups frozen corn, thawed
- 4-1/2 teaspoons Worcestershire sauce
- 1 cup (4 ounces) shredded reduced-fat cheddar cheese
- 12 flour tortillas (8 inches), warmed
- 3 cups shredded lettuce
- 1-1/2 cups chopped fresh tomatoes
- 3/4 cup reduced-fat sour cream

In a large nonstick skillet, cook beef over medium heat until no longer pink; drain. Stir in the beans, corn and Worcestershire sauce. Bring to a boil. Reduce heat; simmer, uncovered, for 4-5 minutes or until heated through. Sprinkle with cheese; cook 1-2 minutes longer.

Spoon about 1/2 cup off center on each tortilla; top with lettuce, tomatoes and sour cream. Roll up. **yield: 12 servings.**

Kim Knight, Hamburg, Pennsylvania
My father shared this recipe with me, and I use it whenever I need a hearty meal. It's
now my sons' favorite. Loaded with sausage, chicken, beans and spinach, this quick
soup is perfect for potlucks and special occasions, too.

italian peasant soup

- 1 pound Italian sausage links, casings removed and cut into 1-inch slices
- 2 medium onions, chopped
- 6 garlic cloves, chopped
- 1 pound boneless skinless chicken breasts, cut into 1-inch cubes
- 2 cans (15 ounces *each*) white kidney *or* cannellini beans, rinsed and drained
- 2 cans (14-1/2 ounces *each*) chicken broth
- 2 cans (14-1/2 ounces *each*) diced tomatoes
- 1 teaspoon dried basil
- 1 teaspoon dried oregano
- 6 cups fresh spinach leaves, chopped

Shredded Parmesan cheese, optional

In a Dutch oven, cook sausage and onions over medium heat until no longer pink. Add garlic; cook 1 minute longer. Drain. Add chicken; cook and stir until no longer pink.

Stir in the beans, broth, tomatoes, basil and oregano. Bring to a boil. Reduce heat; simmer, uncovered, for 10 minutes. Add the spinach and heat just until wilted. Serve with cheese if desired. **yield: 11 servings (2-3/4 quarts).**

salads & sides

super italian
chopped salad
page 174

Lorraine Caland, Thunder Bay, Ontario
You can use any kind of pasta for this creamy toss that bursts with colorful veggies. It's been a mainstay for years now and is perfect for potlucks.

creamy vegetable bow tie toss

12	ounces uncooked bow tie pasta
2	cups sliced fresh mushrooms
2	cups cut fresh asparagus (about 1/2 pound)
2	medium sweet onions, finely chopped
2	medium carrots, sliced
2	medium zucchini, halved and sliced
1	medium sweet yellow pepper, julienned
1/3	cup butter, cubed
2/3	cup chicken broth
1	cup (8 ounces) sour cream
1/2	cup prepared ranch dip
1/2	cup grated Parmesan cheese
1/4	cup minced fresh parsley
2	tablespoons minced fresh basil
1/2	teaspoon salt

Cook pasta according to package directions. Meanwhile, in a large skillet, saute vegetables in butter for 5 minutes. Stir in broth; cook for 3 minutes or until vegetables are crisp-tender.

In a small bowl, combine the sour cream, dip, cheese, parsley, basil and salt; stir into skillet and heat through. Drain pasta; add to the skillet and toss to coat. **yield: 12 servings.**

cheesy noodle casserole

- 2 packages (1 pound *each*) wide egg noodles
- 1/2 cup butter, cubed
- 1/4 cup all-purpose flour
- 1 teaspoon garlic salt
- 1 teaspoon onion salt
- 5 to 6 cups 2% milk
- 2 pounds process cheese (Velveeta), cubed

TOPPING:
- 1/2 cup dry bread crumbs
- 2 tablespoons butter, melted

Cook noodles according to package directions; drain. Meanwhile, in a Dutch oven, melt butter. Stir in the flour, garlic salt and onion salt until smooth; gradually stir in milk. Bring to a boil; cook and stir for 2 minutes or until thickened. Add the cheese; stir until melted. Stir in noodles.

Transfer to two greased shallow 2-qt. baking dishes. Combine the bread crumbs and butter until crumbly; sprinkle over casseroles. Bake, uncovered, at 350° for 25-30 minutes or until golden brown. **yield: 2 casseroles (12 servings each).**

Shirley McKee
Varna, Illinois
This rich and cheesy side dish is an excellent meal extender so I always keep it in mind whenever I feel my menu needs a little boost. It's a quick and easy casserole to fix, and it's always devoured in a hurry no matter where I serve it!

Emily Gedenberg
Battle Ground, Washington
I found this recipe in a family cookbook, and it's been a favorite ever since. Everyone seems to like it, even those who don't normally care for banana bread.

moist banana bread

- 2-1/2 cups all-purpose flour
- 1-1/4 cups sugar
- 2 packages (3.4 ounces *each*) instant vanilla pudding mix
- 1-1/4 teaspoons baking soda
- 1 teaspoon salt
- 1 teaspoon ground cinnamon
- 5 eggs
- 2 cups mashed ripe bananas (4 to 5 medium)
- 1 cup canola oil
- 1 teaspoon vanilla extract
- 1 cup chopped nuts, optional

In a large bowl, combine the first six ingredients. In a large bowl, whisk the eggs, bananas, oil and vanilla. Stir into dry ingredients just until moistened. Stir in nuts if desired

Transfer to two greased 8-in. x 4-in. loaf pans. Bake at 350° for 55-65 minutes or until a toothpick inserted near the center comes out clean. Cool for 10 minutes before removing from pans to wire racks. **yield: 2 loaves (12 slices each).**

next-generation german potato salad

- 4 pounds small red potatoes, quartered
- 10 bacon strips, chopped
- 1 large onion, chopped
- 3 tablespoons chopped celery
- 2 tablespoons chopped green pepper
- 1 tablespoon all-purpose flour
- 1 tablespoon sugar
- 1 teaspoon salt
- 1/2 teaspoon pepper
- 1 cup water
- 1/3 cup white balsamic vinegar

Place the potatoes in a Dutch oven and cover with water. Bring to a boil. Reduce heat; cover and simmer for 15-20 minutes or until tender.

Meanwhile, in a large skillet, cook bacon over medium heat until crisp. Using a slotted spoon, remove to paper towels. In the drippings, saute the onion, celery and green pepper until tender. Stir in the flour, sugar, salt and pepper until blended. Combine water and vinegar; stir into vegetable mixture. Bring to a boil; cook and stir for 2 minutes or until thickened.

Drain potatoes and place in a large serving bowl. Pour dressing over potatoes. Add bacon and toss to coat. Serve warm or at room temperature. Refrigerate leftovers. **yield: 14 servings.**

Mary Shivers
Ada, Oklahoma
My quick-cooking German-style potato salad is a keeper for family reunions. Balsamic vinegar and bacon give it a different taste twist.

Denise Baumert
Dalhart, Texas
My brood can never get enough cucumber slices in the summer. They're crunchy, delicious and simple to make. At picnics or potlucks, I bring a big batch.

refrigerator cucumber slices

- 4 pounds cucumbers (about 6 large), cut into 1/4-inch slices
- 3 medium onions, cut into 1/8-inch slices
- 3 cups sugar
- 3 cups cider vinegar
- 4 teaspoons canning/pickling salt
- 1-1/2 teaspoons mustard seed

In a large container, combine cucumbers and onions. In a large bowl, combine the remaining ingredients, stirring until sugar is dissolved.

Pour over cucumber mixture; mix well. Cover and refrigerate overnight. Refrigerate up to 2 weeks. **yield: about 2-1/2 quarts.**

fancy fruit salad

1-1/2 cups uncooked acini di pepe pasta
1 can (20 ounces) unsweetened pineapple tidbits
1 can (8 ounces) unsweetened crushed pineapple
1 cup sugar
3 tablespoons all-purpose flour
1/2 teaspoon salt
1 can (6 ounces) unsweetened pineapple juice
2 tablespoons orange juice concentrate
3 egg yolks
2 cans (11 ounces *each*) mandarin oranges, drained
1 carton (12 ounces) frozen whipped topping, thawed
2 cups sliced fresh strawberries

Cook pasta according to package directions. Meanwhile, drain pineapple tidbits and crushed pineapple, reserving juice. Set pineapple aside.

In a small saucepan, combine the sugar, flour and salt. Gradually stir in the can of pineapple juice, orange juice concentrate and reserved pineapple juice.

Cook and stir until mixture comes to a boil. Stir a small amount of hot mixture into egg yolks; return all to the pan, stirring constantly. Bring to a gentle boil; cook and stir 2 minutes longer. Transfer mixture to a large bowl and cool to room temperature.

Drain pasta and rinse in cold water; add to sugar mixture. Stir in oranges and reserved pineapple. Fold in whipped topping. Cover and refrigerate until chilled. Just before serving, fold in strawberries. **yield: 14 servings (3/4 cup each).**

editor's note: Acini di pepe are tiny pellets of pasta. This recipe was tested with DaVinci brand pasta. You may substitute 10 ounces of macaroni or other pasta if desired.

Janice Malcolm
Grande Prairie, Alberta
This fruity salad is a great option for special large events, neighborhood barbecues and family gatherings. It keeps well in the refrigerator, so you don't have to be rushing around at the last minute.

pick of the crop

When purchasing strawberries, look for those that are almost completely red, though some whiteness near the leafy cap is acceptable. Refrigerate unwashed strawberries with the caps on until ready to use. Just before using, wash and hull.

chicken pasta salad

1 package (12 ounces) tricolor spiral pasta
2 cups cubed part-skim mozzarella cheese
2 cups cubed cooked chicken
1 large green pepper, chopped
1 large sweet red pepper, chopped
1 cup sliced fresh mushrooms
2 cans (2-1/4 ounces *each*) sliced ripe olives, drained
6 green onions, sliced
1 package (3-1/2 ounces) sliced pepperoni, halved
1/2 cup canola oil
1/3 cup red wine vinegar
1 teaspoon Italian seasoning
1/2 teaspoon garlic powder
1/2 teaspoon salt
1/4 teaspoon pepper

Megan Moore
Memphis, Tennessee
Combining the coolness of a salad and the zesty seasonings of pizza, this salad is perfect for a summer get-together.

Cook pasta according to package directions; rinse with cold water and drain well. In a large serving bowl, combine the cheese, chicken, peppers, mushrooms, olives, green onions, pepperoni and pasta.

In a small bowl, whisk together the remaining ingredients. Pour over salad; toss to coat. Cover and refrigerate until serving. Toss before serving. **yield: 14 servings.**

floret salad

6 cups fresh broccoli florets
6 cups fresh cauliflowerets
3 medium red onions, halved and sliced
2 cups mayonnaise
1 cup (8 ounces) sour cream
1/4 cup packed brown sugar
1/4 cup cider vinegar
1 tablespoon Worcestershire sauce
3 teaspoons dill weed
2 teaspoons salt
Dash Louisiana-style hot sauce

Denise Elder
Hanover, Ontario
Colorful and crunchy, this crowd-pleasing salad can be made a day in advance. Everyone likes the zip in the creamy dressing. Sometimes, I add diced green and red pepper to the mixture or throw in a little celery.

In a large bowl, combine the broccoli, cauliflower and onions. In another large bowl, combine the remaining ingredients. Pour over vegetables; toss to coat. Cover and refrigerate for 4 hours before serving. **yield: 25 servings (2/3 cup each).**

wild rice pilaf

2	cans (14-1/2 ounces *each*) chicken broth
3/4	cup uncooked wild rice
1	cup uncooked long grain rice
1	large onion, chopped
2	medium carrots, halved lengthwise and sliced
1/2	teaspoon dried rosemary, crushed
1/2	cup butter, cubed
1	garlic clove, minced
3	cups fresh broccoli florets
1/4	teaspoon pepper

Dianne Bettin
Truman, Minnesota
I make this rice dish for almost every holiday and often take it to potlucks. Usually, I make the pilaf ahead to allow the flavors to blend and then reheat it in the microwave before serving. This also makes for more room in the oven and less chaos when you are putting out a big meal.

In a large saucepan, bring broth to a boil. Add wild rice; reduce heat. Cover and cook for 30 minutes. Add long grain rice; cook 20-25 minutes longer or until the liquid is absorbed and the rice is tender.

Meanwhile, in a large skillet, saute the onion, carrots and rosemary in butter until vegetables are tender. Add garlic; cook 1 minute longer. Stir in the rice, broccoli and pepper.

Transfer to a greased shallow 2-qt. baking dish. Cover and bake at 350° for 25-30 minutes or until broccoli is crisp-tender. Fluff with a fork before serving. **yield: 10 servings.**

colorful roasted veggies

4	medium carrots, julienned
1-1/2	pounds fresh asparagus, trimmed and halved
1	large green pepper, julienned
1	medium sweet red pepper, julienned
1	medium red onion, sliced and separated into rings
5	cups fresh cauliflowerets
5	cups fresh broccoli florets
1/4	to 1/2 cup olive oil
3	tablespoons lemon juice
3	garlic cloves, minced
1	tablespoon dried rosemary, crushed
1	teaspoon salt
1	teaspoon pepper

In a large bowl, combine the vegetables. In a small bowl, whisk the oil, lemon juice, garlic, rosemary, salt and pepper until blended. Drizzle over vegetables and toss to coat.

Transfer to two greased 15-in. x 10-in. x 1-in. baking pans. Bake, uncovered, at 400° for 20-25 minutes or until tender, stirring occasionally. **yield: 12 servings.**

Diane Harrison
Mechanicsburg,
Pennsylvania
My mom serves this delicious vegetable dish that is pleasantly flavored with rosemary. It is my all-time favorite.

multigrain raisin bread

Debra Van Den Heuvel
Gilman, Wisconsin
After years of searching for the perfect whole grain raisin bread, I whipped up this tasty recipe. My family loves it, and it makes such wonderful French toast.

2	cups raisins
1-1/2	cups water
1/2	cup old-fashioned oats
1	tablespoon active dry yeast
1-1/4	cups warm water (110° to 115°)
1/4	cup honey
2	eggs
3/4	cup nonfat dry milk powder
2	teaspoons salt
1-1/2	teaspoons ground cinnamon
2	cups whole wheat flour
3	to 3-1/2 cups all-purpose flour

In a small saucepan, bring raisins and water to a boil. Reduce heat; cover and simmer for 5 minutes. Drain, reserving 1/2 cup liquid. Stir oats into reserved liquid; set raisins and oat mixture aside.

In a large bowl, dissolve yeast in warm water. Stir in honey; let stand for 5 minutes. Add the eggs, milk powder, salt, cinnamon, whole wheat flour, 1 cup all-purpose flour and oat mixture. Beat on medium speed for 3 minutes. Stir in enough remaining all-purpose flour to form a firm dough. Stir in raisins (dough will be sticky).

Turn onto a lightly floured surface; knead until smooth and elastic, about 6-8 minutes. Place in a bowl coated with cooking spray, turning once to coat the top. Cover and let rise in a warm place until doubled, about 1 hour.

Punch dough down. Turn onto a lightly floured surface; shape into two loaves. Place in two 9-in. x 5-in. loaf pans coated with cooking spray. Cover and let rise until doubled, about 40 minutes.

Bake at 350° for 40-45 minutes or until golden brown. Cover loosely with foil if tops brown too quickly. Remove from pans to wire racks to cool. **yield: 2 loaves (16 slices each).**

storing breads

To store yeast breads, cool loaves completely before placing in an airtight container or resealable storage bag. Yeast bread stays fresh at room temperature for 3 days. For longer storage, freeze bread in a storage bag for 3 months.

honey-mustard potato salad

- 5 pounds red potatoes
- 2 cups chopped celery
- 1 cup chopped sweet red pepper
- 4 hard-cooked eggs, chopped
- 2 green onions, chopped
- 1/2 cup mayonnaise
- 1/2 cup honey mustard
- 1/2 cup prepared mustard
- 1/4 cup sour cream
- 3/4 teaspoon salt
- 1/4 teaspoon pepper

Place potatoes in a saucepan and cover with water. Bring to a boil. Reduce heat; cover and cook for 15-20 minutes or until tender. Drain and cool.

Cut potatoes into quarters; place in a large bowl. Add the celery, red pepper, hard-cooked eggs and onions. In a small bowl, combine the remaining ingredients. Pour over potato mixture and toss to coat. Cover and refrigerate for at least 1 hour. **yield: 16 servings.**

Alicia Quadrozzi
Escondido, California
Whenever there is a picnic or cookout, I am asked to bring this potato salad. It's tangy and enjoyably different.

Betty Claycomb
Alverton, Pennsylvania
Our family gatherings wouldn't be the same without this classic gelatin salad with its lovely fruit layers. Because it stays nice and firm, it travels well and is ideal for taking to covered-dish suppers and charity potlucks.

strawberry-banana gelatin salad

- 1 package (6 ounces) strawberry gelatin
- 1 cup boiling water
- 2 packages (10 ounces *each*) frozen sweetened sliced strawberries, partially thawed
- 1 can (20 ounces) crushed pineapple, undrained
- 1 cup mashed firm bananas (about 3 medium)
- 1/2 to 3/4 cup chopped walnuts
- 2 cups (16 ounces) sour cream
- 2 teaspoons sugar
- 1/2 teaspoon vanilla extract

In a large bowl, dissolve gelatin in water. Stir in strawberries, pineapple, bananas and walnuts. Pour half of the mixture into a 13-in. x 9-in. dish. Refrigerate for 1 hour or until set.

Set the remaining gelatin mixture aside. Combine the sour cream, sugar and vanilla. Spread over the chilled gelatin. Spoon remaining gelatin mixture over top. Chill overnight. **yield: 12-15 servings.**

dijon green beans

1-1/2	pounds fresh green beans, trimmed
2	tablespoons red wine vinegar
2	tablespoons olive oil
2	teaspoons Dijon mustard
1/2	teaspoon salt
1/4	teaspoon pepper
1	cup grape tomatoes, halved
1/2	small red onion, sliced
2	tablespoons grated Parmesan cheese

Jannine Fisk
Malden, Massachusetts
I love this recipe because it combines the freshness of garden green beans with a warm and tangy dressing. It's a wonderful, quick and easy side dish.

Place beans in a large saucepan and cover with water. Bring to a boil. Cook, uncovered, for 8-10 minutes or until crisp-tender.

Meanwhile, for dressing, whisk the vinegar, oil, mustard, salt and pepper in a small bowl. Drain beans; place in a large bowl. Add tomatoes and onion. Drizzle with dressing and toss to coat. Sprinkle with cheese. **yield: 10 servings.**

golden lemon bread

1/2	cup shortening
3/4	cup sugar
2	eggs
1-1/2	cups all-purpose flour
1-1/2	teaspoons baking powder
1/2	teaspoon salt
3/4	cup 2% milk

GLAZE:

1/2	cup confectioners' sugar
2	teaspoons grated lemon peel
2	to 3 tablespoons lemon juice

Marjorie Rose
Albuquerque, New Mexico
This lovely bread, made from my grandmother's recipe, won Best of Show at the New Mexico State Fair. It's so good! My grandchildren love it, too.

In a large bowl, cream shortening and sugar until light and fluffy. Add eggs, one at a time, beating well after each addition. Combine the flour, baking powder and salt; add to creamed mixture alternately with milk.

Pour into a greased 9-in. x 5-in. loaf pan. Bake at 350° for 40-45 minutes or until a toothpick inserted near the center comes out clean. Place pan on a wire rack.

Combine the glaze ingredients; immediately pour over warm bread. Cool completely before removing from pan. **yield: 1 loaf (16 slices).**

antipasto picnic salad

- 1 package (16 ounces) medium pasta shells
- 2 jars (16 ounces *each*) giardiniera
- 1 pound fresh broccoli florets
- 1/2 pound cubed part-skim mozzarella cheese
- 1/2 pound hard salami, cubed
- 1/2 pound deli ham, cubed
- 2 packages (3-1/2 ounces *each*) sliced pepperoni, halved
- 1 large green pepper, cut into chunks
- 1 can (6 ounces) pitted ripe olives, drained

DRESSING:

- 1/2 cup olive oil
- 1/4 cup red wine vinegar
- 2 tablespoons lemon juice
- 1 teaspoon Italian seasoning
- 1 teaspoon coarsely ground pepper
- 1/2 teaspoon salt

Cook pasta according to package directions. Meanwhile, drain giardiniera, reserving 3/4 cup liquid. In a large bowl, combine the giardiniera, broccoli, mozzarella, salami, ham, pepperoni, green pepper and olives. Drain pasta and rinse in cold water; stir into meat mixture.

For dressing, in a small bowl, whisk the oil, vinegar, lemon juice, Italian seasoning, pepper, salt and reserved giardiniera liquid. Pour over salad and toss to coat. Refrigerate salad until serving. **yield: 25 servings.**

---

editor's note: Giardiniera, a pickled vegetable mixture, is available in mild and hot varieties and can be found in the Italian or pickle section of your grocery store.

Michele Larson
Baden, Pennsylvania
Everybody just adores this tempting blend of meats, veggies and pasta. It goes together in no time, serves a crowd and tastes as delicious at room temperature as it does cold. The salad has a wide variety of ingredients, so even kids will find something they like in it!

delicious diary

When you entertain, keep a record of the date, guests and recipes used. Make a note of which dishes were most popular and received the most comments. That way, you can serve a variety of new recipes along with everyone's favorites at the next party.

creamy 'n' fruity gelatin salad

- 2 packages (3 ounces *each*) orange gelatin
- 1 cup boiling water
- 1 pint orange *or* pineapple sherbet
- 1 can (11 ounces) mandarin oranges, drained
- 1 can (8 ounces) crushed pineapple, drained
- 1 cup miniature marshmallows
- 1 cup heavy whipping cream, whipped

In a large bowl, dissolve gelatin in boiling water. Add sherbet; stir until smooth. Stir in the oranges, pineapple and marshmallows. Fold in whipped cream. Pour into a 6-cup serving bowl. Cover and refrigerate for 3-4 hours or until set. **yield: 10 servings.**

Elaine Schmit
Mifflintown, Pennsylvania
I remember looking forward to eating this pretty salad when I was a child. It has all the items little ones would enjoy. My grandmother served it during the holidays and on other special occasions, and my mother did the same.

Kim Molina
Duarte, California
Antipasto ingredients are sliced and diced to make this substantial salad. I like to buy sliced meat from the deli and chop it all up so you can get a bit of everything in each bite.

super italian chopped salad

- 3 cups torn romaine
- 1 can (15 ounces) garbanzo beans *or* chickpeas, rinsed and drained
- 1 jar (6-1/2 ounces) marinated artichoke hearts, drained and chopped
- 1 medium green pepper, chopped
- 2 medium tomatoes, chopped
- 1 can (2-1/4 ounces) sliced ripe olives, drained
- 5 slices deli ham, chopped
- 5 thin slices hard salami, chopped
- 5 slices pepperoni, chopped
- 3 slices provolone cheese, chopped
- 2 green onions, chopped
- 1/4 cup olive oil
- 2 tablespoons red wine vinegar
- 1/4 teaspoon salt
- 1/8 teaspoon pepper
- 2 tablespoons grated Parmesan cheese

Pepperoncinis, optional

In a large bowl, combine the first 11 ingredients. For dressing, in a small bowl, whisk the oil, vinegar, salt and pepper. Pour over salad; toss to coat. Sprinkle with cheese. Top with pepperoncinis if desired. **yield: 10 servings.**

simply-a-must dinner rolls

5-1/2 to 6 cups all-purpose flour
1/2 cup sugar
1 tablespoon quick-rise yeast
2 teaspoons salt
1 cup 2% milk
1/2 cup canola oil
3 eggs
2 tablespoons butter, melted

In a large bowl, combine 3 cups flour, sugar, yeast and salt. In a small saucepan, heat milk and oil to 120°-130°. Add to dry ingredients; beat just until moistened. Add eggs; beat until smooth. Stir in enough remaining flour to form a soft dough (dough will be sticky).

Turn onto a floured surface; knead until smooth and elastic, about 6-8 minutes. Cover and let rest for 10 minutes. Divide dough into thirds. Roll each portion into a 12-in. circle; brush with butter. Cut each circle into 12 wedges.

Roll up wedges from the wide end and place point side down 2 in. apart on baking sheets coated with cooking spray. Curve ends to form crescents. Cover and let rise until nearly doubled, about 30 minutes.

Bake at 400° for 10-12 minutes or until golden brown. Remove from pans to wire racks. **yield: 3 dozen.**

Michelle Minaker
Two Rivers, Wisconsin
I make these fluffy, buttery rolls every year. They always turn out velvety and crisp and any leftovers work wonderfully for sandwiches.

colorful corn and bean salad

1 can (15 ounces) black beans, rinsed and drained
1 jar (13 ounces) corn relish
1/2 cup canned kidney beans, rinsed and drained
1/2 cup quartered cherry tomatoes
1/2 cup chopped celery
1/4 cup chopped sweet orange pepper
1/4 cup sliced pimiento-stuffed olives
2 teaspoons minced fresh parsley

Moore TerryAnn
Vineland, New Jersey
This quick recipe couldn't be any easier.

In a large bowl, combine all ingredients. Cover and refrigerate until serving. **yield: 12 servings.**

hash brown broccoli bake

Jeanette Volker
Walton, Nebraska
Here's a perfect dish for a potluck or holiday buffet. It goes well with fish, poultry, pork or beef. Cheddar cheese can be substituted for Swiss. Often, I double the recipe to serve an extra-large crowd.

4	tablespoons butter, *divided*
2	tablespoons all-purpose flour
1	teaspoon salt
1/8	teaspoon ground nutmeg
1/8	teaspoon pepper
2	cups 2% milk
1	package (8 ounces) cream cheese, cubed
2	cups (8 ounces) shredded Swiss cheese
6	cups frozen shredded hash brown potatoes, thawed
1	package (16 ounces) frozen chopped broccoli, thawed
1/2	cup dry bread crumbs

In a large saucepan, melt 2 tablespoons butter. Stir in the flour, salt, nutmeg and pepper until smooth; gradually add milk. Bring to a boil; cook and stir for 2 minutes or until thickened. Remove from the heat. Add cheeses; stir until melted. Stir in potatoes.

Spoon half of the potato mixture into a greased 2-qt. baking dish. Top with broccoli and remaining potato mixture. Cover and bake at 350° for 35 minutes.

Melt the remaining butter; toss with bread crumbs. Sprinkle over casserole. Bake, uncovered, for 15-20 minutes or until heated through and topping is golden. **yield: 12-14 servings.**

family picnic salad

Barb Hausey
Independence, Missouri
The bountiful potluck at our annual family reunion includes favorites such as this salad. You can substitute Italian dressing or another type to give this dish a tasty twist.

1	can (16 ounces) kidney beans, rinsed and drained
1	can (15 ounces) white *or* shoepeg corn, drained
1	large zucchini, chopped
1	medium cucumber, chopped
1	large tomato, chopped
1	large green pepper, chopped
1	medium red onion, chopped
6	green onions, chopped
1	can (3.8 ounces) sliced ripe olives, drained
1	cup Catalina salad dressing
1-1/2	cups (6 ounces) shredded cheddar cheese
1-1/2	cups corn chips

In a large salad bowl, combine the first nine ingredients. Drizzle with dressing and toss to coat evenly. Stir in cheese and corn chips. Serve immediately. **yield: 10 servings.**

buttery corn bread

2/3 cup butter, softened
1 cup sugar
3 eggs
1-2/3 cups 2% milk
2-1/3 cups all-purpose flour
1 cup cornmeal
4-1/2 teaspoons baking powder
1 teaspoon salt

Nicole Callen
Auburn, California
I got this recipe from a long-time friend several years ago, and it's the one I use most. I love to serve the melt-in-your-mouth corn bread hot from the oven with butter and syrup. It gets rave reviews at covered-dish dinners.

In a large bowl, cream butter and sugar until light and fluffy. Combine the eggs and milk. Combine the flour, cornmeal, baking powder and salt; add to creamed mixture alternately with egg mixture.

Pour into a greased 13-in. x 9-in. baking pan. Bake at 400° for 22-27 minutes or until a toothpick inserted near the center comes out clean. Cut into squares; serve warm. **yield: 12-15 servings.**

tangy four-bean salad

1 can (16 ounces) kidney beans, rinsed and drained
1 can (15 ounces) garbanzo beans *or* chickpeas, rinsed and drained
1 can (14-1/2 ounces) cut green beans, drained
1 can (14-1/2 ounces) cut wax beans, drained
1 cup sliced fresh mushrooms
1 cup chopped green pepper
1 cup chopped onion
DRESSING:
1/2 cup cider vinegar
1/3 cup sugar
1/4 cup canola oil
1 teaspoon celery seed
1/2 teaspoon pepper
1/4 teaspoon salt
1/8 teaspoon dried basil
1/8 teaspoon dried oregano

Sharon Cain
Revelstoke,
British Columbia
This colorful salad is easy to fix, and a no-fuss dressing lends sweet-sour flair. Green pepper and mushrooms help it stand out from all of the other bean medleys.

In a large bowl, combine the beans, mushrooms, green pepper and onion. In a small bowl, whisk the dressing ingredients.

Pour dressing over bean mixture and stir to coat. Cover and refrigerate for at least 4 hours. Serve with a slotted spoon. **yield: 12 servings.**

berry cheesecake muffins

1/3 cup butter, softened
3/4 cup sugar
2 eggs
1/3 cup 2% milk
1-1/2 cups all-purpose flour
1-1/2 teaspoons baking powder
1 teaspoon ground cinnamon

CREAM CHEESE FILLING:

2 packages (3 ounces *each*) cream cheese, softened
1/3 cup sugar
1 egg
3/4 cup fresh raspberries
3/4 cup fresh blueberries

STREUSEL TOPPING:

1/4 cup all-purpose flour
2 tablespoons brown sugar
1/2 teaspoon ground cinnamon
1 tablespoon cold butter

In a large bowl, cream butter and sugar until light and fluffy. Add eggs, one at a time, beating well after each addition. Beat in milk. Combine the flour, baking powder and cinnamon; gradually add to creamed mixture just until moistened. Fill greased or paper-lined muffin cups one-third full.

For filling, in a small bowl, beat the cream cheese, sugar and egg until smooth. Fold in the berries. Drop a rounded tablespoonful into the center of each muffin.

For topping, combine the flour, brown sugar and cinnamon in a small bowl; cut in butter until crumbly. Sprinkle over batter. (Muffin cups will be full.)

Bake at 375° for 25-30 minutes or until a toothpick inserted near the center comes out clean. Cool for 5 minutes before removing from pans to wire racks. Serve warm. Refrigerate leftovers. **yield: 21 muffins.**

Jeanne Bilhimer
Midland, Michigan
I adapted this recipe over the years for my gang, and they think it's wonderful. Not only are the muffins delicious, but they're bursting with fantastic color, too.

apple-walnut sausage stuffing

5	celery ribs, thinly sliced
2	medium onions, chopped
3	teaspoons rubbed sage
2	teaspoons dried thyme
1	cup butter, cubed
3/4	cup grated Parmesan cheese
1/3	cup minced fresh parsley
1	teaspoon salt
1/2	teaspoon pepper
1	pound bulk Italian sausage
16	cups cubed day-old bread
5	medium tart apples, peeled and thinly sliced
1	can (14-1/2 ounces) chicken broth
1-1/2	cups chopped walnuts

Pamela Hewitt
Laguna Niguel, California
Coming from an Italian family, I like to use lots of herbs and seasonings in my cooking. This treasured stuffing features Parmesan cheese, apples and walnuts.

In a large skillet, saute the celery, onions, sage and thyme in butter until vegetables are tender. Transfer to a very large bowl; cool slightly. Stir in the cheese, parsley, salt and pepper; set aside.

In the same skillet, cook sausage over medium heat until no longer pink; drain. Add to celery mixture. Add the bread cubes, apples, broth and walnuts; toss to coat.

Transfer to a greased 3-qt. baking dish (dish will be full). Cover and bake at 350° for 25 minutes. Uncover; bake 10-15 minutes longer or until heated through and lightly browned. **yield 16 servings (3/4 cup each).**

Jill Steiner
Hancock, Minnesota
After sampling these savory beans at our local business' open house, I asked for the recipe. To my surprise, it had started with canned beans and easily gives them a wonderful homemade taste. The beans went over big at our reunion.

country baked beans

4	cans (16 ounces each) baked beans, drained
1	bottle (12 ounces) chili sauce
1	large onion, chopped
1	pound sliced bacon, cooked and crumbled
1	cup packed brown sugar

In a large bowl, combine all ingredients. Pour into a 4-1/2-qt. bean pot or two ungreased 2-qt. baking dishes.

Bake, uncovered, at 350° for 45-60 minutes or until heated through. **yield: 10-12 servings.**

party tortellini salad

1 package (19 ounces) frozen cheese tortellini
2 cups fresh broccoli florets
1 medium sweet red pepper, chopped
1/2 cup pimiento-stuffed olives, halved
3/4 cup reduced-fat red wine vinaigrette
1/2 teaspoon salt

Cook tortellini according to package directions; drain and rinse in cold water.

In a large bowl, combine the tortellini, broccoli, red pepper and olives. Drizzle with dressing and sprinkle with salt; toss to coat. Cover and refrigerate until serving. **yield: 10 servings.**

Mary Wilt
Ipswich, Massachusetts
This easy salad with its crowd-pleasing flavors makes a wonderful addition to cookouts and picnics. It's a favorite with folks of all ages.

special summer berry medley

1 cup sparkling wine *or* white grape juice
1/2 cup sugar
1 tablespoon lemon juice
1-1/2 teaspoons grated lemon peel
1/2 teaspoon vanilla extract
1/8 teaspoon salt
3 cups sliced fresh strawberries
2 cups fresh blueberries
1 cup fresh raspberries
1 cup fresh blackberries
1 tablespoon minced fresh mint

In a small heavy saucepan, bring wine and sugar to a boil. Cook, uncovered, for about 15 minutes or until reduced to 1/2 cup, stirring occasionally. Cool slightly. Stir in the lemon juice and peel, vanilla and salt.

In a large bowl, combine berries and mint. Add syrup and toss gently to coat. Cover and refrigerate until serving. **yield: 12 servings.**

Nancy Whitford
Edwards, New York
No matter how big the meal, guests usually find room for this delightful treat. With its hint of citrus and mint, this medley makes a light side at potlucks. Best of all, it's fast and simple to make, and cleanup is a snap!

bacon potato bake

8	cups thinly sliced peeled red potatoes
2	tablespoons all-purpose flour
2	eggs, lightly beaten
1	cup (8 ounces) sour cream
2	tablespoons butter, melted, *divided*
1-1/2	teaspoons salt
1-1/2	cups (6 ounces) shredded Monterey Jack cheese
1/4	cup dry bread crumbs
8	bacon strips, cooked and crumbled

Helen Haro
Yucaipa, California
This cheesy potato casserole is always popular. It's a nice change from mashed potatoes. With a bread crumb and crumbled bacon topping, it looks as good as it tastes.

Place potatoes in a Dutch oven; cover with water. Bring to a boil. Reduce heat; cover and simmer for 10-15 minutes or until tender. Drain; cool for 10 minutes.

In a small bowl, combine the flour, eggs, sour cream, 1 tablespoon butter and salt. Spoon over potatoes and toss to coat. Place half of the potato mixture in a greased 2-qt. baking dish; top with half of the cheese. Repeat layers.

Toss bread crumbs with remaining butter; sprinkle over the top. Bake, uncovered, at 350° for 1 hour or until a thermometer reads 160° and potatoes are tender. Sprinkle with bacon. **yield: 12 servings.**

holiday lettuce salad

10	cups torn romaine
2	medium red apples, cubed
2	medium pears, cubed
1	cup (4 ounces) shredded Swiss cheese
1/2	cup dried cranberries
6	tablespoons lemon juice
3	tablespoons canola oil
3	tablespoons light corn syrup
1-1/2	teaspoons grated onion
1-1/2	teaspoons Dijon mustard
1/2	teaspoon salt
1/2	cup chopped lightly salted cashews

In a salad bowl, combine the first five ingredients.

For dressing, in a small bowl, whisk the lemon juice, oil, corn syrup, onion, mustard and salt. Pour over romaine mixture; toss to coat. Sprinkle with cashews. **yield: 14 servings.**

Bryan Braack
Eldridge, Iowa
My family often requests that I make this salad for get-togethers. It's healthy and very good; everyone definitely goes back for seconds.

apple 'n' carrot slaw

4 large heads cabbage, shredded
1 pound carrots, shredded
6 medium red apples, finely chopped
3 cups mayonnaise
1/2 cup sugar
1/4 cup white vinegar
3 teaspoons salt
2 teaspoons pepper

In a very large bowl, combine the cabbage, carrots and apples. In a large bowl, combine the mayonnaise, sugar, vinegar, salt and pepper. Pour over the cabbage mixture and toss to coat. Cover and refrigerate until serving. **yield: 42 (3/4-cup) servings.**

Julia Livingston
Frostproof, Florida
This crispy, colorful slaw is a true crowd-pleaser at any picnic or church gathering. The apples add color and a touch of sweetness.

harvest squash medley

Ruth Cowley
Pipe Creek, Texas
To me, cooking is an art, and I love trying new recipes. This one dresses up baked butternut squash, sweet potatoes and apples with citrus and spices.

6 cups water
1 butternut squash, peeled, seeded and cut into 3/4-inch pieces
2 medium sweet potatoes, peeled and cut into 3/4-inch pieces
1/4 cup honey
1/4 cup orange juice
3 tablespoons butter
1 tablespoon grated orange peel
1/2 teaspoon ground cinnamon
1/8 teaspoon ground nutmeg
2 small apples, peeled and sliced
1/2 cup chopped walnuts, toasted

In a large saucepan, bring water to a boil. Add squash and return to a boil. Reduce heat; cover and simmer for 10 minutes. Drain. Place the squash and sweet potatoes in a greased 13-in. x 9-in. baking dish.

In a small saucepan, combine the honey, orange juice, butter, orange peel, cinnamon and nutmeg. Bring to a boil, stirring constantly. Pour over squash and potatoes.

Cover and bake at 350° for 30 minutes, stirring occasionally. Uncover; stir in apples. Bake 30-35 minutes longer or until tender, stirring occasionally. Sprinkle with walnuts. **yield: 10 servings.**

fruited holiday vegetables

- 1 large rutabaga, peeled and cubed
- 3 small red potatoes, cubed
- 3 medium sweet potatoes, peeled and cubed
- 4 teaspoons cornstarch
- 1/2 cup cold water
- 1/2 cup orange juice
- 1 cup prepared mincemeat
- 1/4 cup butter, melted
- 1/4 cup packed dark brown sugar
- 1/4 cup dark corn syrup
- 1/4 teaspoon ground ginger
- 1/4 teaspoon ground cinnamon
- 1-3/4 cups frozen unsweetened sliced peaches, thawed and chopped
- 1 medium tart apple, chopped
- 1 tablespoon lemon juice
- 1/2 cup chopped pecans

Place rutabaga in a Dutch oven; cover with water. Bring to a boil. Reduce heat; cover and simmer for 15 minutes. Add red potatoes and enough additional water to cover. Return to a boil. Reduce heat; cover and simmer for 5 minutes.

Add sweet potatoes and enough additional water to cover. Bring to a boil. Reduce heat; cover and simmer 15 minutes longer or until vegetables are tender.

Meanwhile, in a small saucepan, combine cornstarch and cold water until smooth. Gradually stir in the orange juice. Bring to a boil; cook and stir for 1-2 minutes or until thickened. Stir in the mincemeat, butter, brown sugar, corn syrup, ginger and cinnamon; heat through.

In a large bowl, combine the peaches, apple and lemon juice. Drain vegetables; stir in fruit mixture. Transfer to a greased 4-qt. baking dish. Add mincemeat mixture; stir gently. Sprinkle with pecans. Bake, uncovered, at 325° for 30-35 minutes or until fruit is tender. **yield: 12 servings.**

Paula Marchesi
Lenhartsville,
Pennsylvania
Mom and I made a great team in the kitchen, cooking and baking for hours at a time. I treasure this favorite side dish from her the most.

baked vegetable medley

1 medium head cauliflower, broken into florets
1 bunch broccoli, cut into florets
6 medium carrots, sliced
1 pound sliced fresh mushrooms
1 bunch green onions, sliced
1/4 cup butter, cubed
1 can (10-3/4 ounces) condensed cream of chicken soup, undiluted
1/2 cup milk
1/2 cup process cheese sauce

Linda Vail
Ballwin, Missouri
If you get all the chopping done the night before, it's smooth sailing when company arrives the next day. Just prepare this casserole in advance and bake the next day for dinner.

Place the cauliflower, broccoli and carrots in a steamer basket; place in a large saucepan over 1 in. of water. Bring to a boil; cover and steam for 7-9 minutes or until crisp-tender. Meanwhile, in a large skillet, saute mushrooms and onions in butter until tender.

Drain vegetables. In a large bowl, combine the soup, milk and cheese sauce. Add vegetables and mushroom mixture; toss to coat. Transfer to a greased 2-qt. baking dish. Cover and refrigerate overnight.

Remove from the refrigerator 30 minutes before baking. Bake, uncovered, at 350° for 40-45 minutes or until bubbly. **yield: 12 servings.**

spinach penne toss

2 cups uncooked penne pasta
1 medium sweet red pepper, julienned
1 medium onion, sliced
1 tablespoon plus 1/4 cup olive oil, *divided*
1 package (6 ounces) fresh baby spinach
3/4 cup crumbled cooked bacon
1/2 cup crumbled feta cheese
1/2 cup oil-packed sun-dried tomatoes, chopped
2 tablespoons cider vinegar
1/4 teaspoon pepper
1/8 teaspoon salt

Kierste Wade
Midland, Michigan
Spinach provides a delicious base for all the wonderful flavor combinations found in this hearty salad. It's ideal for so many different occasions, including large buffets and covered-dish events.

Cook pasta according to package directions. Meanwhile, in a large skillet, saute red pepper and onion in 1 tablespoon oil for 3-4 minutes or until tender.

Drain pasta and place in a serving bowl. Add the red pepper mixture, spinach, bacon, feta cheese and tomatoes.

In a small bowl, whisk the vinegar, pepper, salt and remaining oil. Drizzle over pasta mixture; toss to coat. **yield: 10 servings.**

sweet endings

pecan goodie cups

page 194

Patty Courtney, Jonesboro, Texas
The maraschino cherries add colorful flecks to these cookies. As a home economics teacher, I often supplied snacks for large school functions, and these delectable cookies were always popular.

cherry icebox cookies

1	cup butter, softened
1	cup sugar
1/4	cup packed brown sugar
1	egg
1/4	cup maraschino cherry juice
4-1/2	teaspoons lemon juice
1	teaspoon vanilla extract
3-1/4	cups all-purpose flour
1/2	teaspoon baking soda
1/2	teaspoon ground cinnamon
1/4	teaspoon cream of tartar
1/2	cup chopped walnuts
1/2	cup chopped maraschino cherries

In a large bowl, cream butter and sugars until light and fluffy. Beat in the egg, cherry and lemon juices and vanilla. Combine dry ingredients; gradually add to creamed mixture and mix well. Stir in nuts and cherries.

Shape into four 12-in. rolls; wrap each in plastic wrap. Refrigerate for 4 hours or until firm.

Unwrap and cut into 1/4-in. slices. Place 2 in. apart on ungreased baking sheets. Bake at 375° for 8-10 minutes or until the edges begin to brown. Remove cookies to wire racks to cool. **yield: about 6 dozen.**

storing cookies

Store baked cookies in an airtight container at room temperature for 3 days. Freeze cookies for up to 3 months, wrapped in plastic and stacked in an airtight container. Thaw at room temperature.

lemon-lime bars

1 cup butter, softened
1/2 cup confectioners' sugar
2 teaspoons grated lime peel
1-3/4 cups all-purpose flour
1/4 teaspoon salt

FILLING:
4 eggs
1-1/2 cups sugar
1/4 cup all-purpose flour
1/2 teaspoon baking powder
1/3 cup lemon juice
2 teaspoons grated lemon peel

Confectioners' sugar

In a large bowl, cream butter and confectioners' sugar until light and fluffy. Beat in lime peel. Combine flour and salt; gradually add to creamed mixture and mix well.

Press into a greased 13-in. x 9-in. baking dish. Bake at 350° for 13-15 minutes or just until edges are lightly browned.

Meanwhile, in another large bowl, beat eggs and sugar. Combine the flour and baking powder. Gradually add to egg mixture. Stir in lemon juice and peel; beat until frothy. Pour over hot crust.

Bake for 20-25 minutes or until light golden brown. Cool on a wire rack. Dust with confectioners' sugar. Cut into squares. Store in the refrigerator. **yield: 4 dozen.**

Holly Wilkins
Lake Elmore, Vermont
I baked these bars for a luncheon on a hot summer day. A gentleman even made his way to the kitchen just to compliment the cook who made them.

caramel butter-pecan bars

Mary Jean Hlavac
McFarland, Wisconsin
These melt-in-your-mouth bars are simply to die for. They go together in 10 minutes, and even though the chocolate layer takes time to harden (think make-ahead convenience), these treats are definitely worth the effort.

2 cups all-purpose flour
1 cup packed brown sugar
3/4 cup cold butter, cubed
1-1/2 cups chopped pecans
1 jar (12 ounces) caramel ice cream topping, warmed
1 package (11-1/2 ounces) milk chocolate chips

In a large bowl, combine flour and brown sugar; cut in butter until crumbly. Press into an ungreased 13-in. x 9-in. baking dish. Top with pecans. Drizzle caramel topping evenly over pecans.

Bake at 350° for 15-20 minutes or until caramel is bubbly. Place on a wire rack. Sprinkle with chocolate chips. Let stand for 5 minutes. Carefully spread the chips over the caramel layer. Cool at room temperature for at least 6 hours or until chocolate is set. Cut into bars. **yield: 4 dozen.**

pastel tea cookies

1 cup butter, softened
2/3 cup sugar
1 egg
1 teaspoon vanilla extract
2-1/2 cups all-purpose flour
1/2 teaspoon salt
1-1/4 cups confectioners' sugar
2 teaspoons meringue powder
5 teaspoons water
Pastel food coloring

In a large bowl, cream butter and sugar until light and fluffy. Beat in egg and vanilla. Combine flour and salt; gradually add to the creamed mixture. Cover and refrigerate for 1-2 hours until dough is easy to handle.

On a lightly floured surface, roll out dough to 1/8-in. thickness. Cut with floured 2-1/2-in. butterfly or flower cookie cutters. Place 1 in. apart on ungreased baking sheets.

Bake at 350° for 8-10 minutes or until edges are lightly browned. Remove to wire racks to cool.

For glaze, in a small bowl, combine confectioners' sugar and meringue powder; stir in water until smooth. Divide among small bowls; tint pastel colors. Spread over cookies; let stand until set. **yield: 4 dozen.**

Lori Henry
Elkhart, Indiana
These glazed sugar cookies are perfect for nibbling between sips at a tea party, graduation or shower.

cinnamon-sugar crisps

3/4 cup butter, softened
1/3 cup sugar
1/3 cup packed brown sugar
1 egg
1 teaspoon vanilla extract
1-3/4 cups all-purpose flour
1 teaspoon ground cinnamon
1/4 teaspoon salt
2 tablespoons colored sprinkles

In a large bowl, cream butter and sugars until light and fluffy. Beat in egg and vanilla. Combine the flour, cinnamon and salt; gradually add to creamed mixture and mix well. Shape into a 12-in. roll; wrap in plastic wrap. Refrigerate for 2 hours or until firm.

Unwrap and cut into 1/2-in. slices. Place 2 in. apart on ungreased baking sheets. Decorate with sprinkles. Bake at 350° for 10-12 minutes or until lightly browned. Remove to wire racks to cool. **yield: 3-1/2 dozen.**

Kim Marie Van Rheenen
Mendota, Illinois
This slice-and-bake recipe is terrific for folks who don't care for making cutout cookies. I make them throughout the year with different colored sprinkles to match the event.

Linda Hardin-Eldridge, Lake Alfred, Florida

There's always a flurry of activity around the snack bar in my kitchen, especially when I set out a plate of these brownies. Topped with a fluffy chocolaty frosting, they really live up to their name.

brownies from heaven

  1   cup butter, softened
  2   cups sugar
  2   eggs
  1   teaspoon vanilla extract
  2   cups all-purpose flour
1/2   cup baking cocoa
  1   cup chopped walnuts
FROSTING:
1/2   cup butter, softened
3-1/2   cups confectioners' sugar
1/3   cup baking cocoa
1/4   cup milk
  1   teaspoon vanilla extract

In a large bowl, cream butter and sugar until light and fluffy. Add eggs, one at a time, beating well after each addition. Beat in vanilla. Combine flour and cocoa; add to creamed mixture just until combined. Stir in walnuts.

Spread into an ungreased 13-in. x 9-in. baking pan. Bake at 350° for 23-28 minutes or until a toothpick inserted near the center comes out clean. Cool on a wire rack.

For frosting, in a small bowl, beat butter until fluffy. Beat in the confectioners' sugar, cocoa, milk and vanilla until smooth. Spread over brownies. Cut into bars. **yield: 2 dozen.**

chocolate mint surprises

3/4	cup butter, softened
1	cup sugar
1	egg
1	teaspoon vanilla extract
3	ounces unsweetened chocolate, melted and cooled
2-1/2	cups all-purpose flour
1-1/2	teaspoons baking powder
1/2	teaspoon salt

MINT FILLING:

4	cups confectioners' sugar
3	tablespoons butter, softened
1/4	cup evaporated milk
2	to 3 teaspoons peppermint extract
1/2	teaspoon vanilla extract
2	pounds dark chocolate candy coating, melted

In a large bowl, cream butter and sugar until light and fluffy. Beat in egg and vanilla. Add melted chocolate. Combine the flour, baking powder and salt; gradually add to chocolate mixture and mix well. Shape in two 10-in. rolls; wrap each in plastic wrap. Refrigerate for 4 hours or until firm.

Unwrap dough and cut into 1/4-in. slices. Place 2 in. apart on ungreased baking sheets. Bake at 375° for 5-7 minutes or until edges are firm. Remove to wire racks to cool.

For filling, in a small bowl, combine the confectioners' sugar, butter, milk and extracts until smooth. Shape into 1/2-in. balls. Place a ball in the center of each cookie; flatten. Freeze for 30 minutes.

Dip cookies in melted candy coating to completely cover; allow excess to drip off. Place on waxed paper; let stand until set. **yield: about 6 dozen.**

Sheila Kerr
Revelstoke,
British Columbia
I came up with this recipe a few years ago and have shared it with many people. I would often snack on these treats after my baby's middle-of-the-night feeding.

frosty facts

Most cookie doughs can be stored in the freezer. After mixing the dough, chill it in the refrigerator until firm. Shape it into a large ball or square. Wrap in freezer paper, then place in a heavy-duty resealable plastic bag. Freeze for up to 6 months.

chocolate zucchini cake

- 1/2 cup butter, softened
- 1/2 cup canola oil
- 1-3/4 cups sugar
- 2 eggs
- 1 teaspoon vanilla extract
- 2-1/2 cups all-purpose flour
- 1/4 cup baking cocoa
- 1 teaspoon baking soda
- 1/2 teaspoon baking powder
- 1/2 teaspoon ground cinnamon
- 1/2 teaspoon ground cloves
- 1/2 cup buttermilk
- 2 cups shredded zucchini

FROSTING:
- 1 cup flaked coconut
- 6 tablespoons butter, softened
- 2/3 cup packed brown sugar
- 1/2 cup chopped walnuts
- 1/4 cup milk

In a large bowl, beat the butter, oil and sugar until smooth. Add eggs, one at a time, beating well after each addition. Beat in vanilla. Combine the flour, cocoa, baking soda, baking powder, cinnamon and cloves; gradually add to batter alternately with buttermilk, beating well after each addition. Fold in zucchini.

Pour into a greased 13-in. x 9-in. baking pan. Bake at 325° for 45-50 minutes or until a toothpick inserted near the center comes out clean. Cool on a wire rack for 10 minutes.

Meanwhile, in a small bowl, combine the frosting ingredients. Spread over warm cake. Broil 4-6 in. from the heat for 2-3 minutes or until golden brown. Cool completely. **yield: 12-15 servings.**

Lois Holben
Creal Springs, Illinois
Grated zucchini makes this cake really moist, and the topping adds a nice crunch. When zucchini is in season, I shred, measure and freeze it in 2-cup amounts for this favorite recipe.

white chocolate cereal bars

Anne Powers
Munford, Alabama
A friend gave me this recipe that's a different take on the traditional crisp rice goodies. My husband loves them. They're so quick to make, you can prepare them during a TV commercial and you won't miss much of your program.

- 4 cups miniature marshmallows
- 8 ounces white candy coating, coarsely chopped
- 1/4 cup butter, cubed
- 6 cups crisp rice cereal

In a microwave-safe bowl, combine the marshmallows, candy coating and butter. Microwave, uncovered, on high for 2 minutes or until melted, stirring every minute. Add cereal; stir to coat.

Transfer to a greased 13-in. x 9-in. pan; gently press mixture evenly into pan. Cut into squares. **yield: about 3 dozen.**

Vicki Raatz, Waterloo, Wisconsin
The large yield of my recipe makes these cookies perfect for gift giving.

chocolate almond crescents

1-1/4	cups butter, softened
2/3	cup sugar
2	cups finely chopped almonds
1-1/2	teaspoons vanilla extract
2	cups all-purpose flour
1/2	cup baking cocoa
1/8	teaspoon salt
1-1/4	cups semisweet chocolate chips, melted
1	to 2 tablespoons confectioners' sugar

In a large bowl, cream butter and sugar until light and fluffy. Beat in almonds and vanilla. Combine the flour, cocoa and salt; gradually add to creamed mixture and mix well. Cover and refrigerate for 2 hours or until easy to handle.

Roll 2 teaspoonfuls of dough into 2-in. logs. Shape each into a crescent. Place 2 in. apart on ungreased baking sheets. Bake at 350° for 10-12 minutes or until set. Remove crescents to wire racks to cool.

Dip half of each cookie in melted chocolate; allow excess to drip off. Place on waxed paper to harden. Cover dipped sides of cookies with waxed paper; sprinkle undipped sides with confectioners' sugar. Store in an airtight container. **yield: 6 dozen.**

go nuts for almonds

Almonds are a very versatile nuts. They blend well with other items, savory and sweet, and they're delicious eaten as a nutritious snack. They offer a great crunch in recipes.

cherry kolaches

2 packages (1/4 ounce *each*) active dry yeast
1/2 cup warm water (110° to 115°)
2-1/2 cups warm 2% milk (110° to 115°)
3/4 cup sugar
3/4 cup butter, softened
2 teaspoons salt
4 eggs
11 to 11-1/2 cups all-purpose flour

FILLING:

2 cans (21 ounces *each*) cherry pie filling
1/2 cup sugar
2 tablespoons cornstarch
2 tablespoons cold water

TOPPING:

1 package (8 ounces) cream cheese, softened
2/3 cup sugar
1 egg yolk
Melted butter

In a large bowl, dissolve yeast in warm water. Add the milk, sugar, butter, salt, eggs and 5 cups flour; beat until smooth. Stir in enough remaining flour to form a very soft dough. Do not knead. Cover and let rise in a warm place until doubled, about 75 minutes.

Turn onto a well-floured surface. Shape into 1-1/2-in. balls. Place 2 in. apart on greased baking sheets. Cover and let rise until doubled, about 45 minutes.

Meanwhile, in a small saucepan, combine pie filling and sugar. Combine cornstarch and cold water until smooth; gradually stir into filling. Bring to a boil over medium heat. Cook and stir for 1 minute or until thickened; set aside.

For topping, in a large bowl, beat the cream cheese, sugar and egg yolk until smooth. Using the end of a wooden spoon handle, make an indentation in the center of each dough ball; fill with 2 rounded teaspoons of filling. Make a small indentation in center of filling; add 1 teaspoon topping.

Bake at 400° for 10-15 minutes or until lightly browned. Brush melted butter over rolls. Remove from pans to wire racks to cool. Refrigerate leftovers. **yield: about 6 dozen.**

Evelyn Nesiba
Ravenna, Nebraska

I am of Czechoslovakian descent, and baking kolaches is my specialty. These sweet yeast buns with fruit or poppy seed filling are a true Czech tradition. From a young age, I've enjoyed baking, but it wasn't until we retired from farming and moved to town that I started making large quantities of kolaches. I make my fillings from scratch, but you can easily use canned filling instead.

chocolate silk pie

1	unbaked pastry shell (9 inches)
1	jar (7 ounces) marshmallow creme
1	cup (6 ounces) semisweet chocolate chips
1/4	cup butter, cubed
2	ounces unsweetened chocolate
2	tablespoons strong brewed coffee
1	cup heavy whipping cream, whipped

TOPPING:

1	cup heavy whipping cream
2	tablespoons confectioners' sugar

Chocolate curls, optional

Line unpricked pastry shell with a double thickness of heavy-duty foil. Bake at 450° for 8 minutes. Remove foil; bake 5 minutes longer. Cool on a wire rack.

Meanwhile, in a heavy saucepan, combine the marshmallow creme, chocolate chips, butter, unsweetened chocolate and coffee; cook and stir over low heat until chocolate is melted and mixture is smooth. Cool. Fold in whipped cream; pour into crust.

For topping, in a large bowl, beat cream until it begins to thicken. Add confectioners' sugar; beat until stiff peaks form. Spread over filling. Refrigerate for at least 3 hours before serving. Garnish with chocolate curls if desired. **yield: 6-8 servings.**

Mary Relyea
Canastota, New York
This creamy, quick chocolate pie not only melts in your mouth, it also melts any and all resistance to dessert!

pecan goody cups

3/4	cup butter, softened
2	packages (3 ounces *each*) cream cheese, softened
2	cups all-purpose flour

FILLING:

1-1/2	cups packed brown sugar
2	eggs
1	tablespoon butter, melted
48	pecan halves

In a large bowl, beat butter and cream cheese until light and fluffy. Gradually add flour, beating until mixture forms a ball. Cover and refrigerate for 15 minutes. For filling, in a small bowl, combine the brown sugar, eggs and butter.

Roll dough into 1-in. balls. Press onto the bottoms and up the sides of greased miniature muffin cups. Spoon filling into cups; top each with a pecan half.

Bake at 350° for 20-25 minutes or until golden brown. Cool for 2-3 minutes before removing from pans to wire racks. **yield: 4 dozen.**

Janice Hose
Hagerstown, Maryland
These miniature tarts feature whole pecans, a caramel-like filling, and a butter and cream cheese crust that is almost impossible to ignore!

Mary Ann Bostic, Sinks Grove, West Virginia
This pie always receives rave reviews from family and friends. I think it's especially good when fresh peaches are in season.

creamy peach pie

Pastry for double-crust pie (9 inches)
- 3/4 cup plus 1 tablespoon sugar, *divided*
- 3 tablespoons cornstarch
- 1/2 teaspoon ground nutmeg
- 1/4 teaspoon ground ginger
- 1/4 teaspoon ground cinnamon
- 4 tablespoons heavy whipping cream, *divided*
- 1 tablespoon lemon juice
- 1/2 teaspoon almond extract
- 7 cups sliced peeled peaches (about 7 medium)

Line a 9-in. pie plate with bottom pastry; trim even with edge of plate. Set aside. In a bowl, combine 3/4 cup sugar, cornstarch, nutmeg, ginger and cinnamon; stir in 3 tablespoons cream, lemon juice and extract. Add the peaches; toss gently. Pour into the crust.

Roll out remaining pastry to fit top of pie; make decorative cutouts in pastry. Place top crust over filling; trim, seal and flute edges. Brush pastry and cutouts with remaining cream. Place cutouts on top of the pie; sprinkle with the remaining sugar.

Cover edges loosely with foil. Bake at 400° for 40 minutes. Remove foil; bake 8-12 minutes longer or until crust is golden brown and filling is bubbly. Cool on a wire rack. Refrigerate leftovers. **yield: 6-8 servings.**

peanut butter chocolate cupcakes

1	package (3 ounces) cream cheese, softened
1/4	cup creamy peanut butter
2	tablespoons sugar
1	tablespoon 2% milk

BATTER:

2	cups sugar
1-3/4	cups all-purpose flour
1/2	cup baking cocoa
1-1/2	teaspoons baking powder
1	teaspoon salt
1/4	teaspoon baking soda
2	eggs
1	cup water
1	cup 2% milk
1/2	cup canola oil
2	teaspoons vanilla extract

FROSTING:

1/3	cup butter, softened
2	cups confectioners' sugar
6	tablespoons baking cocoa
3	to 4 tablespoons 2% milk

In a small bowl, beat cream cheese, peanut butter, sugar and milk until smooth; set aside.

In a large bowl, combine sugar, flour, cocoa, baking powder, salt and baking soda. In another bowl, whisk the eggs, water, milk, oil and vanilla. Stir into dry ingredients just until moistened (batter will be thin).

Fill paper-lined jumbo muffin cups half full with batter. Drop scant tablespoonfuls of peanut butter mixture into center of each; cover with remaining batter.

Bake at 350° for 25-30 minutes or until a toothpick inserted into cake comes out clean. Cool 10 minutes; remove from pans to wire racks. Cool completely.

In a large bowl, combine frosting ingredients until smooth; frost the cupcakes. Store cupcakes in the refrigerator. **yield: 1 dozen jumbo cupcakes.**

Julie Small
Claremont,
New Hampshire
I didn't have any luck finding a peanut butter-filled chocolate cupcake, which are my two favorite flavors. Instead, I made my favorite chocolate cupcake recipe, and then I experimented with the filling until I found one I liked.

orange tea cake

7	eggs, *separated*
1-3/4	cups all-purpose flour
1/2	teaspoon salt
1-1/2	cups sugar, *divided*
6	tablespoons orange juice
4-1/2	teaspoons grated orange peel
3/4	teaspoon confectioners' sugar

Let eggs stand at room temperature for 30 minutes. Sift flour and salt; set aside. In a large bowl, beat yolks until slightly thickened. Gradually add 1/2 cup sugar, beating until thick and lemon-colored. Blend in orange juice and peel. Add dry ingredients to yolk mixture; mix well.

In another bowl, beat egg whites on medium speed until soft peaks form. Gradually beat in remaining sugar, about 1 tablespoon at a time, on high until stiff glossy peaks form and sugar is dissolved. Fold a fourth of egg whites into the batter, then fold in remaining whites.

Gently spoon into an ungreased 10-in. tube pan. Cut through batter with a knife to remove air pockets. Bake on the lowest oven rack at 350° for 30-35 minutes or until cake springs back when lightly touched. Immediately invert pan onto a wire rack; cool completely, about 1 hour.

Run a knife around sides of cake and remove to a serving plate. Dust with confectioners' sugar. **yield: 12 servings.**

Beth Duerr
North Tonawanda,
New York
This from-scratch sponge cake has a hint of orange in every bite and is wonderful served with a cup of hot tea. It doesn't need frosting.

cherry cream trifle

1	package (18-1/4 ounces) yellow cake mix
2	packages (3.4 ounces *each*) instant vanilla pudding mix
2	cans (21 ounces *each*) cherry pie filling
2	cans (20 ounces *each*) crushed pineapple, drained
2	cartons (16 ounces *each*) frozen whipped topping, thawed
2	cups chopped pecans

Prepare and bake cake according to package directions for a 13-in. x 9-in. pan. Cool on a wire rack. Meanwhile, prepare pudding according to package directions.

Cut cake into 1-1/2-in. cubes; place a third of the cubes in an 8-qt. punch bowl. Top with a third of the pie filling, pineapple, pudding, whipped topping and pecans; repeat layers twice. Cover and refrigerate until serving. **yield: 25-30 servings.**

Juanita Davis
Martin, Tennessee
Not only is this dessert cool and creamy, it's a conversation piece when presented in a punch bowl!

Josie Bochek, Sturgeon Bay, Wisconsin
Here's a recipe for a traditional sweet and nutty Greek pastry. It's a tasty end to any large gathering.

walnut baklava

4	cups finely chopped walnuts
1/4	cup sugar
1	tablespoon ground cinnamon
1	cup butter, melted
40	sheets phyllo dough (14 inches x 9 inches)

SYRUP:

1	cup sugar
1/2	cup water
1/4	cup honey
1	teaspoon lemon juice
1	teaspoon vanilla extract

In a small bowl, combine the walnuts, sugar and cinnamon; set aside. Grease two 13-in. x 9-in. baking dishes with some of the melted butter. Unroll phyllo dough sheets (keep dough covered with plastic wrap while assembling).

Place one sheet of phyllo in a baking dish; brush with butter. Top with a second sheet; brush with butter. Fold long ends under to fit the dish. Sprinkle with about 2 tablespoons nut mixture. Repeat 18 times, layering two sheets, brushing with butter and sprinkling with nut mixture. Top with remaining dough; brush with butter. Cut into 2-in. diamonds with a sharp knife.

Bake at 350° for 45-55 minutes or until golden brown. Meanwhile, in a saucepan, combine the syrup ingredients; bring to a boil. Reduce heat; simmer, uncovered, for 10 minutes. Pour over warm baklava. Cool on a wire rack. **yield: 3 dozen.**

editor's note: This recipe was tested with Athenos phyllo dough. The phyllo sheets measure 14-in. x 9-in.

coconut carrot cake

- 2 cups sugar
- 1 cup canola oil
- 4 eggs
- 4 cups all-purpose flour
- 2 teaspoons baking powder
- 2 teaspoons ground cinnamon
- 1-1/2 teaspoons baking soda
- 1 teaspoon salt
- 1 can (8 ounces) crushed pineapple
- 2 cups grated carrots
- 1-1/2 cups flaked coconut

FROSTING:
- 1 package (8 ounces) cream cheese, softened
- 1/2 cup butter, softened
- 1 teaspoon vanilla extract
- 2-1/2 cups confectioners' sugar

Orange paste food coloring

Parsley sprig

In a large bowl, beat the sugar, oil and eggs until well blended. In another large bowl, combine the flour, baking powder, cinnamon, baking soda and salt; gradually beat into sugar mixture until blended. Drain pineapple, reserving juice; set juice aside. Stir in the pineapple, carrots and coconut (batter will be thick).

Transfer to three greased and floured 9-in. round baking pans. Bake at 350° for 35-40 minutes or until a toothpick inserted near the center comes out clean. Cool for 10 minutes before removing from pans to wire racks.

For frosting, in a large bowl, beat the cream cheese, butter and vanilla until fluffy. Gradually add confectioners' sugar and enough of the reserved pineapple juice to achieve desired spreading consistency. Tint 1/4 cup frosting orange; place in a small resealable plastic bag. Cut a small hole in a corner of the bag; set aside.

Place one cake layer on a serving plate; spread with a third of the white frosting. Repeat layers twice. With orange frosting, pipe carrots on top; add parsley sprig for carrot top. Cover and store in the refrigerator **yield: 12-14 servings.**

Shirley Braithewaite
Onaway, Alberta
I found this cake recipe in a cookbook many years ago. It's easy to make, and everyone just loves its moistness. It's impressive when prepared in three layers.

chunky apple cake

Debi Benson
Bakersfield, California
*This tender, moist cake is full
of old-fashioned comfort, and
the yummy brown-sugar sauce
makes it special. For a festive
occasion, top with a dollop of
whipped cream.*

1/2	cup butter, softened
2	cups sugar
2	eggs
1/2	teaspoon vanilla extract
2	cups all-purpose flour
1-1/2	teaspoons ground cinnamon
1	teaspoon ground nutmeg
1/2	teaspoon salt
1/2	teaspoon baking soda
6	cups chopped peeled tart apples

BUTTERSCOTCH SAUCE:

1/2	cup packed brown sugar
1/4	cup butter, cubed
1/2	cup heavy whipping cream

In a large bowl, cream butter and sugar until light and fluffy. Add eggs, one at a time, beating well after each addition. Beat in vanilla. Combine the flour, cinnamon, nutmeg, salt and baking soda; gradually add to creamed mixture and mix well (batter will be stiff). Stir in apples until well combined.

Spread into a greased 13-in. x 9-in. baking dish. Bake at 350° for 40-45 minutes or until top is lightly browned and springs back when lightly touched. Cool for 30 minutes before serving.

Meanwhile, in a small saucepan, combine brown sugar and butter. Cook over medium heat until butter is melted. Gradually add cream. Bring to a slow boil over medium heat, stirring constantly. Remove from the heat. Serve with cake. **yield: 12-14 servings.**

slow cooker ease

If you decide to bring Chunky Apple Cake to a potluck, keep the delicious Butterscotch Sauce warm in a slow cooker. Then guests can easily top each slice of cake just as they like. You may want to have whipped topping on hand, too.

super brownies

- 1/2 cup butter, cubed
- 1-1/2 cups sugar
- 4-2/3 cups (28 ounces) semisweet chocolate chips, *divided*
- 3 tablespoons hot water
- 4 eggs
- 5 teaspoons vanilla extract
- 1-1/2 cups all-purpose flour
- 1/2 teaspoon baking soda
- 1/2 teaspoon salt
- 2 cups coarsely chopped macadamia nuts *or* pecans, *divided*

In a large saucepan, melt butter with sugar over medium heat. Remove from the heat; stir in 2 cups of the chocolate chips until they are melted.

Pour into a large bowl; beat in water. Add eggs, one at a time, beating well after each addition. Add vanilla. Combine the flour, baking soda and salt; beat into the chocolate mixture until blended. Stir in 2 cups chocolate chips and 1 cup nuts.

Pour into a greased 13-in. x 9-in. baking pan. Sprinkle with remaining chips and nuts. Bake at 325° for 55 minutes or until the center is set (do not overbake). Cool on a wire rack. **yield: about 3-1/2 dozen.**

Bernice Muilenburg
Molalla, Oregon
Loaded with macadamia nuts, these chunky, bite-size treats never fail to catch attention on a buffet table. If you prefer, replace the macadamia nuts with pecans.

mocha nut balls

- 1 cup butter, softened
- 1/2 cup sugar
- 2 teaspoons vanilla extract
- 1-3/4 cups all-purpose flour
- 1/3 cup baking cocoa
- 1 tablespoon instant coffee granules
- 1 cup finely chopped pecans *or* walnuts
- Confectioners' sugar

Janet Sullivan
Buffalo, New York
These yummy, flavorful cookies are so addictive, I always know I have to make a double batch. The family demands they get a share.

In a large bowl, cream butter and sugar until light and fluffy. Beat in vanilla. Combine the flour, cocoa and coffee granules; gradually add to creamed mixture and mix well. Stir in pecans. Roll into 1-in. balls. Place 2 in. apart on ungreased baking sheets.

Bake at 325° for 14-16 minutes or until firm. Cool on pans for 1-2 minutes before removing to wire racks. Roll warm cookies in confectioners' sugar. **yield: 4-1/2 dozen.**

festive fruit tart

Pastry for single-crust pie (9 inches)
- 1 package (8 ounces) cream cheese, softened
- 3 tablespoons sugar
- 1 teaspoon vanilla extract
- 3/4 teaspoon almond extract, *divided*
- 1 cup fresh blueberries
- 1 cup fresh raspberries
- 1 medium ripe peach *or* nectarine, peeled and sliced
- 2 tablespoons apricot preserves

Press pastry onto the bottom and up the sides of an ungreased 9-in. tart pan with a removable bottom; trim edges. Generously prick the bottom with a fork. Bake at 450° for 10-12 minutes or until golden brown. Cool completely on a wire rack.

In a small bowl, beat the cream cheese, sugar, vanilla and 1/2 teaspoon almond extract until smooth; spread over crust. Arrange fruit over cream cheese mixture.

In a microwave, heat preserves and remaining extract, uncovered, on high for 20-30 seconds or until warm. Brush over fruit. Store in the refrigerator. **yield: 12 servings.**

Nancy Adams
Hancock, New Hampshire
"Wow!" is what you'll hear when you contribute this impressive dessert. The tart is not only pretty, it's also very easy to make.

chewy coconut cookies

- 3/4 cup butter-flavored shortening
- 1/2 cup peanut butter
- 1 cup sugar
- 1 cup packed brown sugar
- 3 eggs
- 1/2 cup mashed ripe banana
- 1 teaspoon vanilla extract
- 1/2 teaspoon almond extract
- 2-1/2 cups all-purpose flour
- 1 teaspoon baking soda
- 1 teaspoon salt
- 1/2 teaspoon baking powder
- 1 cup flaked coconut

Nick Robeson
Casper, Wyoming
These yummy cookies are sure to keep guests coming to the dessert table for seconds.

In a large bowl, cream the shortening, peanut butter and sugars until light and fluffy. Add eggs, one at a time, beating well after each addition. Beat in the banana and extracts. Combine the flour, baking soda, salt and baking powder; gradually add to creamed mixture and mix well. Stir in coconut.

Drop by heaping teaspoonfuls 2 in. apart onto lightly greased baking sheets. Bake at 350° for 12-14 minutes or until edges are lightly browned. Remove to wire racks. **yield: about 5-1/2 dozen.**

LeAnn Sager, Fairmont, Minnesota
This recipe makes one of my family's favorite pies. It is served at many get-togethers and potlucks.

cherry-apple lattice pie

1/2	cup dried cherries
1/4	cup unsweetened apple juice
2	tablespoons plus 1/2 cup sugar, *divided*
2-1/4	teaspoons ground cinnamon, *divided*
2	tablespoons cornstarch
6	cups thinly sliced peeled tart apples
1	teaspoon vanilla extract
1	package (15 ounces) refrigerated pie pastry
1	egg white

In a small microwave-safe bowl, combine cherries and apple juice. Cover and microwave on high until heated through; set aside.

In a small bowl, combine 2 tablespoons sugar and 1/4 teaspoon cinnamon; set aside for topping. In a large bowl, combine cornstarch with the remaining sugar and cinnamon. Stir in the apples, vanilla and reserved cherry mixture.

Line a 9-in. deep-dish pie plate with bottom crust; trim pastry even with edge of plate. Add filling. With remaining pastry, make a lattice crust. Seal and flute edges. Beat egg white until foamy; brush over lattice top. Sprinkle with reserved cinnamon-sugar.

Cover edges loosely with foil. Bake at 450° for 15 minutes. Reduce heat to 350° and remove foil. Bake 30-45 minutes longer or until crust is golden brown and filling is bubbly. Cool on a wire rack. **yield: 8 servings.**

fluted edges

To flute the edges of a pie crust, position your thumb on the inside of the crust. Place thumb and index finger of your other hand outside the crust, and then pinch pastry around thumb to form a "V" and seal dough together.

mocha bundt cake

1-1/2	cups butter
12	ounces bittersweet chocolate
2-1/4	cups sugar
3	eggs
2	cups strong brewed coffee
2	teaspoons rum extract
1-1/2	teaspoons vanilla extract
3	cups all-purpose flour
1-1/2	teaspoons baking soda
3/4	teaspoon salt

Confectioners' sugar
Whipped cream, optional

In a microwave, melt butter and chocolate; stir until smooth. Transfer to a large bowl. Beat in sugar until smooth. Add eggs, one at a time, beating well after each addition. Beat in the coffee and extracts. Combine the flour, baking soda and salt; gradually add to the chocolate mixture.

Pour into a greased and floured 10-in. fluted tube pan. Bake at 325° for 55-65 minutes or until a toothpick inserted near the center comes out clean. Cool for 10 minutes before inverting onto a wire rack to cool completely.

Dust with confectioners' sugar. Serve with whipped cream if desired. **yield: 12-16 servings.**

Mark Trinklein
Cedarburg, Wisconsin
Bittersweet chocolate and strong brewed coffee pair up well to deliver the distinctive taste in this moist cake. A quick dusting of confectioners' sugar is all you need to top the delightful treat.

travel tip

Taking Mocha Bundt Cake to a potluck or covered-dish event? Set the dessert on a serving platter, and carefully cover it with a clean fluted pan. Use plastic wrap to secure the cake to the platter if desired. Your cake will make it to the party easily!

candy bar freezer dessert

- 2 cups graham cracker crumbs
- 1 cup crushed saltines (about 30 crackers)
- 1/2 cup butter, melted
- 2 cups cold 2% milk
- 2 packages (3.4 ounces *each*) instant vanilla pudding mix
- 4 cups butter pecan ice cream, softened
- 1 carton (8 ounces) frozen whipped topping, thawed
- 1 Butterfinger candy bar (2.1 ounces), chopped

In a large bowl, combine the cracker crumbs and butter. Pat three-fourths of the mixture into an ungreased 13-in. x 9-in. dish. Cover and refrigerate.

In a large bowl, whisk milk and pudding mixes for 2 minutes or until thickened. Stir in ice cream until blended. Spread over crust. Spread whipped topping over pudding layer.

In a small bowl, combine chopped candy bar and remaining crumb mixture; sprinkle over whipped topping. Cover and freeze for at least 2 hours. **yield: 12-15 servings.**

Melissa Heberer
Hoskins, Nebraska
I combine butter pecan ice cream and instant pudding to create this sweet frozen treat. A crushed Butterfinger candy bar adds a fun crunch to the tasty topping.

springtime strawberry bars

- 1 cup butter, softened
- 1-1/2 cups sugar
- 2 eggs
- 1 teaspoon grated lemon peel
- 3-1/4 cups all-purpose flour, *divided*
- 3/4 cup slivered almonds, chopped
- 1 teaspoon baking powder
- 1/2 teaspoon salt
- 1 jar (12 ounces) strawberry preserves

Marna Heitz
Farley, Iowa
Warmer weather calls for a lighter dessert such as these popular fruity bars. The recipe makes a big batch, so they are simply perfect for bake sales and large gatherings.

In a large bowl, cream butter and sugar until light and fluffy. Add eggs, one at a time, beating well after each addition. Beat in lemon peel. Combine 3 cups flour, almonds, baking powder and salt; gradually add to creamed mixture until mixture resembles coarse crumbs (do not over mix).

Set aside 1 cup of dough. Press the remaining dough into a greased 15-in. x 10-in. x 1-in. baking pan. Spread preserves to within 1/4 in. of edges. Combine the reserved dough with the remaining flour; sprinkle over preserves.

Bake at 350° for 25-30 minutes or until lightly browned. Cool on wire rack. Cut into bars. **yield: about 3 dozen.**

Rachel Krupp, Perkiomenville, Pennsylvania
What makes these tender banana cupcakes extra special is the ground nutmeg. They're so amazingly good, I get requests for them all the time.

walnut banana cupcakes

1/4	cup butter, softened
3/4	cup sugar
2	eggs
1/2	cup mashed ripe banana
1	teaspoon vanilla extract
1	cup all-purpose flour
1/2	teaspoon baking soda
1/2	teaspoon ground nutmeg
1/4	teaspoon salt
1/4	cup sour cream

CREAM CHEESE FROSTING:

4	ounces cream cheese, softened
1/2	teaspoon vanilla extract
1-3/4	cups confectioners' sugar
3	tablespoons chopped walnuts

In a large bowl, cream butter and sugar until light and fluffy. Add eggs, one at a time, beating well after each addition. Beat in banana and vanilla. Combine the flour, baking soda, nutmeg and salt; gradually add to creamed mixture alternately with sour cream, mixing well after each addition.

Fill paper-lined muffin cups half full. Bake at 350° for 18-22 minutes or until a toothpick inserted near the center comes out c ean. Cool for 10 minutes before removing from pan to a wire rack to cool completely.

For frosting, in a small bowl, beat cream cheese and vanilla until smooth. Gradually beat in confectioners' sugar. Frost cupcakes; sprinkle with walnuts. Store in the refrigerator. **yield: 1 dozen.**

hot berries 'n' brownie ice cream cake

1 package fudge brownie mix (13-inch x 9-inch pan size)
1/4 cup water
1/4 cup unsweetened applesauce
1/4 cup canola oil
2 eggs
1 carton (1-3/4 quarts) reduced-fat no-sugar-added vanilla ice cream, softened

BERRY SAUCE:
2 tablespoons butter
1/3 cup sugar
1/4 cup honey
2 tablespoons lime juice
1 tablespoon balsamic vinegar
1 teaspoon ground cinnamon
1/4 to 1/2 teaspoon cayenne pepper
1 quart fresh strawberries, hulled and sliced
2 cups fresh blueberries
2 cups fresh raspberries

Prepare brownie mix using water, applesauce, oil and eggs. Bake according to package directions; cool completely on a wire rack.

Crumble brownies into 1-in. pieces; sprinkle half into a 13-in. x 9-in. dish coated with cooking spray. Spread evenly with ice cream. Press remaining brownie pieces into ice cream. Cover and freeze for 1 hour or until firm.

Remove from the freezer 5 minutes before serving. For sauce, in a large skillet, melt butter over medium heat. Stir in the sugar, honey, lime juice, vinegar, cinnamon and cayenne. Add the berries; cook for 3-5 minutes or until heated through, stirring occasionally. Cut the cake into squares; top with the hot berry sauce. **yield: 24 servings.**

Allene Bary-Cooper
Wichita Falls, Texas
This decadent dessert is a taste of Heaven. The hot mixed-berry topping seeps through the brownie layer into the cool vanilla ice cream for a chilled cake folks love.

soft and easy

To soften ice cream before using it in recipes such as this, transfer the ice cream from the freezer to the refrigerator 20-30 minutes before using. You can also let the ice cream stand at room temperature for 10-15 minutes, checking on it periodically.

deluxe marshmallow brownies

1	cup butter, cubed
4	ounces unsweetened chocolate, coarsely chopped
2	cups sugar
4	eggs
2	teaspoons vanilla extract
1-1/2	cups all-purpose flour
1-1/2	teaspoons baking powder
1	cup chopped walnuts *or* pecans

TOPPING:

1/2	cup butter, cubed
4	ounces unsweetened chocolate, coarsely chopped
1	cup sugar
1	can (5 ounces) evaporated milk
3-3/4	cups confectioners' sugar
3	teaspoons vanilla extract
4	cups miniature marshmallows

In a microwave, melt butter and chocolate; stir until smooth. Cool. In a large bowl, combine the sugar, eggs, vanilla and melted chocolate. Combine flour and baking powder; add to chocolate mixture and beat just until b ended. Fold in nuts.

Spread into a greased 15-in. x 10-in. x 1-in. baking pan. Bake at 325° for 25-30 minutes or until a toothpick inserted near the center comes out clean.

Meanwhile, in a large heavy saucepan, melt butter and chocolate. Stir in sugar and milk. Cook over low heat for 20 minutes, stirring frequently. Gradually whisk in confectioners' sugar until smooth. Remove from the heat; stir in vanilla.

Place marshmallows over warm brownies; pour warm topping over marshmallows. Cool on a wire rack for at least 2 hours before cutting. **yield: about 3 dozen.**

Martha Stine
Johnstown, Pennsylvania
I found this recipe in a garden club cookbook many years ago. I always serve these at Fourth of July picnics and at church suppers.

frozen raspberry delight

Nancy Whitford
Edwards, New York
This pretty, make-ahead dessert is a light, refreshing ending to a summer meal. I first made it for my aunt's 85th birthday dinner, and everyone loved it!

  2   cups crushed chocolate wafers
1/4 cup sugar
1/3 cup butter, melted
FILLING:
  1   cup hot fudge ice cream topping
  1   quart vanilla ice cream, softened
  1   pint raspberry sherbet, softened
  1   package (10 ounces) frozen sweetened raspberries, thawed and drained
  1   carton (8 ounces) frozen whipped topping, thawed

In a large bowl, combine the wafer crumbs, sugar and butter; set aside 1/4 cup. Press the remaining crumb mixture into a 13-in. x 9-in. dish. Cover and refrigerate for 15 minutes.

Place hot fudge topping in a microwave-safe bowl; cover and microwave on high for 15-20 seconds. Spread over crust.

Spoon ice cream over fudge layer. Place spoonfuls of sherbet over ice cream; cut through sherbet with a knife to swirl. Top with raspberries. Spread with whipped topping; sprinkle with reserved crumb mixture.

Cover and freeze for 2-3 hours or overnight. Remove from the freezer 15 minutes before serving. **yield: 12-15 servings.**

coffee ice cream pie

  2   ounces unsweetened chocolate
1/4 cup butter, cubed
  1   can (5 ounces) evaporated milk
1/2 cup sugar
  1   pint coffee ice cream, softened
  1   chocolate crumb crust (8 inches)
  1   carton (8 ounces) frozen whipped topping, thawed
1/4 cup chopped pecans

In a heavy saucepan, melt chocolate and butter over low heat. Stir in milk and sugar. Bring to a boil over medium heat, stirring constantly. Cook and stir for 3-4 minutes or until thickened. Remove from the heat; cool completely.

Spoon ice cream into crust. Stir sauce; spread over ice cream. Top with whipped topping; sprinkle with pecans. Freeze the pie until firm. Remove from the freezer 15 minutes before serving. **yield: 8 servings.**

Verna Brown
Turner Station, Kentucky
While coffee ice cream is great, I sometimes vary the flavor of this all-time family favorite. It's one dreamy treat that is always high on requests for dessert contributions.

orange refrigerator cake

- 1 package (4.6 ounces) cook-and-serve vanilla pudding mix
- 1 envelope unflavored gelatin
- 1 cup orange juice
- 1 tablespoon grated orange peel
- 2 loaf-shaped angel food cakes (10-1/2 ounces *each*)
- 2 cups heavy whipping cream, whipped

Marietta Martin
Brazil, Indiana
This refreshing dessert will disappear in a hurry at your next get-together. My mother used this recipe more than 60 years ago, but she called it "Icebox Cake" because we didn't have a refrigerator.

Prepare pudding according to package directions; set aside. In a small saucepan, sprinkle gelatin over orange juice; let stand for 1 minute. Cook and stir over low heat until gelatin is completely dissolved. Stir into pudding. Add orange peel. Transfer to a large bowl. Cover and refrigerate for 2 hours or until cooled.

Cut one angel food cake in half widthwise. Save one half for another use. Cut remaining half into eight slices. Cut second loaf into 16 slices.

Arrange half of the cake slices in an ungreased 13-in. x 9-in. dish. Fold whipped cream into pudding; spread half over the cake slices. Repeat layers. Cover and refrigerate overnight or until set. **yield: 12 servings.**

chewy apple oatmeal cookies

- 1 cup butter, softened
- 1 cup packed brown sugar
- 1/2 cup sugar
- 2 eggs
- 1 teaspoon vanilla extract
- 1-1/2 cups all-purpose flour
- 2 teaspoons ground cinnamon
- 1 teaspoon baking soda
- 1/4 teaspoon salt
- 3 cups old-fashioned oats
- 1/2 cup chopped dried apples

In a large bowl, cream butter and sugars until light and fluffy. Beat in eggs and vanilla. Combine the flour, cinnamon, baking soda and salt; gradually add to creamed mixture, beating well after each addition. Stir in oats and apples.

Drop by rounded tablespoonfuls 2 in. apart onto ungreased baking sheets. Bake at 350° for 10-12 minutes or until golden brown. Let cookies stand for 1 minute before removing to wire racks. **yield: 4 dozen.**

Jan Marshall
Fenton, Missouri
My family has always loved oatmeal raisin cookies, but I wanted to try something new with the classic recipe. We enjoy apples, and I thought the dried fruit would make a good tasting cookie.

Deanne Causey, Midland, Texas
Since I don't care for traditional pie crust, I usually eat only the filling of pie. That changed when I discovered this recipe. Boasting a luscious cheesecake flavor, this unique pie gets creative with phyllo dough.

berry cheesecake pie

8	sheets phyllo dough (14 inches x 9 inches)
6	tablespoons butter, melted
2	packages (8 ounces *each*) cream cheese, softened
1/2	cup sugar
1	teaspoon vanilla extract
2	eggs, lightly beaten
2	cups fresh *or* frozen blueberries
1/2	cup strawberry jelly
1	cup whipped topping

Sliced fresh strawberries and additional blueberries, optional

Place one phyllo sheet in a greased 9-in. pie plate; brush with butter. Repeat seven times; trim edges. (Keep remaining phyllo covered with plastic wrap and a damp towel to prevent it from drying out.)

Bake at 425° for 6-8 minutes or until edges are lightly browned (center will puff up). Cool on a wire rack.

For filling, in a small bowl, beat the cream cheese, sugar and vanilla until smooth. Add eggs; beat on low speed just until combined. Fold in blueberries. Spoon into crust.

Bake at 350° for 10 minutes; cover edges with foil to prevent overbrowning. Bake 23-27 minutes longer or until center is almost set. Cool on a wire rack for 1 hour. Refrigerate until chilled.

In a small bowl, beat jelly until smooth; spread over filling. Spread with whipped topping. Garnish with strawberries and additional blueberries if desired. **yield: 6-8 servings.**

Rachel Greenawalt Keller, Roanoke, Virginia
I grew up in Lancaster County, Pennsylvania and spent a lot of time in the kitchen with my mom and grandmother making Pennsylvania Dutch classics. This very scrumptious recipe, which combines two of our favorite flavors, is one I adapted.

peanut butter squares

3/4   cup cold butter, cubed
2   ounces semisweet chocolate
1-1/2   cups graham cracker crumbs (about 24 squares)
1   cup flaked coconut
1/2   cup chopped salted peanuts
1/4   cup toasted wheat germ

FILLING:
2   packages (8 ounces *each*) cream cheese, softened
3/4   cup sugar
2/3   cup chunky peanut butter
1   teaspoon vanilla extract

TOPPING:
4   ounces semisweet chocolate, chopped
1/4   cup butter, cubed

In a microwave-safe bowl, melt butter and chocolate; stir until smooth. Stir in the cracker crumbs, coconut, peanuts and wheat germ. Press into a greased 13-in. x 9-in. pan. Cover and refrigerate for at least 30 minutes.

In a small bowl, combine filling ingredients. Spread over crust. Cover and refrigerate for at least 30 minutes.

In a microwave, melt the chocolate and butter; stir until smooth. Pour over filling. Cover and refrigerate for at least 30 minutes or until topping is set. Cut into squares. Refrigerate leftovers. **yield: 4 dozen.**

chocolate chip banana cream pie

- 1 tube (16-1/2 ounces) refrigerated chocolate chip cookie dough
- 1/3 cup sugar
- 1/4 cup cornstarch
- 1/8 teaspoon salt
- 2-1/3 cups 2% milk
- 5 egg yolks, lightly beaten
- 2 tablespoons butter
- 2 teaspoons vanilla extract, *divided*
- 3 medium firm bananas
- 1-1/2 cups heavy whipping cream
- 3 tablespoons confectioners' sugar

Cut cookie dough in half widthwise. Let one portion stand at room temperature for 5-10 minutes to soften (return the other half to the refrigerator for another use).

Press dough onto the bottom and up the sides of an ungreased 9-in. pie plate. Bake at 375° for 11-12 minutes or until lightly browned. Cool on a wire rack.

In a large saucepan, combine the sugar, cornstarch and salt. Stir in milk until smooth. Cook and stir over medium-high heat until thickened and bubbly. Reduce heat; cook and stir 2 minutes longer. Remove from the heat. Stir a small amount of hot filling into egg yolks; return all to the pan, stirring constantly. Bring to a gentle boil; cook and stir 2 minutes longer. Remove from the heat; stir in butter and 1 teaspoon vanilla.

Spread 1 cup filling into prepared crust. Slice bananas; arrange over filling. Pour remaining filling over bananas. Refrigerate for 2 hours or until set.

In a large bowl, beat cream until it begins to thicken. Add confectioners' sugar and remaining vanilla; beat until stiff peaks form. Spread over pie. Refrigerate for 1 hour or until chilled. Refrigerate leftovers. **yield: 6-8 servings.**

Taylor Carroll
Parkesburg, Pennsylvania
Here's a rich treat that's always a hit. The filling, brimming with bananas, is refreshing, and the easy cookie crust provides a chocolaty crunch. Even a small slice will satisfy the largest sweet tooth you know!

triple layer brownie cake

Barbara Dean
Littleton, Colorado
A little of this rich brownie cake goes a long way, so you'll have plenty to share with grateful friends and family members. It's a sure way to satisfy chocolate lovers.

1-1/2   cups butter
    6   ounces unsweetened chocolate, chopped
    3   cups sugar
    5   eggs
1-1/2   teaspoons vanilla extract
1-1/2   cups all-purpose flour
  3/4   teaspoon salt
FROSTING:
   16   ounces semisweet chocolate, chopped
    3   cups heavy whipping cream
  1/2   cup sugar, optional
    2   milk chocolate candy bars (1.55 ounces *each*), shaved

In a large microwave-safe bowl, melt butter and chocolate; stir until smooth. Stir in sugar. Add eggs, one at a time, beating well after each addition. Stir in vanilla, flour and salt.

Pour into three greased and floured 9-in. round baking pans. Bake at 350° for 23-25 minutes or until a toothpick inserted near the center comes out clean. Cool for 10 minutes; remove from pan to a wire rack to cool completely.

For frosting, melt chocolate in a heavy saucepan over medium heat. Gradually stir in cream and sugar if desired, until well blended. Heat to a gentle boil; boil and stir for 1 minute. Remove from the heat; transfer to a large bowl. Refrigerate for 2-3 hours or until mixture reaches a pudding-like consistency, stirring a few times.

Beat frosting until soft peaks form. Immediately spread between layers and over top and sides of cake. Sprinkle with shaved chocolate. Store in the refrigerator. **yield: 16-20 servings.**

great garnishes

Leave a chocolate bar out until it's warm but not melted. With a vegetable peeler, draw along the flat side of the chocolate bar, making a curl. Move the curls onto the dessert with a toothpick, not your hands, to avoid melting the chocolate.

for a
crowd

antipasto-stuffed
baguettes
page 220

Gareth Craner, Minden, Nevada
People love these hearty little sandwich wedges. The recipe is wonderful for a party, and the bites can be made the day before.

mini muffuletta

1	jar (10 ounces) pimiento-stuffed olives, drained and chopped
2	cans (4-1/4 ounces *each*) chopped ripe olives
2	tablespoons balsamic vinegar
1	tablespoon red wine vinegar
1	tablespoon olive oil
3	garlic cloves, minced
1	teaspoon dried basil
1	teaspoon dried oregano
6	French rolls, split
1/2	pound thinly sliced hard salami
1/4	pound sliced provolone cheese
1/2	pound thinly sliced cotto salami
1/4	pound sliced part-skim mozzarella cheese

In a large bowl, combine the first eight ingredients; set aside. Hollow out tops and bottoms of rolls, leaving 3/4-in. shells (discard removed bread or save for another use).

Spread olive mixture over tops and bottoms of rolls. On roll bottoms, layer the hard salami, provolone cheese, cotto salami and mozzarella cheese. Replace tops.

Wrap tightly in plastic wrap. Refrigerate overnight. Cut each into six wedges; secure with toothpicks. **yield: 3 dozen.**

what's a muffuletta?

Traditionally, a muffuletta refers to a sandwich made with a large round roll of Italian bread split in half and filled with layers of salami, ham and an olive salad.

shredded beef 'n' slaw sandwiches

- 4 pounds beef stew meat, cut into 1-inch cubes
- 2 cups water
- 2 cups ketchup
- 1/2 to 3/4 cup Worcestershire sauce
- 2 tablespoons lemon juice
- 2 tablespoons prepared horseradish
- 1 tablespoon prepared mustard
- 2 teaspoons salt
- 8 cups shredded cabbage
- 30 sandwich buns, split

In a Dutch oven, bring beef and water to a boil. Reduce heat; cover and simmer for 2 hours or until tender.

Remove beef with a slotted spoon; shred with two forks and set aside. Skim the fat from cooking liquid. Stir in the ketchup, Worcestershire sauce, lemon juice, horseradish, mustard and salt. Add the shredded beef and cabbage. Bring to a boil. Reduce heat; cover and simmer for 45 minutes or until cabbage is tender.

Spoon 1/3 cup onto each sandwich bun. **yield: 30 sandwiches.**

Mary Johnson
Whitehouse, Ohio
I have served these tangy, robust sandwiches for family gatherings and to many coworkers. They have always gone over quite well.

Ruth Ann Stelfox
Raymond, Alberta
A friend of mine served this scrumptious, comforting dish at her wedding. I liked it so much, I asked for the recipe. The potatoes and ham taste great covered in a creamy cheese sauce.

scalloped potatoes and ham

- 2 cans (10-3/4 ounces *each*) condensed cream of mushroom soup, undiluted
- 2 cans (10-3/4 ounces *each*) condensed cream of celery soup, undiluted
- 1 can (10-3/4 ounces) condensed cheddar cheese soup, undiluted
- 1 can (12 ounces) evaporated milk
- 10 pounds medium potatoes, peeled and thinly sliced
- 5 pounds fully cooked ham, cubed
- 4 cups (16 ounces) shredded cheddar cheese

In two large bowls, combine the soups and milk. Add potatoes and ham; toss to coat. Divide among four greased 13-in. x 9-in. baking dishes.

Cover and bake at 325° for 1-1/4 hours or until potatoes are tender. Uncover; sprinkle with cheese. Bake 5-10 minutes longer or until cheese is melted. **yield: 4 casseroles (10 servings each).**

spruced-up cheese spread

1 jar (4 ounces) diced pimientos, drained, *divided*
1 small onion, grated
1 cup mayonnaise
1 to 2 tablespoons prepared mustard
1 tablespoon Worcestershire sauce
1 teaspoon celery seed
1/2 teaspoon paprika
1/4 teaspoon garlic salt
3 cups (12 ounces) finely shredded sharp cheddar cheese
2 tablespoons finely chopped pecans
Minced fresh parsley
Assorted crackers

Set aside 2 tablespoons pimientos for topping. In a large bowl, combine the remaining pimientos and the next seven ingredients. Stir in cheese.

Transfer to a serving bowl; sprinkle with pecans, parsley and reserved pimientos. Serve with crackers. **yield: 4 cups.**

Judy Grimes
Brandon, Mississippi
A neighbor who's a wonderful cook is the one who gave me the recipe for this zippy cracker spread. It's easy to shape into a Christmas tree for a festive get-together.

buttermilk pan rolls

18 to 23 cups all-purpose flour
1 cup buttermilk blend powder
1/2 cup sugar
2 tablespoons salt
4-1/2 teaspoons active dry yeast
1 teaspoon baking soda
7 cups warm water (120° to 130°)
1 cup vegetable oil

In several large bowls, combine 15 cups flour, buttermilk powder, sugar, salt, yeast and baking soda. Add water and oil. Beat until smooth. Stir in enough remaining flour to form a soft dough.

Turn onto a floured surface; knead until smooth and elastic, about 10 minutes. Place in several large greased bowls, turning once to grease top. Cover and let rise in a warm place until doubled, about 1-1/4 hours.

Punch dough down. Divide into 80 pieces. Shape each into a ball. Place in two greased 15-in. x 10-in. x 1-in. baking pans. Cover and let rise until doubled, about 30 minutes.

Bake at 375° for 20-30 minutes or until lightly browned. Remove from pans to wire racks. Serve warm. **yield: 80 rolls.**

Elaine Kellum
Anaktuvuk Pass, Alaska
These rolls are a perfect addition to any meal! They are tender and taste best when warmed in the oven.

Norma Harder, Saskatoon, Saskatchewan
This classic potato dish makes enough for 24 hungry people. It's great with ham and other meats. Guests always seem to remark on its rich, creamy sauce and buttery crumb topping.

creamed potato casseroles

10	pounds medium potatoes (about 30)
2/3	cup plus 3 tablespoons butter, *divided*
2/3	cup all-purpose flour
5	cups chicken broth
5	cups half-and-half cream
8	egg yolks, lightly beaten
1-1/2	cups minced fresh parsley
3	teaspoons salt
3/4	teaspoon pepper
1/4	teaspoon cayenne pepper
1	cup seasoned bread crumbs

Place potatoes in a large stockpot; cover with water. Bring to a boil. Reduce heat; cover and simmer for 15-20 minutes or until crisp-tender. Drain and rinse in cold water. When cool enough to handle, peel potatoes and cut into 1/4-in. slices; set aside.

In a large saucepan, melt 2/3 cup butter. Stir in flour until smooth; gradually add broth and cream. Bring to a boil; cook and stir for 2 minutes or until thickened. Remove from the heat. Stir 1 cup hot cream mixture into egg yolks; return all to the pan, stirring constantly. Add the parsley, salt, pepper and cayenne. Bring to a gentle boil; cook and stir 2 minutes longer. Remove from the heat.

Spread 1 cup sauce into each of two 3-qt. baking dishes. Top with a third of the potato slices. Repeat layers twice. Spread with remaining sauce. Melt remaining butter; toss with bread crumbs. Sprinkle over casseroles. Bake, uncovered, at 375° for 40-45 minutes or until bubbly. **yield: 2 casseroles (12 servings each).**

antipasto-stuffed baguettes

1 can (2-1/4 ounces) sliced ripe olives, drained
2 tablespoons olive oil
1 teaspoon lemon juice
1 garlic clove, minced
1/8 teaspoon *each* dried basil, thyme, marjoram and rosemary, crushed
2 French bread baguettes (8 ounces *each*)
1 package (4 ounces) crumbled feta cheese
1/4 pound thinly sliced Genoa salami
1 cup fresh baby spinach
1 jar (7-1/4 ounces) roasted red peppers, drained and chopped
1 can (14 ounces) water-packed artichoke hearts, rinsed, drained and quartered

In a blender, combine the olives, oil, lemon juice, garlic and herbs; cover and process until olives are chopped. Set aside 1/3 cup olive mixture (refrigerate remaining mixture for another use).

Cut the top third off each baguette; carefully hollow out bottoms, leaving a 1/4-in. shell (discard the removed bread or save for another use).

Spread olive mixture in the bottom of each loaf. Sprinkle with feta cheese. Fold salami slices in half and place over cheese. Top with the spinach, red peppers and artichokes, pressing down as necessary. Replace bread tops. Wrap loaves tightly in foil. Refrigerate for at least 3 hours or overnight.

Serve cold, or place foil-wrapped loaves on a baking sheet and bake at 350° for 20-25 minutes or until heated through. Cut into slices; secure with a toothpick. **yield: 3 dozen.**

editor's note: 1/3 cup purchased tapenade (olive paste) may be substituted for the olive mixture.

Dianne Holmgren
Prescott, Arizona
These Italian-style sandwiches can be served as an appetizer or even as a light lunch. A homemade olive paste makes every bite delicious.

small size, big hit

Mini sandwiches are great additions to potlucks since many like small serving sizes. Secure your sandwiches with colorful toothpicks before arranging them on a platter. They'll look great and be easier to eat!

home-style roast beef

- 1 beef rump roast *or* bottom round roast (10 to 12 pounds)
- 1 can (14-1/2 ounces) chicken broth
- 1 can (10-1/4 ounces) beef gravy
- 1 can (10-3/4 ounces) condensed cream of celery soup, undiluted
- 1/4 cup water
- 1/4 cup Worcestershire sauce
- 1/4 cup soy sauce
- 3 tablespoons dried parsley flakes
- 3 tablespoons dill weed
- 2 tablespoons dried thyme
- 4-1/2 teaspoons garlic powder
- 1 teaspoon celery salt
- Pepper to taste
- 1 large onion, sliced 1/4 inch thick
- 8 bacon strips
- 1/4 cup butter, cubed

Place roast in a large roasting pan with fat side up. In a small bowl, combine the broth, gravy, soup, water, Worcestershire sauce and soy sauce; pour over roast. Sprinkle with seasonings. Arrange onion slices over roast. Place bacon strips diagonally over onion. Dot with butter.

Bake, uncovered, at 325° for 2-1/2 to 3-1/2 hours or until the meat reaches desired doneness (for medium-rare, a meat thermometer should read 145°; medium, 160°; well-done, 170°). Let stand for 15 minutes before slicing. **yield: 25-30 servings.**

Sandra Furman-Krajewski
Amsterdam, New York
A very moist roast, this beef gains richness from the gravy while the bacon gives it a great flavor. For variety, you can slice the roast and serve it over rice with gravy...or even cube it and mix it with noodles, gravy and vegetables if you'd like to turn it into a casserole.

glazed carrots for a crowd

Bonnie Milner
DeRidder, Louisiana
Whenever our church group plans a gathering, I am undoubtedly asked to bring these carrots. I never complain because I enjoy them as much as everyone else.

- 3 cups sugar
- 1 cup light corn syrup
- 1/2 cup butter, cubed
- 1/4 cup thawed orange juice concentrate
- 1 teaspoon salt
- 2 cans (no. 10 size) baby carrots, drained *or* 12 pounds medium carrots, sliced and cooked

In a large saucepan, combine the first five ingredients; bring to a boil over medium heat. Boil for 5 minutes, stirring occasionally. Place carrots in two 13-in. x 9-in. baking pans.

Pour sugar mixture over carrots. Bake, uncovered, at 350° for 30-40 minutes or until heated through. **yield: 45 servings.**

Faith Jensen, Meridian, Idaho
With the classic combination of chocolate and peanut butter, it's no surprise these are
my family's favorite cookies.

peanut butter cup cookies

1	cup butter, softened
2/3	cup peanut butter
1	cup sugar
1	cup packed brown sugar
2	eggs
2	teaspoons vanilla extract
2-1/4	cups all-purpose flour
1	teaspoon baking soda
1/2	teaspoon salt
2	cups (12 ounces) semisweet chocolate chips
2	cups chopped peanut butter cups (about six 1.6-ounce packages)

In a large bowl, cream the butter, peanut butter and sugars until light and fluffy. Beat in eggs and vanilla. Combine the flour, baking soda and salt; gradually add to creamed mixture and mix well. Stir in chocolate chips and peanut butter cups.

Drop by rounded tablespoonfuls 2 in. apart onto ungreased baking sheets. Bake at 350° for 10-12 minutes or until edges are lightly browned. Cool for 2 minutes before removing to wire racks. **yield: 7-1/2 dozen.**

spicy nacho bake

- 2 pounds ground beef
- 2 large onions, chopped
- 2 large green peppers, chopped
- 2 cans (28 ounces *each*) diced tomatoes, undrained
- 2 cans (16 ounces *each*) hot chili beans, undrained
- 2 cans (15 ounces *each*) black beans, rinsed and drained
- 2 cans (11 ounces *each*) whole kernel corn, drained
- 2 cans (8 ounces *each*) tomato sauce
- 2 envelopes taco seasoning
- 2 packages (13 ounces *each*) spicy nacho tortilla chips
- 4 cups (16 ounces) shredded cheddar cheese

Anita Wilson
Mansfield, Ohio
I made this hearty, layered Southwestern casserole for a dinner meeting once; and now, I'm asked to bring it every time we have a potluck. Everybody loves the hearty ground beef and bean filling.

In a Dutch oven, cook the beef, onions and green peppers over medium heat until meat is no longer pink; drain. Stir in the tomatoes, beans, corn, tomato sauce and taco seasoning. Bring to a boil. Reduce heat; simmer, uncovered, for 30 minutes.

In each of two greased 13-in. x 9-in. baking dishes, layer with 5 cups of chips and 4-2/3 cups of meat mixture. Repeat layers. Top each with 4 cups of chips and 2 cups of cheese.

Bake, uncovered, at 350° for 20-25 minutes or until golden brown. **yield: 2 casseroles (15 servings each).**

stroganoff for a crowd

- 20 pounds ground beef
- 5 large onions, chopped
- 7 cans (26 ounces *each*) condensed cream of mushroom soup, undiluted
- 3 quarts milk
- 1/2 cup Worcestershire sauce
- 3 tablespoons garlic powder
- 2 tablespoons salt
- 1 tablespoon pepper
- 1 teaspoon paprika
- 5 pints sour cream

Hot cooked noodles

In several large stockpots, cook beef and onions over medium heat until meat is no longer pink; drain. In a several large bowls, combine the soup, milk, Worcestershire sauce, garlic powder, salt, pepper and paprika, add to beef mixture. Bring to a boil. Reduce heat and keep warm. Just before serving, stir in sour cream; heat through but do not boil. Serve with noodles. **yield: 70 servings (1 cup each).**

Ada Lower
Minot, North Dakota
This creamy dish is perfect for a chilly day. Don't expect to have any leftovers after you serve this one!

maple-ginger root vegetables

     5   medium parsnips, peeled and sliced
     5   small carrots, sliced
     3   medium turnips, peeled and cubed
     1   large sweet potato, peeled and cubed
     1   small rutabaga, peeled and cubed
     1   large sweet onion, cut into wedges
     1   small red onion, cut into wedges
     2   tablespoons olive oil
     1   tablespoon minced fresh gingerroot
     1   teaspoon salt
   1/2   teaspoon pepper
     1   cup maple syrup

Place the first seven ingredients in a large resealable plastic bag; add the oil, ginger, salt and pepper. Seal bag and shake to coat. Arrange vegetables in a single layer in two 15-in. x 10-in. x 1-in. baking pans coated with cooking spray.

Bake, uncovered, at 425° for 25 minutes, stirring once. Drizzle with syrup. Bake 20-25 minutes longer or until vegetables are tender, stirring once. **yield: 24 servings.**

Kelli Ritz
Innisfail, Alberta
My family loves this recipe because it brings out the fabulous flavors of the vegetables. Even my children enjoy it…they really like the drizzle of maple syrup! It's a tasty way to introduce kids to turnips and rutabaga.

calico salad

    12   packages (16 ounces *each*) frozen corn, thawed
    12   packages (16 ounces *each*) frozen peas, thawed
    12   cans (8 ounces *each*) sliced water chestnuts, drained
     3   cups chopped green onions
     3   jars (4 ounces *each*) diced pimientos, drained
     6   cups mayonnaise
 2-1/4   cups grated Parmesan cheese
 2-1/4   cups milk
   3/4   cup lemon juice
     2   tablespoons salt
 1-1/2   teaspoons pepper
     6   cups slivered almonds, toasted

Bernice Knutson
Danbury, Iowa
Here's a top-rated salad perfect for potlucks or family parties. Its colorful blend of corn, peas and pimentos makes it easy to spot on the buffet table, and the gang will simply love the crunch of the water chestnuts and the almonds.

In several large bowls, combine the corn, peas, water chestnuts, onions and pimientos.

In another large bowl, combine the mayonnaise, cheese, milk, lemon juice, salt and pepper. Pour over vegetables; toss to coat. Cover and chill for at least 2 hours. Just before serving, add almonds and toss to combine. **yield: 128 servings (3/4 cup each).**

Carol Earl, Brewster, New York
The original recipe for this roulade called for tomatoes, which our son is allergic to. I substituted artichokes and mushrooms with wonderful results.

turkey breast roulade

- 3 jars (7-1/2 ounces *each*) marinated artichoke hearts, drained and chopped
- 3 cans (4 ounces *each*) mushroom stems and pieces, drained and chopped
- 3 tablespoons chopped sweet onion
- 3 boneless turkey breast halves (3 to 3-1/2 pounds *each*)
- 2-1/4 pounds thinly sliced deli ham
- 1 cup butter, melted
- 1-1/2 teaspoons dried thyme

In a large bowl, combine the artichokes, mushrooms and onion; set aside. With skin side down, cut a lengthwise slit through the thickest portion of each turkey breast to within 1/2 in. of bottom. Open the turkey breasts so they lie flat; cover with plastic wrap. Flatten to 3/4- to 1-in. thickness; remove plastic.

Place ham slices over turkey to within 1 in. of edges. Spoon vegetable mixture lengthwise down center of the ham. Roll each turkey breast, starting from a side where the fold is in the center. Secure with kitchen string at 3-in. intervals.

Place the turkey rolls seam side down in one greased 15-in. x 10-in. x 1-in. baking pan and one 13-in. x 9-in. baking pan.

In a small bowl, combine the butter and thyme; spoon over the turkey rolls. Bake, uncovered, at 350° for 1-1/4 to 1-3/4 hours or until meat thermometer reads 170°, basting frequently. Cover and let stand for 10 minutes before slicing. **yield: 24-30 servings.**

Ruth Ann Stelfox
Raymond, Alberta
These treats are perfect for folks who like both chocolate and vanilla cookies because it gives them the best of both worlds. They're an appealing addition to any cookie tray, and they're usually the first to disappear at gatherings.

double delights

CHOCOLATE DOUGH:
- 1 cup butter, softened
- 1-1/2 cups sugar
- 2 eggs
- 2 teaspoons vanilla extract
- 2 cups all-purpose flour
- 2/3 cup baking cocoa
- 3/4 teaspoon baking soda
- 1/2 teaspoon salt
- 1 cup coarsely chopped pecans
- 5 ounces white baking chocolate, chopped

VANILLA DOUGH:
- 1 cup butter, softened
- 1-1/2 cups sugar
- 2 eggs
- 2 teaspoons vanilla extract
- 2-3/4 cups all-purpose flour
- 2 teaspoons cream of tartar
- 1 teaspoon baking soda
- 1/2 teaspoon salt
- 1 cup coarsely chopped pecans
- 4 ounces German sweet chocolate, chopped

For chocolate dough, in a large bowl, cream butter and sugar until light and fluffy. Beat in eggs and vanilla. Combine the flour, cocoa, baking soda and salt; gradually add to creamed mixture and mix well. Stir in pecans and white chocolate.

For vanilla dough, in another large bowl, cream butter and sugar until light and fluffy. Beat in eggs and vanilla. Combine the flour, cream of tartar, baking soda and salt; gradually add to creamed mixture and mix well. Stir in pecans and German chocolate. Cover and refrigerate both doughs for 2 hours.

Divide both doughs in half. Shape each portion into a 12-in. roll; wrap in plastic wrap. Refrigerate for 3 hours or until firm.

Unwrap and cut each roll in half lengthwise. Place a chocolate half and vanilla half together, pressing to form a log; wrap in plastic wrap. Refrigerate for 1 hour or until the dough holds together when cut.

Using a serrated knife, cut into 1/4-in. slices. Place 2 in. apart on greased baking sheets. Bake at 350° for 8-10 minutes or until set. Remove to wire racks to cool. **yield: about 15 dozen.**

chili for a crowd

- 5 pounds ground beef
- 3 large onions, chopped
- 5 celery ribs, chopped
- 2 cans (28 ounces *each*) diced tomatoes, undrained
- 2 cans (16 ounces *each*) kidney beans, rinsed and drained
- 1 can (28 ounces) pork and beans
- 2 cans (10-3/4 ounces *each*) condensed tomato soup, undiluted
- 2-2/3 cups water
- 1/4 cup chili powder
- 3 teaspoons salt
- 2 teaspoons garlic powder
- 2 teaspoons seasoned salt
- 2 teaspoons pepper
- 1 teaspoon ground cumin
- 1 teaspoon *each* dried thyme, oregano and rosemary, crushed
- 1/2 teaspoon cayenne pepper

Linda Boehme
Fairmont, Minnesota
A coworker made this hearty and well-seasoned chili for a potluck at work, and I just had to have the recipe. It freezes nicely, too.

In a large stockpot, cook the beef, onions and celery over medium heat until meat is no longer pink; drain. Stir in the remaining ingredients. Bring to a boil. Reduce heat; simmer, uncovered, for 1 hour. **yield: 24 servings (1 cup each).**

Jacquie Olson
West Linn, Oregon
This is a simple and satisfying soup that my family has always enjoyed. It goes great with a grilled sandwich.

chunky chicken rice soup

- 4 cans (14-1/2 ounces *each*) chicken broth
- 2 cups water
- 2 packages (16 ounces *each*) frozen mixed vegetables, thawed
- 2 packages (6 ounces *each*) grilled chicken strips, cut into 1/2-inch cubes
- 1 teaspoon poultry seasoning
- 1/2 teaspoon pepper
- 4 cups uncooked instant rice
- 2 tablespoons minced fresh parsley

In a large saucepan, combine the first six ingredients; bring to a boil over medium heat. Reduce heat; cover and simmer for 5 minutes. Stir in rice and parsley. Remove from heat; cover and let stand for 5 minutes. **yield: 12 servings.**

Marcia Severson, Hallock, Minnesota
This quick-to-fix soup feeds a lot of hungry people. The tender sirloin pieces and diced veggies make a very satisfying meal.

hearty beef soup

4	pounds beef top sirloin steak, cut into 1/2-inch cubes
4	cups chopped onions
1/4	cup butter
4	quarts hot water
4	cups sliced carrots
4	cups cubed peeled potatoes
2	cups chopped cabbage
1	cup chopped celery
1	large green pepper, chopped
8	teaspoons beef bouillon granules
1	tablespoon seasoned salt
1	teaspoon dried basil
1	teaspoon pepper
4	bay leaves
6	cups tomato juice

In two Dutch ovens, brown beef and onions in butter in batches; drain. Add the water, vegetables and seasonings; bring to a boil. Reduce heat; cover and simmer for 20 minutes.

Add tomato juice; cover and simmer 10 minutes longer or until the beef and vegetables are tender. Discard bay leaves. **yield: 32 servings (8 quarts).**

traditional holiday stuffing

1 package (12 ounces) reduced-fat bulk pork sausage *or* breakfast turkey sausage links, casings removed
3 celery ribs, chopped
1 large onion, chopped
2 tablespoons reduced-fat mayonnaise
2 tablespoons prepared mustard
4 teaspoons rubbed sage
1 tablespoon poultry seasoning
2 loaves (16 ounces *each*) day-old white bread, cubed
1 loaf (16 ounces) day-old whole wheat bread, cubed
3 eggs, lightly beaten
2 cans (14-1/2 ounces *each*) reduced-sodium chicken broth

In a large nonstick skillet coated with cooking spray, cook the sausage, celery and onion over medium heat until meat is no longer pink; drain. Remove from the heat; stir in the mayonnaise, mustard, sage and poultry seasoning.

Place bread cubes in a large bowl; add sausage mixture. Combine eggs and broth; pour over bread cubes and stir gently to combine. Transfer to two 3-qt. baking dishes coated with cooking spray.

Cover and bake at 350° for 30 minutes. Uncover; bake 12-18 minutes longer or until lightly browned and a thermometer reads 160°. **yield: 24 servings.**

editor's note: If using this recipe to stuff poultry, replace the eggs with 3/4 cup egg substitute. Bake until a meat thermometer reads 180° for poultry and 165° for stuffing. Allow 3/4 cup stuffing per pound of turkey. Bake the remaining stuffing as directed.

Lorraine Brauckhoff
Zolfo Springs, Florida
Sausage and sage add a gourmet taste to this stuffing. It's perfect for large family gatherings, but you can also save some to reheat for later.

stuffing strategies

In general, when you want a drier dressing, use prepackaged dry bread cubes and limit the amount of liquid. For a moist stuffing, add melted butter to the liquid because the butter won't evaporate when the side dish is heated.

meat loaf for a mob

8	eggs, lightly beaten
1	can (46 ounces) V8 juice
2	large onions, finely chopped
4	celery ribs, finely chopped
4-1/4	cups seasoned bread crumbs
2	envelopes onion soup mix
2	teaspoons pepper
8	pounds ground beef
3/4	cup ketchup
1/3	cup packed brown sugar
1/4	cup prepared mustard

In a very large bowl, combine the eggs, V8 juice, onions, celery, bread crumbs, soup mix and pepper. Crumble beef over mixture and mix well,

Shape into four loaves; place each loaf in a greased 13-in. x 9-in. baking dish. Bake, uncovered, at 350° for 45 minutes.

Meanwhile, combine the ketchup, brown sugar and mustard. Spread over loaves. Bake 15 minutes longer until no pink remains and a meat thermometer reads 160°. **yield: 4 meat loaves.**

Niki Reese Eschen
Santa Maris, California
Our synagogue has two teams that alternate with churches of various denominations and civic organizations to provide meals at a homeless shelter. This tasty, satisfying meat loaf is very well liked every time I prepare it.

Donna Sternthal
Sharpsville, Pennsylvania
The whole group will munch up these "top dogs" in a jiffy. Mom and I make them for get-togethers. Leftovers are no problem—there are none!

coney dogs

2	pounds ground beef
3	small onions, chopped
3	cups water
1	can (12 ounces) tomato paste
5	teaspoons chili powder
2	teaspoons rubbed sage
2	teaspoons salt
1	teaspoon pepper
1/2	teaspoon garlic salt
1/2	teaspoon dried oregano
1/4	teaspoon cayenne pepper
24	hot dogs, cooked
24	hot dog buns

Shredded cheddar cheese, optional

In a Dutch oven, cook beef and onions over medium heat until meat is no longer pink; drain. Stir in the water, tomato paste and the seasonings. Cover and simmer for 30 minutes, stirring occasionally. Serve on hot dogs in buns; sprinkle with cheese if desired. **yield: 24 servings.**

Ellen Borst, Park Falls, Wisconsin
I combined my grandmother's apple crisp topping with a traditional cherry pie recipe to come up with these flavorful bars.

cherry streusel bars

- 4 cups all-purpose flour, *divided*
- 2 teaspoons sugar
- 1 teaspoon salt
- 3/4 cup butter-flavored shortening
- 1 egg
- 1/4 cup water
- 1-1/2 teaspoons cider vinegar
- 2 cans (21 ounces *each*) cherry pie filling
- 1 tablespoon grated orange peel
- 1-1/4 cups packed brown sugar
- 1/2 teaspoon ground cinnamon
- 1 cup cold butter, cubed

In a large bowl, combine 2 cups flour, sugar and salt; cut in shortening until crumbly. In another bowl, whisk the egg, water and vinegar. Stir into flour mixture with a fork until a soft ball forms.

On a lightly floured surface, roll out dough into a 15-in. x 10-in. rectangle. Transfer to a greased 15-in. x 10-in. x 1-in. baking pan. Bake at 400° for 6-8 minutes or until firm and dry to the touch.

Meanwhile, combine pie filling and orange peel; set aside. In a large bowl, combine the brown sugar, cinnamon and remaining flour; cut in the butter until crumbly.

Spread cherry mixture over crust. Sprinkle with crumb mixture. Bake at 400° for 20-25 minutes or until golden brown. Cool on a wire rack for 20 minutes before cutting. **yield: about 2-1/2 dozen.**

Debra Weiers, Silver Lake, Minnesota
I use apples from our own apple trees to make this dessert. It's a big hit at group gatherings as well as with my family.

apple pie bars

     5 cups all-purpose flour
   1/4 cup sugar
   1/2 teaspoon salt
     2 cups shortening
     4 egg yolks, beaten
   2/3 cup milk
FILLING:
     1 cup crisp rice cereal
     8 cups sliced peeled tart apples (about 9 medium)
     1 cup sugar
     1 teaspoon all-purpose flour
   1/2 teaspoon ground cinnamon
     2 egg whites, lightly beaten
     1 cup confectioners' sugar
     1 to 2 tablespoons milk

In a large bowl, combine the flour, sugar and salt; cut in the shortening until crumbly.

Combine egg yolks and milk; gradually add to crumb mixture, tossing with a fork until dough forms a ball. Divide in half.

On a lightly floured surface, roll each portion into a 15-in. x 10-in. rectangle. Line a 15-in. x 10-in. x 1-in. baking pan with one rectangle; sprinkle with cereal.

Arrange apples over cereal. Combine the sugar, flour and cinnamon; sprinkle over apples. Top with remaining pastry; cut slits in top. Brush with egg whites.

Bake at 350° for 50-55 minutes or until golden brown. Cool completely on a wire rack. In a bowl, combine confectioners' sugar and enough milk to achieve drizzling consistency. Drizzle over bars. Store in the refrigerator. **yield: 3-4 dozen.**

chicken supreme with gravy

1-1/2 bunches celery, diced (about 6 cups)
   6 medium onions, diced (about 4 cups)
   2 cups butter, cubed
   3 loaves day-old white bread (1-1/2 pounds *each*), cut into 1-inch cubes
   3 tablespoons salt
   3 tablespoons rubbed sage
   1 tablespoon baking powder
   2 teaspoons pepper
 12 eggs
  9 cups milk
 24 cups diced cooked chicken (about 6 chickens)
  3 cans (14-1/2 ounces *each*) chicken broth

GRAVY:
  8 cans (10-3/4 ounces *each*) condensed cream of chicken and mushroom soup, undiluted
  9 to 10 cups water

In a Dutch oven, saute celery and onions in butter. Meanwhile, in a large bowl, combine the bread, salt, sage, baking powder and pepper; toss to coat. Stir in celery mixture. Beat eggs and milk; add to bread mixture.

Divide half of the chicken among four 13-in. x 9-in. greased baking dishes. Cover with half of the bread mixture. Repeat layers. Pour broth into each dish. Cover and bake at 325° for 70 minutes or until hot and bubbly; uncover and bake 10-15 minutes longer.

For gravy, in a Dutch oven, combine soup and water. Bring to a boil. Reduce heat; simmer, uncovered, for 10 minutes. Serve with chicken. **yield: 70-80 servings.**

Bernice Hartje
Cavalier, North Dakota
A group of friends and I have met often throughout the years to swap our favorite recipes. This tried-and-true dish has always been well received.

simply scale it back a bit

If the yield for Chicken Supreme With Gravy is too much, cut the ingredients in half. Then freeze one casserole to enjoy later (with freshly prepared gravy).

coconut chocolate cake

2	cups all-purpose flour
2	cups sugar
1	teaspoon baking soda
1/2	teaspoon salt
1	cup butter, cubed
1	cup water
1/4	cup baking cocoa
2	eggs
1/2	cup buttermilk
1	teaspoon vanilla extract

TOPPING:

1	can (12 ounces) evaporated milk, *divided*
1-1/4	cups sugar, *divided*
20	large marshmallows
1	package (14 ounces) coconut
2	cups slivered almonds, toasted, *divided*
1/2	cup butter, cubed
1	cup semisweet chocolate chips

In a large bowl, combine the flour, sugar, baking soda and salt. In a small saucepan, combine the butter, water and cocoa. Cook and stir until butter is melted; add to dry ingredients. Combine the eggs, buttermilk and vanilla; add to chocolate mixture and mix well.

Pour into a greased 15-in. x 10-in. x 1-in. baking pan. Bake at 350° for 20-25 minutes or until a toothpick inserted near the center comes out clean.

Meanwhile, in a large saucepan, combine 1 cup evaporated milk, 3/4 cup sugar and marshmallows; cook and stir until marshmallows are melted. Remove from heat; stir in coconut. Immediately sprinkle 1 cup almonds over cake. Spread coconut mixture over top. Sprinkle with remaining almonds (pan will be full).

In a small saucepan, combine butter with remaining milk and sugar. Cook and stir until butter is melted. Remove from the heat; stir in chocolate chips until melted. Drizzle over almonds. Cool on a wire rack. **yield: 35 servings.**

Dorothy West
Nacogdoches, Texas
I hope other families enjoy this cake as much as my gang does. I've given almost 100 copies of this recipe to others who have tried the cake and liked it for larger gatherings.

picnic chicken

- 3 eggs
- 3 tablespoons water
- 1-1/2 cups dry bread crumbs
- 2 teaspoons paprika
- 1 teaspoon salt
- 1/2 teaspoon *each* dried marjoram, thyme and rosemary, crushed
- 1/2 teaspoon pepper
- 1 cup butter, melted
- 12 chicken drumsticks
- 12 bone-in chicken thighs

CREAMY LEEK DIP:
- 1 cup heavy whipping cream
- 1-1/2 cups plain yogurt
- 1 envelope leek soup mix
- 1 cup (4 ounces) shredded Colby cheese

In a shallow bowl, whisk eggs and water. In another shallow bowl, combine bread crumbs and seasonings. Divide butter between two 13-in. x 9-in. baking dishes.

Dip chicken pieces in egg mixture, then coat with crumb mixture. Place in prepared pans. Bake, uncovered, at 375° for 1 hour or until juices run clear, turning once. Cool for 30 minutes; refrigerate until chilled.

For dip, in a small bowl, beat cream until stiff peaks form. In another bowl, combine the yogurt, soup mix and cheese; fold in whipped cream. Cover and refrigerate until serving. Serve with cold chicken. **yield: 24 servings (4 cups dip).**

Ami Okasinski
Memphis, Tennessee
I made this well-seasoned chicken one evening for dinner and served it hot from the oven. While raiding the fridge the next day, I discovered how delicious it was cold and created the simple leek dip to go with it.

frozen strawberry pie

- 1 package (8 ounces) cream cheese, softened
- 1 cup sugar
- 1 teaspoon vanilla extract
- 4 cups chopped fresh strawberries
- 1 carton (12 ounces) frozen whipped topping, thawed
- 1/2 cup chopped pecans, toasted
- 2 chocolate crumb crusts (9 inches)

Awynne Thurstenson
Siloam Springs, Arkansas
This recipe makes two attractive pies using store-bought chocolate crumb crust. I work full-time, so I like the fact that this yummy pie can be made ahead. I serve each slice with a dollop of whipped cream, a strawberry and a few chocolate curls.

In a large bowl, beat the cream cheese, sugar and vanilla until smooth. Stir in strawberries. Fold in whipped topping and pecans. Pour into crusts.

Cover and freeze the pies for 3-4 hours or until firm. Remove pies from the freezer 15-20 minutes before serving. **yield: 2 pies (6 servings each).**

mac 'n' cheese for a bunch

3 packages (two 16 ounces, one 7 ounces) elbow macaroni
1-1/4 cups butter, *divided*
3/4 cup all-purpose flour
2 teaspoons salt
3 quarts milk
3 pounds sharp cheddar cheese, shredded
1-1/2 cups dry bread crumbs

Cook macaroni according to package directions until almost tender. Meanwhile, in a large stockpot, melt 1 cup butter. Stir in flour and salt until smooth. Gradually stir in milk. Bring to a boil; cook and stir for 2 minutes or until thickened. Reduce heat. Add cheese, stirring until melted. Drain macaroni; stir into sauce.

Transfer to three greased 13-in. x 9-in. baking dishes. Melt the remaining butter; toss with the bread crumbs. Sprinkle over the three casseroles.

Bake, uncovered, at 350° for 35-40 minutes or until golden brown. **yield: 36 servings (1 cup each).**

Dixie Terry
Goreville, Illinois
You'll delight many taste buds with this rich and comforting dish. Tender macaroni is covered in a very creamy homemade cheese sauce, and then topped with golden bread crumbs. It's a true crowd-pleaser wherever I take it!

pasta bean soup

6 large onions, chopped
2/3 cup olive oil
18 garlic cloves, minced
12 cans (16 ounces *each*) kidney beans, rinsed and drained
4 cans (28 ounces *each*) Italian crushed tomatoes
3 cartons (32 ounces *each*) chicken broth
1/4 to 1/3 cup dried oregano
4 tablespoons salt
1 to 2 teaspoons pepper
3 packages (1 pound *each*) spaghetti, cut into fourths
Grated Parmesan cheese, optional

In several stockpots, saute onions in oil until tender. Add garlic; cook and 1 minute longer. Stir in the beans, tomatoes, broth, oregano, salt and pepper. Bring to a boil. Reduce heat; cover and simmer for 30-35 minutes.

Cook spaghetti according to package directions; drain. Just before serving the soup, stir in spaghetti. Serve with cheese if desired. **yield: 45-55 servings.**

Edward Reis
Phoenix, Arizona
This hearty Italian-style recipe proved very popular when I made it for about 90 people who attended our church's special "Souper Sunday" one January.

Susan Seymar, Valatie, New York
This Southwest-style lasagna will satisfy a hungry crowd. It can be stretched with extra beans, and it's oh-so easy to put together. People love it!

corn tortilla chicken lasagna

- 36 corn tortillas (6 inches)
- 6 cups shredded *or* cubed cooked chicken breast
- 2 cans (one 28 ounces, one 16 ounces) kidney beans, rinsed and drained
- 3 jars (16 ounces *each*) salsa
- 3 cups (24 ounces) sour cream
- 3 large green peppers, chopped
- 3 cans (3.8 ounces *each*) sliced ripe olives, drained
- 3 cups (12 ounces) shredded Monterey Jack cheese
- 3 cups (12 ounces) shredded cheddar cheese

In each of two greased 13-in. x 9-in. baking dishes, arrange six tortillas. Top each with 1 cup chicken, 2/3 cup kidney beans, 1 cup salsa, 1/2 cup sour cream, 1/2 cup green pepper, about 1/3 cup olives, 1/2 cup Monterey Jack cheese and 1/2 cup cheddar cheese. Repeat layers twice.

Cover and bake at 350° for 25 minutes. Uncover; bake 10-15 minutes longer or until cheese is melted. Let stand for 10 minutes before serving. **yield: 2 casseroles (12 servings each).**

baked pork chimichangas

- 1 pound dried pinto beans
- 1 boneless pork loin roast (3 pounds), trimmed
- 3 cans (4 ounces *each*) chopped green chilies
- 1 large onion, chopped
- 1/3 cup chili powder
- 1/2 cup reduced-sodium chicken broth
- 30 flour tortillas (6 inches)
- 4 cups (16 ounces) shredded reduced-fat cheddar cheese
- 2 cups picante sauce
- 1 egg white
- 2 teaspoons water

Place beans in a soup kettle; add water to cover by 2 in. Bring to a boil; boil for 2 minutes. Remove from the heat; cover and let stand for 1 hour. Drain and rinse beans, discarding liquid.

Place roast in a Dutch oven. In a bowl, combine chilies, onion, chili powder and beans. Spoon over roast. Cover and bake at 325° for 1-1/2 hours. Stir in broth; cover and bake 30-45 minutes longer or until a meat thermometer reads 160°. Increase oven temperature to 350°.

Remove meat and shred with two forks; set aside. Mash bean mixture; stir in shredded pork. Spoon 1/3 cup mixture down the center of each tortilla; top with 2 tablespoons cheese and 1 tablespoon picante sauce. Fold sides and ends over filling and roll up. Place seam side down on two 15-in. x 10-in. x 1-in. baking pans coated with cooking spray.

In a bowl, whisk egg white and water; brush over top. Bake, uncovered, at 350° for 25-30 minutes or until heated through. Serve immediately or cool, wrap and freeze for up to 3 months.

To use frozen chimichangas: Place chimichangas on a baking sheet coated with cooking spray. Bake at 400° for 10-15 minutes or until heated through. **yield: 2-1/2 dozen.**

LaDonna Reed
Ponca City, Oklahoma
Lean shredded pork and pinto beans combine with south-of-the-border ingredients such as green chilies and picante sauce in these chimichangas. Since my recipe makes a lot, I can freeze them for nights when I don't feel like cooking or don't have time to cook.

classic potato salad for 50

15 pounds potatoes, peeled and cubed
4 cups mayonnaise
1 cup sweet pickle relish
1/4 cup prepared mustard
1 jar (4 ounces) diced pimientos, drained
2 tablespoons salt
1 tablespoon sugar
2 teaspoons pepper
6 celery ribs, chopped
8 hard-cooked eggs, chopped
1 small onion, chopped

Paprika and green pepper rings, optional

Place potatoes in two large stockpots and cover with water. Bring to a boil. Reduce heat; cover and simmer for 10-15 minutes or until tender. Drain and cool to room temperature.

In a large bowl, combine the mayonnaise, relish, mustard, pimientos, salt, sugar and pepper. Divide the potatoes, celery, eggs and onion between two very large bowls; add mayonnaise mixture. Stir to combine.

Cover salad and refrigerate for at least 1 hour. Garnish with the paprika and the green pepper rings if desired. **yield: 50 servings (3/4 cup each).**

Dixie Terry
Goreville, Illinois
With creamy chunks of potato and crunchy bits of veggies, this traditional potato salad will gain rave reviews from your gang. It's perfect for family gatherings or potlucks during the summer.

fruit slush

1 can (46 ounces) pineapple juice
8 cups water
1 can (12 ounces) frozen lemonade concentrate, thawed
1 can (12 ounces) frozen orange juice concentrate, thawed
4 cups sugar
2 cups fresh *or* frozen unsweetened raspberries
2 envelopes unsweetened cherry soft drink mix *or* other red flavor of your choice

ADDITIONAL INGREDIENT:
Grapefruit *or* citrus soda

In a 6-qt. container, combine the first seven ingredients. Cover and freeze for 12 hours, stirring every 2 hours. May be frozen for up to 3 months.

For each serving: Place 1/2 cup fruit slush in a glass. Add 1/2 cup soda. **yield: about 5 quarts.**

Darlene White
Hobson, Montana
I mix up this sweet fruity slush using juices, berries and soft drink mix. Then I store it in the freezer for unexpected company. Simply pour a little citrus soda over scoops of the colorful mixture for frosty and refreshing beverages.

Sharon Nichols, Brookings, South Dakota
Family and friends will munch this fun mix of crackers, nuts and ranch dressing by the handfuls! Everyone is sure to find something they like. Mix it up with other snack ingredients to vary the flavors.

cracker snack mix

- 12 cups original flavor Bugles
- 6 cups miniature pretzels
- 1 package (11 ounces) miniature butter-flavored crackers
- 1 package (10 ounces) Wheat Thins
- 1 package (9-1/4 ounces) Cheese Nips
- 1 package (7-1/2 ounces) nacho cheese Bugles
- 1 package (6 ounces) miniature Parmesan fish-shaped crackers
- 1 cup mixed nuts *or* peanuts
- 1 bottle (10 *or* 12 ounces) butter-flavored popcorn oil
- 2 envelopes ranch salad dressing mix

In a very large bowl, combine the first eight ingredients. In a small bowl, combine oil and salad dressing mix. Pour over cracker mixture; toss to coat evenly.

Transfer to four ungreased 15-in. x 10-in. x 1-in. baking pans. Bake at 250° for 45 minutes, stirring every 15 minutes. Cool completely, stirring several times. **yield: about 8 quarts.**

fudge ripple brownies

- 1 cup butter, softened
- 2 cups sugar
- 4 eggs
- 2 ounces unsweetened chocolate, melted
- 2 teaspoons vanilla extract
- 1-1/2 cups all-purpose flour
- 1 teaspoon baking powder
- 1 teaspoon salt
- 1 cup chopped walnuts

FROSTING:
- 1/3 cup butter
- 3 cups confectioners' sugar
- 1-1/2 teaspoons vanilla extract
- 4 to 5 tablespoons heavy whipping cream

TOPPING:
- 1 tablespoon butter
- 1 ounce unsweetened chocolate
- 1 tablespoon confectioners' sugar

In a large bowl, cream butter and sugar until light and fluffy. Add eggs, one at a time, beating well after each addition. Beat in chocolate and vanilla. Combine the flour, baking powder and salt; add to creamed mixture and mix well. Stir in nuts.

Spread into a greased 15-in. x 10-in. x 1-in. baking pan. Bake at 350° for 25-30 minutes or until a toothpick inserted near the center comes out clean. Cool on a wire rack.

For frosting, cook and stir butter in a saucepan over medium heat for 6-7 minutes or until golden brown. Pour into a large bowl; add the confectioners' sugar, vanilla and enough cream to achieve spreading consistency. Frost cooled brownies.

For topping, melt chocolate and butter in a microwave; stir until smooth. Add confectioners' sugar; stir until smooth. Drizzle over frosting. Cut into bars. **yield: 4 dozen.**

Bobi Raab
St. Paul, Minnesota
Now that I'm retired and a new grandmother, I'm always looking for special treats to serve my grandchildren. These brownies have a rich chocolate taste and yummy brown butter frosting they adore.

brownie basics

For delicious brownies, start by measuring the ingredients accurately; avoid overmixing the batter. Use dull aluminum baking pans or glass baking dishes, and check your brownies when the minimum baking time has been reached.

chocolate chip oatmeal cookies

1	cup butter, softened
3/4	cup sugar
3/4	cup packed brown sugar
2	eggs
1	teaspoon vanilla extract
3	cups quick-cooking oats
1-1/2	cups all-purpose flour
1	package (3.4 ounces) instant vanilla pudding mix
1	teaspoon baking soda
1	teaspoon salt
2	cups (12 ounces) semisweet chocolate chips
1	cup chopped nuts

Diane Neth
Menno, South Dakota
Crazy about chocolate chips? This chewy cookie has plenty, not to mention lots of heart-healthy oatmeal. The gang will come back repeatedly for another taste…so this big batch is perfect.

In a large bowl, cream butter and sugars until light and fluffy. Beat in eggs and vanilla. Combine the oats, flour, pudding mix, baking soda and salt; gradually add to creamed mixture and mix well. Stir in chocolate chips and nuts.

Drop by rounded teaspoonfuls 2 in. apart onto ungreased baking sheets. Bake at 375° for 10-12 minutes or until lightly browned. Remove to wire racks. **yield: about 7 dozen.**

citrus cranberry tea

4	quarts water
1-1/2	cups sugar
6	cinnamon sticks (3 inches)
8	cups cranberry juice
4	cups orange juice
1/3	cup lemon juice

In a Dutch oven, combine the water, sugar and cinnamon. Bring to a boil; reduce heat. Cover and simmer for 25 minutes.

Discard cinnamon sticks. Stir juices into syrup mixture. Serve warm. **yield: 32 servings (8 quarts).**

editor's note: This recipe does not contain tea.

Pat Habiger
Spearville, Kansas
I stir up holiday spirit with this hot brew that's full of tangy fruit flavor.

Betsy Sams, Jamesville, New York
When planning your next fiesta, look no further than this hearty, pretty salsa. The succulent seasoning includes coriander, cumin, garlic and cilantro, and your crowd will definitely say, "Ole!"

salsa for a crowd

 4 cans (14-1/2 ounces *each*) diced tomatoes
 4 large tomatoes, chopped
 2 cups frozen corn, thawed
 1 can (15 ounces) black beans, rinsed and drained
 1 medium sweet onion, finely chopped
 1/3 cup lime juice
 1/4 cup minced fresh cilantro
 2 tablespoons cider vinegar
 2 tablespoons hot pepper sauce
 1 garlic clove, minced
 1 tablespoon coriander seeds, crushed
 1 tablespoon ground cumin
 1 teaspoon salt
 1 teaspoon coarsely ground pepper
Chopped jalapeno pepper, optional
Corn chips *or* tortilla chips

Place two undrained cans of tomatoes in a large bowl; drain the two remaining cans and add tomatoes to the bowl.

Stir in the chopped fresh tomatoes, corn, beans, onion, lime juice, cilantro, vinegar, pepper sauce, garlic and seasonings. Stir in the jalapeno if desired. Cover and refrigerate until serving. Serve with chips. **yield: 56 servings (1/4 cup each).**

hearty spaghetti sauce

- 8 bacon strips
- 8 pounds ground beef
- 4 large onions, chopped
- 2 large green peppers, diced
- 1 pound sliced fresh mushrooms
- 1/2 cup olive oil
- 16 garlic cloves, minced
- 1/2 cup all-purpose flour
- 6 cans (28 ounces *each*) diced tomatoes
- 2 cans (12 ounces each) tomato paste
- 2 cups water
- 1 cup white wine vinegar
- 6 tablespoons sugar
- 3 tablespoons Worcestershire sauce
- 2 tablespoons dried celery flakes
- 2 tablespoons dried oregano
- 2 tablespoons dried basil
- 4 teaspoons salt
- 2 teaspoons celery salt
- 2 teaspoons cayenne pepper

Hot cooked spaghetti

In a large stockpot, cook bacon over medium heat until crisp. Remove to paper towels to drain. Cook beef over medium heat in drippings until meat is no longer pink; drain. Remove beef and keep warm.

In the same pot, saute the onions, peppers and mushrooms in oil for 5 minutes or until onions are tender. Add garlic; cook 2 minutes longer.

Stir in flour until blended. Stir in the tomatoes, tomato paste, water, vinegar, sugar, Worcestershire sauce and seasonings. Crumble bacon; return bacon and beef to pan. Bring to a boil. Reduce heat; simmer, uncovered, for 2 hours, stirring occasionally. Serve with spaghetti. **yield: 38 servings (1 cup each).**

Margaret Malinowski
Queen Creek, Arizona
This hearty, old-fashioned spaghetti sauce will satisfy even the largest appetite. It may look like a lot of work, but it goes together fast and smells delicious as it cooks.

recipe
indexes

turkey enchilada
casserole
page 130

general recipe index

Refer to this index for a complete general listing of all the recipes in this book.

appetizers

Cold Appetizers
Antipasto-Stuffed Baguettes, 220
Asparagus Ham Roll-Ups, 17
Easy Party Bruschetta, 21
Italian Subs, 150
Mini Muffuletta, 216
Picnic Stuffed Eggs, 23
Shrimp Cocktail, 20
Tangy Marinated Mushrooms, 26

Dips & Spreads
Asiago Chicken Spread, 10
Caramel Apple Dip, 21
Chili con Queso Dip, 155
Cowboy Beef Dip, 22
Garlic Garbanzo Bean Spread, 20
Hot Chili Cheese Dip, 6
Salsa for a Crowd, 243
Special Cheese Balls, 14
Spicy Crab Dip, 24
Spruced-Up Cheese Spread, 218
Warm Ham and Cheese Spread, 8
Watermelon Salsa, 13

Hot Appetizers
Bacon-Cheddar Biscuit Snackers, 12
Chicken Skewers with Cool
   Avocado Sauce, 7
Chili Ham Cups, 18
Crab Crescents, 146
Crab Wonton Cups, 11
Cranberry Chili Meatballs, 147
Crispy Baked Wontons, 19
Honey Garlic Ribs, 8
Honey-Mustard Chicken Wings, 23
Honey-Tangerine Chicken
   Skewers, 25
Olive-Onion Cheese Bread, 154
Pepperoni Pinwheels, 15
Pepperoni Roll-Ups, 143

Pigs in a Blanket, 9
Raspberry Barbecue Wings, 17
Saucy Asian Meatballs, 24
Sausage-Stuffed Mushrooms, 10
Seafood Cakes, 161
Sour Cream and Beef Turnovers, 16
Spinach Bacon Tartlets, 148
Spinach-Corn Bread Bites, 14

Snacks
Chocolate Wheat Cereal Snacks, 7
Confetti Snack Mix, 16
Cracker Snack Mix, 240
Texas Snack Mix, 12

apples
Apple 'n' Carrot Slaw, 182
Apple Citrus Cider, 25
Apple Country Ribs, 111
Apple Cream Cheese Pie, 146
Apple Pie Bars, 232
Apple-Walnut Sausage Stuffing, 179
Big-Yield Chicken Salad, 77
Caramel Apple Dip, 21
Cherry-Apple Lattice Pie, 203
Chewy Apple Oatmeal
   Cookies, 210
Chunky Apple Cake, 200
Harvest Squash Medley, 182
Holiday Lettuce Salad, 181
Thanksgiving Cabbage Salad, 143

asparagus
Asparagus Ham Roll-Ups, 17
Colorful Roasted Veggies, 169
Creamy Vegetable Bow Tie Toss, 164

avocados
Almond-Avocado Tossed Salad, 145
Chicken Skewers with Cool
   Avocado Sauce, 7

bacon
Bacon-Cheddar Biscuit Snackers, 12
Bacon Potato Bake, 181
Bacon-Wrapped Beef Patties, 53
Breakfast Burritos, 32
Country Baked Beans, 179
Hash Brown Egg Brunch, 35
Hearty Spaghetti Sauce, 244
Next-Generation German Potato
   Salad, 166
Sausage Bacon Bites, 29
Spinach Bacon Tartlets, 148
Spinach Penne Toss, 184

bananas
Banana-Pecan Sweet Rolls, 34
Chewy Coconut Cookies, 202
Chocolate Chip Banana Cream
   Pie, 213
Moist Banana Bread, 165
Strawberry-Banana Gelatin
   Salad, 171
Walnut Banana Cupcakes, 206

bars & brownies
Almost a Candy Bar, 160
Apple Pie Bars, 232
Brownies from Heaven, 189
Caramel Butter-Pecan Bars, 187
Cherry Streusel Bars, 231
Deluxe Marshmallow Brownies, 208
Frosted Cake Brownies, 157
Fudge Ripple Brownies, 241
Hot Berries 'n' Brownie Ice
   Cream Cake, 207
Lemon-Lime Bars, 187
Peanut Butter Squares, 212
Springtime Strawberry Bars, 205
Super Brownies, 201

Triple Layer Brownie Cake, 214
White Chocolate Cereal Bars, 191

beans & lentils

Baked Pork Chimichangas, 238
Chili for a Crowd, 227
Colorful Corn and Bean Salad, 175
Corn Tortilla Chicken Lasagna, 237
Country Baked Beans, 179
Creole Black Beans 'n' Sausage, 97
Family Picnic Salad, 176
Fancy Bean Salad, 151
Firehouse Chili, 70
Flavorful Southwestern Chili, 156
Garlic Garbanzo Bean Spread, 20
Ham and Bean Soup, 69
Hearty Beef Enchiladas, 92
Hot Chili Cheese Dip, 6
Italian Peasant Soup, 162
Pasta Bean Soup, 236
Pork and Pinto Beans, 107
Salsa for a Crowd, 243
Southwest Rib Roast with Salsa, 114
Spicy Nacho Bake, 223
Spicy Pork Chili, 54
Taco Dogs, 89
Tangy Four-Bean Salad, 177
Tender Beef 'n' Bean Stew, 108
Turkey Enchilada Casserole, 130
White Chicken Chili, 67

beef
(also see ground beef)
Beef Brisket with Mop Sauce, 79
Hearty Beef Soup, 228
Herbed Beef Tenderloin, 155
Home-Style Roast Beef, 221
Irish Beef Stew, 78
Italian Beef, 54
Italian Pot Roast, 94
Mixed Grill Fajitas, 103
Mushroom-Blue Cheese
 Tenderloin, 80
Panhandle Beef Brisket, 87

Reuben Sandwiches, 58
Shredded Beef 'n' Slaw
 Sandwiches, 217
Shredded Beef Sandwiches, 61
Sirloin Roast with Gravy, 104
Southwest Rib Roast with Salsa, 114
Special Sandwich Loaves, 57
Tender Beef 'n' Bean Stew, 108

beverages

Apple Citrus Cider, 25
Bubbly Cranberry Punch, 19
Citrus Cranberry Tea, 242
Fruit Slush, 239
Fruity Iced Tea, 22
Golden Fruit Punch, 17
Homemade Lemonade, 9
Hot Buttered Coffee, 15
Lemon-Lime Punch, 26

breads & muffins
(also see breakfast & brunch)
Almond Berry Muffins, 39
Banana-Pecan Sweet Rolls, 34
Berry Cheesecake Muffins, 178
Buttermilk Pan Rolls, 218
Buttery Corn Bread, 177
Cherry Kolaches, 193
Chicago-Style Deep-Dish
 Pizza, 83
Golden Lemon Bread, 172
Ezekiel Bread, 41
Festive Fruit Ladder, 38
Moist Banana Bread, 165
Multigrain Raisin Bread, 170
Raspberry-Filled Poppy Seed
 Muffins, 33
Simply-a-Must Dinner Rolls, 175

breakfast & brunch
(also see breads & muffins,
eggs, oats & granola)
Chocolate Pecan Waffles, 36
Hot Fruit Compote, 39
Mocha-Cinnamon Coffee Cake, 40

Orlando Orange Fritters, 32
Pennsylvania Dutch Potato
 Doughnuts, 43
Raspberry-Rhubarb Coffee Cake, 30
Sage Breakfast Patties, 37
Sausage Bacon Bites, 29
Strawberry Syrup, 40
Whole-Grain Waffle Mix, 42

broccoli & cauliflower

Antipasto Picnic Salad, 173
Baked Vegetable Medley, 184
Bow Tie Ham Bake, 142
Broccoli Chicken Lasagna, 116
Colorful Roasted Veggies, 169
Creamy Turkey Casserole, 117
Floret Salad, 168
Hash Brown Broccoli Bake, 176
Party Tortellini Salad, 180
Wild Rice Pilaf, 169

cabbage & sauerkraut

Apple 'n' Carrot Slaw, 182
Bavarian Pork Loin, 81
Cabbage Roll Casserole, 137
Hearty Beef Soup, 228
Minestrone with Italian Sausage, 65
Polish Reuben Casserole, 128
Reuben Sandwiches, 58
Shredded Beef 'n' Slaw
 Sandwiches, 217
Thanksgiving Cabbage Salad, 143

cakes & cupcakes

Chocolate Peanut Butter Cake, 144
Chocolate Peanut Butter
 Cupcakes, 196
Chocolate Zucchini Cake, 191
Chunky Apple Cake, 200
Coconut Carrot Cake, 199
Coconut Chocolate Cake, 234
Hot Berries 'n' Brownie Ice
 Cream Cake, 207
Mocha Bundt Cake, 204
Orange Refrigerator Cake, 210

cakes & cupcakes (continued)

Orange Tea Cake, 197
Raspberry Lemon Torte, 159
Triple Layer Brownie Cake, 214
Walnut Banana Cupcakes, 206

caramel

Caramel Apple Dip, 21
Caramel Butter-Pecan Bars, 187

cheese

Antipasto Picnic Salad, 173
Asiago Chicken Spread, 10
Bacon-Cheddar Biscuit
    Snackers, 12
Baked Ziti Casserole, 131
Cheese Sausage Strata, 36
Cheesy Corn Chowder, 50
Cheesy Noodle Casserole, 165
Cheesy Rigatoni Bake, 127
Cheesy Sausage Penne, 125
Chili con Queso Dip, 155
Eggplant Parmigiana, 140
Hot Chili Cheese Dip, 6
Hot Colby Ham Sandwiches, 48
Italian Subs, 150
Mac 'n' Cheese for a Bunch, 236
Mini Muffuletta, 216
Monterey Quiche, 44
Mushroom-Blue Cheese
    Tenderloin, 80
Olive-Onion Cheese Bread, 154
Pinwheel Pizza Loaf, 90
Special Cheese Balls, 14
Spicy Nacho Bake, 223
Spinach Cheese Enchiladas, 89
Spruced-Up Cheese Spread, 218
Warm Ham and Cheese Spread, 8

cherries

Cherry-Apple Lattice Pie, 203
Cherry Cream Trifle, 197
Cherry Icebox Cookies, 186
Cherry Kolaches, 193
Cherry Streusel Bars, 231

chicken

Amish Chicken Corn Soup, 62
Asiago Chicken Spread, 10
Big-Yield Chicken Salad, 77
Biscuit-Topped Lemon Chicken, 135
Broccoli Chicken Lasagna, 116
Chicken Macaroni Casserole, 125
Chicken Noodle Casserole, 120
Chicken Pasta Salad, 168
Chicken Skewers with Cool
    Avocado Sauce, 7
Chicken Stuffing Casserole, 159
Chicken Supreme with Gravy, 233
Chunky Chicken Rice Soup, 227
Colorful Chicken 'n' Squash Soup, 46
Corn Tortilla Chicken Lasagna, 237
Creamy Chicken Noodle Bake, 129
Firefighter's Chicken Spaghetti, 132
Golden Baked Chicken, 97
Hearty Chicken Lasagna, 110
Home-Style Chicken Potpie, 91
Honey-Lime Roasted Chicken, 105
Honey-Mustard Chicken Wings, 23
Honey-Tangerine Chicken
    Skewers, 25
Italian Peasant Soup, 162
Make-Ahead Chicken Bake, 121
Mixed Grill Fajitas, 103
Kentucky Grilled Chicken, 86
New Orleans Jambalaya, 75
Pecan Chicken Casserole, 139
Picnic Chicken, 235
Pineapple Pepper Chicken, 100
Raspberry Barbecue Wings, 17
Raspberry Chicken Sandwiches, 153
White Chicken Chili, 67

chocolate

Almost a Candy Bar, 160
Brownies from Heaven, 189
Chocolate Almond Crescents, 192
Chocolate Chip Banana Cream Pie, 213
Chocolate Chip Oatmeal Cookies, 242
Chocolate Mint Surprises, 190

Chocolate Peanut Butter Cake, 144
Chocolate Peanut Butter
    Cupcakes, 196
Chocolate Pecan Waffles, 36
Chocolate Silk Pie, 194
Chocolate Wheat Cereal Snacks, 7
Chocolate Zucchini Cake, 191
Coconut Chocolate Cake, 234
Coffee Ice Cream Pie, 209
Deluxe Marshmallow Brownies, 208
Double Delights, 226
Frosted Cake Brownies, 157
Fudge Ripple Brownies, 241
Hot Berries 'n' Brownie Ice Cream
    Cake, 207
Mocha Bundt Cake, 204
Mocha-Cinnamon Coffee Cake, 40
Mocha Nut Balls, 201
Peanut Butter Cup Cookies, 222
Peanut Butter Squares, 212
Super Brownies, 201
Triple Layer Brownie Cake, 214
White Chocolate Cereal Bars, 191

cookies
(also see bars & brownies)

Cherry Icebox Cookies, 186
Chewy Apple Oatmeal Cookies, 210
Chewy Coconut Cookies, 202
Chocolate Almond Crescents, 192
Chocolate Chip Oatmeal
    Cookies, 242
Chocolate Mint Surprises, 190
Cinnamon-Sugar Crisps, 188
Double Delights, 226
Mocha Nut Balls, 201
Pastel Tea Cookies, 188
Peanut Butter Chippers, 160
Peanut Butter Cup Cookies, 222
Pecan Goodie Cups, 194

corn

Amish Chicken Corn Soup, 62
Calico Salad, 224
Casserole for a Crowd, 118

Cheesy Corn Chowder, 50
Colorful Corn and Bean Salad, 175
Corn-Stuffed Crown Roast, 112
Family Picnic Salad, 176
Fancy Bean Salad, 151
Salsa for a Crowd, 243
Spinach-Corn Bread Bites, 14
Tender Beef 'n' Bean Stew, 108

cranberries

Bubbly Cranberry Punch, 19
Citrus Cranberry Tea, 242
Cranberry Chili Meatballs, 147
Thanksgiving Cabbage Salad, 143

desserts

(also see bars & brownies, cakes &
cupcakes, cookies, pies & tarts)
Candy Bar Freezer Dessert, 205
Cherry Cream Trifle, 197
Frozen Raspberry Delight, 209
Walnut Baklava, 198

eggs

Breakfast Burritos, 32
Cheese Sausage Strata, 36
Egg Scramble, 31
Hash Brown Egg Brunch, 35
Make-Ahead Chicken Bake, 121
Mini Sausage Quiches, 37
Monterey Quiche, 44
Picnic Stuffed Eggs, 23

fish & seafood

Angel Hair Pasta with Tuna, 85
Angel Hair Shrimp Bake, 122
Crab Crescents, 146
Crab Wonton Cups, 11
Honey-Mustard Glazed
    Salmon, 157
Hot Crab Hero, 48
Louisiana Shrimp, 73
New Orleans Jambalaya, 75
Paella, 96
Pecan Salmon Casserole, 133

Rich Clam Chowder, 55
Seafood Cakes, 161
Shrimp Cocktail, 20
Spicy Crab Dip, 24

fruit

(also see specific kinds)
Apricot-Glazed Turkey Breast, 72
Berry Cheesecake Muffins, 178
Berry Cheesecake Pie, 211
Christmas Fruit Kabobs, 44
Creamy 'n' Fruity Gelatin Salad, 174
Creamy Peach Pie, 195
Fancy Fruit Salad, 167
Festive Fruit Ladder, 38
Festive Fruit Tart, 202
Fruit-Glazed Spiral Ham, 106
Fruit Slush, 239
Fruited Holiday Vegetables, 183
Fruity Iced Tea, 22
Golden Fruit Punch, 11
Hawaiian Fruit Salad, 29
Hot Berries 'n' Brownie Ice Cream
    Cake, 207
Hot Fruit Compote, 39
Special Summer Berry Medley, 180
Watermelon Salsa, 13

grilled recipes

Apple Country Ribs, 111
Bacon-Wrapped Beef Patties, 53
Chicken Skewers with Cool
    Avocado Sauce, 7
Garlic-Onion Turkey Burgers, 52
Kentucky Grilled Chicken, 86
Mixed Grill Fajitas, 103
Pepper-Lime Pork Kabobs, 94
Raspberry Chicken Sandwiches, 153
Sweet 'n' Spicy Country Ribs, 95
Turkey Brats with Slaw, 73

ground beef

Bacon-Wrapped Beef Patties, 53
Beefy Tomato Pasta Soup, 49
Cabbage Roll Casserole, 137

California Casserole, 134
Casserole for a Crowd, 118
Chili for a Crowd, 227
Chuck Wagon Wraps, 161
Coney Dogs, 230
Cowboy Beef Dip, 22
Deep-Dish Beef Bake, 117
Fake Steak, 85
Fiesta Lasagna, 98
Firehouse Chili, 70
Flavorful Southwestern Chili, 156
French Canadian Meat Pie, 109
Garlic-Onion Turkey Burgers, 52
Greek Tacos, 151
Ground Beef Spiral Bake, 131
Hamburger Noodle Casserole, 119
Hamburger Vegetable Soup, 59
Hearty Beef Enchiladas, 92
Hearty Spaghetti Sauce, 244
Hickory-Smoked Cheeseburgers, 58
Italian Pasta Bake, 74
Italian Wedding Soup, 60
Meat Loaf for a Mob, 230
Meatball Sub Sandwiches, 47
Pigs in a Blanket, 9
Pinwheel Pizza Loaf, 90
Pizza Hot Dish, 121
Sloppy Joe Pizza, 90
Sour Cream and Beef Turnovers, 16
Spicy Goulash, 77
Spicy Nacho Bake, 223
Steak Sauce Sloppy Joes, 145
Stroganoff for a Crowd, 223
Sun-Dried Tomato Meat Loaf, 88
Supreme Pizza Casserole, 123
Taco-Filled Pasta Shells, 84
Texas-Style Lasagna, 128
Three-Meat Spaghetti Sauce, 102
Vegetable Beef Soup, 144
Zesty Sloppy Joes, 70

ham

Antipasto Picnic Salad, 173
Asparagus Ham Roll-Ups, 17

ham (continued)

Boston Subs, 53
Bow Tie Ham Bake, 142
Broccoli Chicken Lasagna, 116
Chili Ham Cups, 18
Egg Scramble, 31
Focaccia Sandwich, 64
Fruit-Glazed Spiral Ham, 106
Ham and Bean Soup, 69
Ham & Shells Casserole, 124
Ham Barbecue, 47
Hawaiian Pizza Pasta, 126
Honey-Glazed Ham, 79
Hot Colby Ham Sandwiches, 48
Italian Subs, 150
New Orleans Jambalaya, 75
Pinwheel Pizza Loaf, 90
Sausage Ham Loaves, 105
Scalloped Potatoes and Ham, 217
Super Italian Chopped Salad, 174
Turkey Breast Roulade, 225
Warm Ham and Cheese Spread, 8

lamb

Lemon-Herb Leg of Lamb, 92

lemons & limes

Biscuit-Topped Lemon Chicken, 136
Golden Lemon Bread, 172
Homemade Lemonade, 9
Lemon Berry Pie, 152
Lemon-Herb Leg of Lamb, 92
Lemon-Lime Bars, 187
Lemon-Lime Punch, 26
Louisiana Shrimp, 73
Honey-Lime Roasted Chicken, 105
Pepper-Lime Pork Kabobs, 94
Raspberry Lemon Torte, 159

meat loaf & meatballs

Cranberry Chili Meatballs, 147
Fake Steak, 85
Italian Wedding Soup, 60
Meat Loaf for a Mob, 230
Meatball Sub Sandwiches, 47
Pinwheel Pizza Loaf, 90
Saucy Asian Meatballs, 24
Sausage Ham Loaves, 105
Sun-Dried Tomato Meat Loaf, 88
Turkey Meat Loaf, 99

mushrooms

Chicken Noodle Casserole, 120
Classic Turkey Tetrazzini, 138
Creamy Vegetable Bow Tie Toss, 164
Hearty Spaghetti Sauce, 244
Irish Beef Stew, 78
Mushroom Barley Soup, 68
Mushroom-Blue Cheese Tenderloin, 80
Sausage-Stuffed Mushrooms, 10
Tangy Marinated Mushrooms, 26
Turkey Breast Roulade, 225

nuts & peanut butter

Almond-Avocado Tossed Salad, 145
Almond Berry Muffins, 39
Almost a Candy Bar, 160
Apple-Walnut Sausage
  Stuffing, 179
Banana-Pecan Sweet Rolls, 34
Caramel Butter-Pecan Bars, 187
Chocolate Almond Crescents, 192
Chocolate Peanut Butter
  Cake, 144
Chocolate Peanut Butter
  Cupcakes, 196
Chocolate Pecan Waffles, 36
Cracker Snack Mix, 240
Double Delights, 226
Fudge Ripple Brownies, 241
Mocha Nut Balls, 201
Peanut Butter Chippers, 160
Peanut Butter Cup Cookies, 222
Peanut Butter Squares, 212
Pecan Chicken Casserole, 139
Pecan Goodie Cups, 194
Pecan Salmon Casserole, 133
Super Brownies, 201
Turkey Pecan Enchiladas, 76

Walnut Baklava, 198
Walnut Banana Cupcakes, 206

oats & granola

Baked Oatmeal, 31
Chewy Apple Oatmeal Cookies, 210
Chocolate Chip Oatmeal Cookies, 242
Good-Morning Granola, 28

oranges

Honey-Tangerine Chicken Skewers, 25
Orange Refrigerator Cake, 210
Orange Tea Cake, 197
Orlando Orange Fritters, 32

pasta

Angel Hair Pasta with Tuna, 85
Angel Hair Shrimp Bake, 122
Antipasto Picnic Salad, 173
Baked Ziti Casserole, 131
Beefy Tomato Pasta Soup, 49
Bow Tie Ham Bake, 142
Broccoli Chicken Lasagna, 116
California Casserole, 134
Casserole for a Crowd, 118
Cheesy Noodle Casserole, 165
Cheesy Rigatoni Bake, 127
Cheesy Sausage Penne, 125
Chicken Macaroni Casserole, 125
Chicken Noodle Casserole, 120
Chicken Pasta Salad, 168
Classic Turkey Tetrazzini, 138
Creamy Chicken Noodle Bake, 129
Creamy Vegetable Bow Tie Toss, 164
Eggplant Sausage Casserole, 135
Fancy Fruit Salad, 167
Fiesta Lasagna, 98
Firefighter's Chicken Spaghetti, 132
Ground Beef Spiral Bake, 131
Ham & Shells Casserole, 124
Hamburger Noodle Casserole, 119
Hawaiian Pizza Pasta, 126
Hearty Chicken Lasagna, 110
Hearty Spaghetti Sauce, 244

Italian Pasta Bake, 74
Mac 'n' Cheese for a Bunch, 236
Party Tortellini Salad, 180
Pasta Bean Soup, 236
Pecan Salmon Casserole, 133
Pizza Hot Dish, 121
Polish Reuben Casserole, 128
Spicy Goulash, 77
Spinach Penne Toss, 184
Stroganoff for a Crowd, 223
Supreme Pizza Casserole, 123
Taco-Filled Pasta Shells, 84
Three-Meat Spaghetti Sauce, 102
Tortellini Spinach Casserole, 158
Turkey Pasta Soup, 62

pepperoni

Antipasto Picnic Salad, 173
Chicago-Style Deep-Dish Pizza, 83
Chicken Pasta Salad, 168
Pepperoni Pinwheels, 15
Pepperoni Roll-Ups, 143
Supreme Pizza Casserole, 123
Three-Meat Spaghetti Sauce, 102

peppers

Chili con Queso Dip, 155
Chili Ham Cups, 18
Pepper-Lime Pork Kabobs, 94
Pineapple Pepper Chicken, 100
Sausage Pepper Calzones, 63

pies & tarts

Apple Cream Cheese Pie, 146
Berry Cheesecake Pie, 211
Cherry-Apple Lattice Pie, 203
Chocolate Chip Banana Cream Pie, 213
Chocolate Silk Pie, 194
Coffee Ice Cream Pie, 209
Creamy Peach Pie, 195
Festive Fruit Tart, 202
Frozen Strawberry Pie, 235
Lemon Berry Pie, 152

pineapple

Cherry Cream Trifle, 197
Creamy 'n' Fruity Gelatin Salad, 174
Fancy Fruit Salad, 167
Fruit-Glazed Spiral Ham, 106
Hawaiian Fruit Salad, 29
Hawaiian Pizza Pasta, 125
Pineapple Pepper Chicken, 100
Pork Burgers Deluxe, 147

pork

(also see bacon, pepperoni,
sausage & hot dogs)

Antipasto-Stuffed Baguettes, 220
Apple Country Ribs, 111
Baked Pork Chimichangas, 238
Bavarian Pork Loin, 81
Corn-Stuffed Crown Roast, 112
Crispy Baked Wontons, 19
Cuban Pork Roast, 86
French Canadian Meat Pie, 109
Honey Garlic Ribs, 8
Marinated Pork Loin, 82
Mini Muffuletta, 216
New Orleans Jambalaya, 75
Pepper-Lime Pork Kabobs, 94
Pork and Pinto Beans, 107
Pork Burgers Deluxe, 147
Pulled Pork Subs, 51
Roasted Garlic Pork Supper, 106
Sage Breakfast Patties, 37
Spicy Pork Chili, 54
Sweet 'n' Spicy Country Ribs, 95

potatoes & sweet potatoes

Bacon Potato Bake, 181
Classic Potato Salad for 50, 239
Creamed Potato Casseroles, 219
Egg Scramble, 31
Flavorful Mashed Potatoes, 149
French Canadian Meat Pie, 109
Fruited Holiday Vegetables, 183
Harvest Squash Medley, 182
Hash Brown Broccoli Bake, 176

Hash Brown Egg Brunch, 35
Honey-Mustard Potato Salad, 171
Irish Beef Stew, 78
Next-Generation German Potato
Salad, 166
Pennsylvania Dutch Potato
Doughnuts, 43
Roasted Garlic Pork Supper, 106
Scalloped Potatoes and Ham, 217
Vegetable Beef Soup, 144

raspberries

Berry Cheesecake Muffins, 178
Frozen Raspberry Delight, 209
Fruit Slush, 239
Hot Berries 'n' Brownie Ice
Cream Cake, 207
Raspberry Barbecue Wings, 17
Raspberry Chicken Sandwiches, 153
Raspberry-Filled Poppy Seed
Muffins, 33
Raspberry Lemon Torte, 159
Raspberry-Rhubarb Coffee Cake, 30
Special Summer Berry Medley, 180

rice & barley

Baked Rice with Sausage, 122
Cabbage Roll Casserole, 137
Chunky Chicken Rice Soup, 227
Mushroom Barley Soup, 68
Paella, 96
Vegetable Barley Soup, 56
Wild Rice Pilaf, 169

salads

Almond-Avocado Tossed Salad, 145
Antipasto Picnic Salad, 173
Apple 'n' Carrot Slaw, 182
Big-Yield Chicken Salad, 77
Calico Salad, 224
Chicken Pasta Salad, 168
Christmas Fruit Kabobs, 44
Classic Potato Salad for 50, 239
Colorful Corn and Bean Salad, 175
Creamy 'n' Fruity Gelatin Salad, 174

salads (continued)

Family Picnic Salad, 176
Fancy Fruit Salad, 167
Floret Salad, 168
Hawaiian Fruit Salad, 29
Holiday Lettuce Salad, 181
Honey-Mustard Potato Salad, 171
Next-Generation German Potato Salad, 166
Party Tortellini Salad, 180
Refrigerator Cucumber Slices, 166
Special Summer Berry Medley, 180
Spinach Penne Toss, 184
Strawberry-Banana Gelatin Salad, 171
Super Italian Chopped Salad, 174
Tangy Four-Bean Salad, 177
Thanksgiving Cabbage Salad, 143
Turkey Brats with Slaw, 73

sandwiches, burgers & wraps

Antipasto-Stuffed Baguettes, 220
Bacon-Wrapped Beef Patties, 53
Boston Subs, 53
Breakfast Burritos, 32
Coney Dogs, 230
Chuck Wagon Wraps, 161
Focaccia Sandwich, 64
Garlic-Onion Turkey Burgers, 52
Ham Barbecue, 47
Hickory-Smoked Cheeseburgers, 58
Hot Colby Ham Sandwiches, 48
Hot Crab Hero, 48
Italian Beef, 54
Italian Sausage Hoagies, 50
Italian Subs, 150
Meatball Sub Sandwiches, 47
Mini Muffuletta, 216
Mixed Grill Fajitas, 103
Pork Burgers Deluxe, 147
Pulled Pork Subs, 51
Raspberry Chicken Sandwiches, 153
Reuben Sandwiches, 58
Sausage Pepper Calzones, 63

Shredded Beef 'n' Slaw Sandwiches, 217
Shredded Beef Sandwiches, 61
Special Sandwich Loaves, 57
Steak Sauce Sloppy Joes, 145
Turkey Focaccia Sandwich, 156
Turkey Sloppy Joes, 59
Zesty Sloppy Joes, 70

sausage & hot dogs

Apple-Walnut Sausage Stuffing, 179
Baked Rice with Sausage, 122
Cheese Sausage Strata, 36
Cheesy Sausage Penne, 125
Chicago-Style Deep-Dish Pizza, 83
Coney Dogs, 230
Creole Black Beans 'n' Sausage, 97
Eggplant Sausage Casserole, 135
Italian Peasant Soup, 162
Italian Sausage Hoagies, 50
Italian Wedding Soup, 60
Minestrone with Italian Sausage, 65
Mini Sausage Quiches, 37
Mixed Grill Fajitas, 103
Paella, 96
Pigs in a Blanket, 9
Polish Reuben Casserole, 128
Sausage and Kale Soup, 66
Sausage Bacon Bites, 29
Sausage Ham Loaves, 105
Sausage-Stuffed Mushrooms, 10
Taco Dogs, 89
Three-Meat Spaghetti Sauce, 102
Traditional Holiday Stuffing, 229

side dishes

Apple-Walnut Sausage Stuffing, 179
Bacon Potato Bake, 181
Baked Vegetable Medley, 184
Cheesy Noodle Casserole, 165
Colorful Roasted Veggies, 169
Corn-Stuffed Crown Roast, 112
Country Baked Beans, 179

Creamed Potato Casseroles, 219
Creamy Spinach Casserole, 150
Creamy Vegetable Bow Tie Toss, 164
Dijon Green Beans, 172
Fancy Bean Salad, 151
Flavorful Mashed Potatoes, 149
Fruited Holiday Vegetables, 183
Glazed Carrots for a Crowd, 221
Harvest Squash Medley, 182
Hash Brown Broccoli Bake, 176
Holiday Peas, 148
Mac 'n' Cheese for a Bunch, 236
Maple-Ginger Root Vegetables, 224
Scalloped Potatoes and Ham, 217
Simple Sautéed Zucchini, 152
Traditional Holiday Stuffing, 229
Wild Rice Pilaf, 169

slow cooker recipes

Bavarian Pork Loin, 81
Creole Black Beans 'n' Sausage, 97
Ham Barbecue, 47
Hash Brown Egg Brunch, 35
Honey-Glazed Ham, 79
Hot Chili Cheese Dip, 6
Italian Beef, 54
Italian Sausage Hoagies, 50
Pork and Pinto Beans, 107
Pulled Pork Subs, 51
Shredded Beef Sandwiches, 61
Sirloin Roast with Gravy, 104
Spicy Goulash, 77
Tender Beef 'n' Bean Stew, 108
Turkey Sloppy Joes, 59

soups & chili

Amish Chicken Corn Soup, 62
Beefy Tomato Pasta Soup, 49
Cheesy Corn Chowder, 50
Chili for a Crowd, 227
Chunky Chicken Rice Soup, 227
Colorful Chicken 'n' Squash Soup, 46
Firehouse Chili, 70
Flavorful Southwestern Chili, 156

Ham and Bean Soup, 69
Hamburger Vegetable Soup, 59
Hearty Beef Soup, 228
Italian Peasant Soup, 162
Italian Wedding Soup, 60
Minestrone with Italian Sausage, 65
Mushroom Barley Soup, 68
Pasta Bean Soup, 236
Rich Clam Chowder, 55
Sausage and Kale Soup, 66
Spicy Pork Chili, 54
Turkey Pasta Soup, 62
Vegetable Barley Soup, 56
Vegetable Beef Soup, 144
White Chicken Chili, 67

spinach & kale

Almond-Avocado Tossed Salad, 145
Antipasto-Stuffed Baguettes, 220
Colorful Chicken 'n' Squash
   Soup, 46
Creamy Spinach Casserole, 150
Greek Tacos, 151
Ham & Shells Casserole, 124
Italian Wedding Soup, 60
Sausage and Kale Soup, 66
Spinach Bacon Tartlets, 148
Spinach Cheese Enchiladas, 89
Spinach-Corn Bread Bites, 14
Spinach Penne Toss, 184
Tortellini Spinach Casserole, 158
Turkey Meat Loaf, 99

strawberries

Almond Berry Muffins, 39
Frozen Strawberry Pie, 235
Hot Berries 'n' Brownie Ice Cream
   Cake, 207
Lemon Berry Pie, 152
Special Summer Berry Medley, 180
Springtime Strawberry Bars, 205
Strawberry-Banana Gelatin
   Salad, 171
Strawberry Syrup, 40

tomatoes

Beefy Tomato Pasta Soup, 49
Deep-Dish Beef Bake, 117
Easy Party Bruschetta, 21
Greek Tacos, 151
Hearty Spaghetti Sauce, 244
Salsa for a Crowd, 243
Southwest Rib Roast with Salsa, 114
Sun-Dried Tomato Meat Loaf, 88

turkey

Apricot-Glazed Turkey Breast, 72
Classic Turkey Tetrazzini, 138
Creamy Turkey Casserole, 117
Crispy Baked Wontons, 19
Focaccia Sandwich, 64
Garlic-Onion Turkey Burgers, 52
Paella, 96
Rosemary Turkey Breast, 74
Sage Breakfast Patties, 37
Saucy Asian Meatballs, 24
Sausage Pepper Calzones, 63
Special Sandwich Loaves, 57
Turkey Brats with Slaw, 73
Turkey Breast Roulade, 225
Turkey Enchilada Casserole, 130
Turkey Focaccia Sandwich, 156
Turkey Meat Loaf, 99
Turkey Pasta Soup, 62
Turkey Pecan Enchiladas, 76
Turkey Potpies, 93
Turkey Sloppy Joes, 59
Turkey Stew with Dumplings, 113
Turkey Stir-Fry Supper, 101

vegetables
(also see specific kinds)

Apple 'n' Carrot Slaw, 132
Baked Vegetable Medley, 184
Calico Salad, 224
Chunky Chicken Rice Soup, 227
Coconut Carrot Cake, 199
Colorful Roasted Veggies, 169

Creamy Vegetable Bow Tie
   Toss, 164
Dijon Green Beans, 172
Eggplant Parmigiana, 140
Eggplant Sausage Casserole, 135
Fruited Holiday Vegetables, 183
Glazed Carrots for a Crowd, 221
Hamburger Vegetable Soup, 59
Hearty Beef Soup, 228
Holiday Peas, 148
Home-Style Chicken Potpie, 91
Maple-Ginger Root Vegetables, 224
Minestrone with Italian Sausage, 65
Refrigerator Cucumber Slices, 166
Roasted Garlic Pork Supper, 106
Super Italian Chopped Salad, 174
Tangy Four-Bean Salad, 177
Turkey Potpies, 93
Turkey Stew with Dumplings, 113
Turkey Stir-Fry Supper, 101
Vegetable Barley Soup, 56
Vegetable Beef Soup, 144

zucchini & squash

Chocolate Zucchini Cake, 191
Colorful Chicken 'n' Squash
   Soup, 46
Creamy Vegetable Bow Tie
   Toss, 164
Family Picnic Salad, 176
Harvest Squash Medley, 182
Minestrone with Italian
   Sausage, 65
Simple Sauteed Zucchini, 152

alphabetical recipe index

Refer to this index for a complete alphabetical listing cf all the recipes in this book.

a

Almond-Avocado Tossed Salad, 145
Almond Berry Muffins, 39
Almost a Candy Bar, 160
Amish Chicken Corn Soup, 62
Angel Hair Pasta with Tuna, 85
Angel Hair Shrimp Bake, 122
Antipasto Picnic Salad, 173
Antipasto-Stuffed Baguettes, 220
Apple 'n' Carrot Slaw, 182
Apple Citrus Cider, 25
Apple Country Ribs, 111
Apple Cream Cheese Pie, 146
Apple Pie Bars, 232
Apple-Walnut Sausage Stuffing, 179
Apricot-Glazed Turkey Breast, 72
Asiago Chicken Spread, 10
Asparagus Ham Roll-Ups, 17

b

Bacon-Cheddar Biscuit Snackers, 12
Bacon Potato Bake, 181
Bacon-Wrapped Beef Patties, 53
Baked Oatmeal, 31
Baked Pork Chimichangas, 238
Baked Rice with Sausage, 122
Baked Vegetable Medley, 184
Baked Ziti Casserole, 131
Banana-Pecan Sweet Rolls, 34
Bavarian Pork Loin, 81
Beef Brisket with Mop Sauce, 79
Beefy Tomato Pasta Soup, 49
Berry Cheesecake Muffins, 178
Berry Cheesecake Pie, 211
Big-Yield Chicken Salad, 77
Biscuit-Topped Lemon Chicken, 136
Boston Subs, 53
Bow Tie Ham Bake, 142
Breakfast Burritos, 32

Broccoli Chicken Lasagna, 116
Brownies from Heaven, 189
Bubbly Cranberry Punch, 19
Buttermilk Pan Rolls, 218
Buttery Corn Bread, 177

c

Cabbage Roll Casserole, 137
Calico Salad, 224
California Casserole, 134
Candy Bar Freezer Dessert, 205
Caramel Apple Dip, 21
Caramel Butter-Pecan Bars, 187
Casserole for a Crowd, 118
Cheese Sausage Strata, 36
Cheesy Corn Chowder, 50
Cheesy Noodle Casserole, 165
Cheesy Rigatoni Bake, 127
Cheesy Sausage Penne, 125
Cherry-Apple Lattice Pie, 203
Cherry Cream Trifle, 197
Cherry Icebox Cookies, 186
Cherry Kolaches, 193
Cherry Streusel Bars, 231
Chewy Apple Oatmeal Cookies, 210
Chewy Coconut Cookies, 202
Chicago-Style Deep-Dish Pizza, 83
Chicken Macaroni Casserole, 125
Chicken Noodle Casserole, 120
Chicken Pasta Salad, 168
Chicken Skewers with Cool
    Avocado Sauce, 7
Chicken Stuffing Casserole, 159
Chicken Supreme with Gravy, 233
Chili con Queso Dip, 155
Chili for a Crowd, 227
Chili Ham Cups, 18
Chocolate Almond Crescents, 192
Chocolate Chip Banana Cream
    Pie, 213

Chocolate Chip Oatmeal
    Cookies, 242
Chocolate Mint Surprises, 190
Chocolate Peanut Butter Cake, 144
Chocolate Peanut Butter
    Cupcakes, 196
Chocolate Pecan Waffles, 36
Chocolate Silk Pie, 194
Chocolate Wheat Cereal Snacks, 7
Chocolate Zucchini Cake, 191
Christmas Fruit Kabobs, 44
Chuck Wagon Wraps, 161
Chunky Apple Cake, 200
Chunky Chicken Rice Soup, 227
Cinnamon-Sugar Crisps, 188
Citrus Cranberry Tea, 242
Classic Potato Salad for 50, 239
Classic Turkey Tetrazzini, 138
Coconut Carrot Cake, 199
Coconut Chocolate Cake, 234
Coffee Ice Cream Pie, 209
Colorful Chicken 'n' Squash
    Soup, 46
Colorful Corn and Bean Salad, 175
Colorful Roasted Veggies, 169
Coney Dogs, 230
Confetti Snack Mix, 16
Corn-Stuffed Crown Roast, 112
Corn Tortilla Chicken
    Lasagna, 237
Country Baked Beans, 179
Cowboy Beef Dip, 22
Crab Crescents, 146
Crab Wonton Cups, 11
Cracker Snack Mix, 240
Cranberry Chili Meatballs, 147
Creamed Potato Casseroles, 219
Creamy 'n' Fruity Gelatin Salad, 174
Creamy Chicken Noodle Bake, 129
Creamy Peach Pie, 195

Creamy Spinach Casserole, 150
Creamy Turkey Casserole, 117
Creamy Vegetable Bow Tie
   Toss, 164
Creole Black Beans 'n' Sausage, 97
Crispy Baked Wontons, 19
Cuban Pork Roast, 86

d

Deep-Dish Beef Bake, 117
Deluxe Marshmallow Brownies, 208
Dijon Green Beans, 172
Double Delights, 226

e

Easy Party Bruschetta, 21
Egg Scramble, 31
Eggplant Parmigiana, 140
Eggplant Sausage Casserole, 135
Ezekiel Bread, 41

f

Fake Steak, 85
Family Picnic Salad, 176
Fancy Bean Salad, 151
Fancy Fruit Salad, 167
Festive Fruit Ladder, 38
Festive Fruit Tart, 202
Fiesta Lasagna, 98
Firefighter's Chicken Spaghetti, 132
Firehouse Chili, 70
Flavorful Mashed Potatoes, 149
Flavorful Southwestern Chili, 156
Floret Salad, 168
Focaccia Sandwich, 64
French Canadian Meat Pie, 109
Frosted Cake Brownies, 157
Frozen Raspberry Delight, 209
Frozen Strawberry Pie, 235
Fruit-Glazed Spiral Ham, 106
Fruit Slush, 239
Fruited Holiday Vegetables, 183
Fruity Iced Tea, 22
Fudge Ripple Brownies, 241

g

Garlic Garbanzo Bean Spread, 20
Garlic-Onion Turkey Burgers, 52

Glazed Carrots for a Crowd, 221
Golden Baked Chicken, 97
Golden Fruit Punch, 11
Golden Lemon Bread, 172
Good-Morning Granola, 28
Greek Tacos, 151
Ground Beef Spiral Bake, 131

h

Ham and Bean Soup, 69
Ham & Shells Casserole, 124
Ham Barbecue, 47
Hamburger Noodle Casserole, 119
Hamburger Vegetable Soup, 59
Harvest Squash Medley, 182
Hash Brown Broccoli Bake, 176
Hash Brown Egg Brunch, 35
Hawaiian Fruit Salad, 29
Hawaiian Pizza Pasta, 126
Hearty Beef Enchiladas, 92
Hearty Beef Soup, 228
Hearty Chicken Lasagna, 110
Hearty Spaghetti Sauce, 244
Herbed Beef Tenderloin, 155
Hickory-Smoked Cheeseburgers, 58
Holiday Lettuce Salad, 181
Holiday Peas, 148
Homemade Lemonade, 9
Home-Style Chicken Potpie, 91
Home-Style Roast Beef, 221
Homemade Lemonade, 9
Honey Garlic Ribs, 8
Honey-Glazed Ham, 79
Honey-Lime Roasted Chicken, 105
Honey-Mustard Chicken Wings, 23
Honey-Mustard Glazed Salmon, 157
Honey-Mustard Potato Salad, 171
Honey-Tangerine Chicken
   Skewers, 25
Hot Berries 'n' Brownie Ice Cream
   Cake, 207
Hot Buttered Coffee, 15
Hot Chili Cheese Dip, 6
Hot Colby Ham Sandwiches, 48
Hot Crab Hero, 48
Hot Fruit Compote, 39

i

Irish Beef Stew, 78
Italian Beef, 54
Italian Pasta Bake, 74
Italian Peasant Soup, 162
Italian Pot Roast, 94
Italian Sausage Hoagies, 50
Italian Subs, 150
Italian Wedding Soup, 60

k

Kentucky Grilled Chicken, 86

l

Lemon Berry Pie, 152
Lemon-Herb Leg of Lamb, 92
Lemon-Lime Bars, 187
Lemon-Lime Punch, 26
Louisiana Shrimp, 73

m

Mac 'n' Cheese for a Bunch, 236
Make-Ahead Chicken Bake, 121
Maple-Ginger Root Vegetables, 224
Marinated Pork Loin, 82
Meat Loaf for a Mob, 230
Meatball Sub Sandwiches, 47
Minestrone with Italian Sausage, 65
Mini Muffuletta, 216
Mini Sausage Quiches, 37
Mixed Grill Fajitas, 103
Mocha Bundt Cake, 204
Mocha-Cinnamon Coffee Cake, 40
Mocha Nut Balls, 201
Moist Banana Bread, 165
Monterey Quiche, 44
Multigrain Raisin Bread, 170
Mushroom Barley Soup, 68
Mushroom-Blue Cheese
   Tenderloin, 80

n

New Orleans Jambalaya, 75
Next-Generation German Potato
   Salad, 166

o

Olive-Onion Cheese Bread, 154
Orange Refrigerator Cake, 210

Orange Tea Cake, 197
Orlando Orange Fritters, 32

p

Paella, 96
Panhandle Beef Brisket, 87
Party Tortellini Salad, 180
Pasta Bean Soup, 236
Pastel Tea Cookies, 188
Peanut Butter Chippers, 160
Peanut Butter Cup Cookies, 222
Peanut Butter Squares, 212
Pecan Chicken Casserole, 139
Pecan Goodie Cups, 194
Pecan Salmon Casserole, 133
Pennsylvania Dutch Potato
    Doughnuts, 43
Pepper-Lime Pork Kabobs, 94
Pepperoni Pinwheels, 15
Pepperoni Roll-Ups, 143
Picnic Chicken, 235
Picnic Stuffed Eggs, 23
Pigs in a Blanket, 9
Pineapple Pepper Chicken, 100
Pinwheel Pizza Loaf, 90
Pizza Hot Dish, 121
Polish Reuben Casserole, 128
Pork and Pinto Beans, 107
Pork Burgers Deluxe, 147
Pulled Pork Subs, 51

r

Raspberry Barbecue Wings, 17
Raspberry Chicken Sandwiches, 153
Raspberry-Filled Poppy Seed
    Muffins, 33
Raspberry Lemon Torte, 159
Raspberry-Rhubarb Coffee Cake, 30
Refrigerator Cucumber Slices, 166
Reuben Sandwiches, 58
Rich Clam Chowder, 55
Roasted Garlic Pork Supper, 106
Rosemary Turkey Breast, 74

s

Sage Breakfast Patties, 37
Salsa for a Crowd, 243

Saucy Asian Meatballs, 24
Sausage and Kale Soup, 66
Sausage Bacon Bites, 29
Sausage Ham Loaves, 105
Sausage Pepper Calzones, 63
Sausage-Stuffed Mushrooms, 10
Scalloped Potatoes and Ham, 217
Seafood Cakes, 161
Shredded Beef 'n' Slaw
    Sandwiches, 217
Shredded Beef Sandwiches, 61
Shrimp Cocktail, 20
Simple Sauteed Zucchini, 152
Simply-a-Must Dinner Rolls, 175
Sirloin Roast with Gravy, 104
Sloppy Joe Pizza, 90
Sour Cream and Beef Turnovers, 16
Southwest Rib Roast with Salsa, 114
Special Cheese Balls, 14
Special Sandwich Loaves, 57
Special Summer Berry Medley, 180
Spicy Crab Dip, 24
Spicy Goulash, 77
Spicy Nacho Bake, 223
Spicy Pork Chili, 54
Spinach Bacon Tartlets, 148
Spinach Cheese Enchiladas, 89
Spinach-Corn Bread Bites, 14
Spinach Penne Toss, 184
Springtime Strawberry Bars, 205
Spruced-Up Cheese Spread, 218
Steak Sauce Sloppy Joes, 145
Strawberry-Banana Gelatin
    Salad, 171
Strawberry Syrup, 40
Stroganoff for a Crowd, 223
Sun-Dried Tomato Meat Loaf, 88
Super Brownies, 201
Super Italian Chopped Salad, 174
Supreme Pizza Casserole, 123
Sweet 'n' Spicy Country Ribs, 95

t

Taco Dogs, 89
Taco-Filled Pasta Shells, 84
Tangy Four-Bean Salad, 177

Tangy Marinated Mushrooms, 26
Tender Beef 'n' Bean Stew, 108
Texas Snack Mix, 12
Texas-Style Lasagna, 128
Thanksgiving Cabbage Salad, 143
Three-Meat Spaghetti Sauce, 102
Tortellini Spinach Casserole, 158
Traditional Holiday Stuffing, 229
Triple Layer Brownie Cake, 214
Turkey Brats with Slaw, 73
Turkey Breast Roulade, 225
Turkey Enchilada Casserole, 130
Turkey Focaccia Sandwich, 156
Turkey Meat Loaf, 99
Turkey Pasta Soup, 62
Turkey Pecan Enchiladas, 76
Turkey Potpies, 93
Turkey Sloppy Joes, 59
Turkey Stew with Dumplings, 113
Turkey Stir-Fry Supper, 101

v

Vegetable Barley Soup, 56
Vegetable Beef Soup, 144

w

Walnut Baklava, 198
Walnut Banana Cupcakes, 206
Warm Ham and Cheese Spread, 8
Watermelon Salsa, 13
White Chicken Chili, 67
White Chocolate Cereal Bars, 191
Whole-Grain Waffle Mix, 42
Wild Rice Pilaf, 169

z

Zesty Sloppy Joes, 70